BUDDHIST DI

Ven. Piyadassi Thera, Ven. Ñânatiloka Mahâthera, and Ven. Ñânaponika Thera in front of the Forest Hermitage, Udawattakele, Kandy, Sri Lanka (1956).

BUDDHIST DICTIONARY

A MANUAL OF BUDDHIST TERMS AND DOCTRINES

BY VEN. NYANATILOKA

EDITED BY VEN. NYANAPONIKA

Buddhist Publication Society Inc.
P.O. Box 61
54 Sangharaja Mawatha
Kandy, Sri Lanka
E-mail: bps@bps.lk
Web site: http://www.bps.lk
Tel: 0094 81 223 7283—Fax: 0094 81 222 3679

Copyright © by Buddhist Publication Society - 2011
First BPS edition 1952
Reprint 1956
Third edition 1972 (Revised and enlarged by Ven. Nyanaponika)
Forth edition 1980 (with minor revisions by Ven. Nyanaponika)
Reprint 1988, 1997, 2004, 2011, 2016

National Library and Documentation Service Board-
Cataloguing-In-Publication Data

Nyanaponika Thera
Buddhist Dictionary/Nyanatiloka Thera - Kandy: Buddhist Publication Society, 2004 - 272 pp.; 13cm.
ISBN 955-24-0019-8
i. 294.303 DDC 21 ii. Title

1. Buddhism - Dictionary

ISBN 955-24-0019-8

Typeset at Silkworm Books, Chiang Mai, Thailand.

Printed by
Ajith Printers (Pvt) Ltd.
342, Old Kesbewa Rd, Ratnapitiya, Boralasgamuwa.

PREFACE
TO THE FIRST EDITION

As a first attempt of an authentic dictionary of Buddhist doctrinal terms, used in the Pali Canon and its Commentaries, this present manual will fill a real gap felt by many students of Buddhism. It provides the reader not with a mere superficial enumeration of important Pali terms and their English equivalents, but offers him precise and authentic definitions and explanations of canonical and post-canonical terms and doctrines, based on sutta, Abhidhamma Piṭaka (Canon) and commentary, and illustrated by numerous quotations taken from these sources, so that, if anyone wishes, he could, by intelligently joining together the different articles, produce without difficulty a complete exposition of the entire teachings of Buddhism.

As already pointed out by the author in the preface to his *Guide through the Abhidhamma-Piṭaka* (Colombo 1938), there are found in the Abhidhamma Canon numerous technical terms not met with in the Sutta Canon; and again other terms are found only in the Commentaries and not in Sutta and Abhidhamma. The author therefore has made a first attempt—without, however, laying any claim to absolute reliability or completeness in this by no means easy undertaking—to indicate in the Appendix all the terms that in the oldest sutta texts are either not found at all, or at least not in the same form or meaning, and to set forth how far these are deviations from the older texts, or further developments.

In this connection, the author wishes to state that the often quoted Patisambhidā-Magga, as well as Niddesa, Buddhavaṃsa and Cariyapitaka, though included in the Khuddaka Nikāya of the Sutta Piṭaka, nevertheless bear throughout the character of Commentaries, and though apparently older than the Sutta Commentaries handed down to us in Buddhaghosa's version, must doubtless belong to a later period of origin than the Abhidhamma Canon.

In rendering the terms into English, I often had to differ considerably from the interpretation of Western scholars, and to introduce quite new words. A great number of such earlier translations must be considered partly as totally incorrect, partly as misleading, or at the very least ambiguous. Incorrect are, for instance, the English renderings of *nāma-rūpa* by 'name and form'; *javana* (impulsion, i.e., the karmic impulsive moments) by 'apperception', etc.

The expositions concerning the true nature of the Eightfold Path, the Four Noble Truths, the *paṭiccasamuppāda* and the five groups of existence—

doctrines which, with regard to their true nature, have been often misunderstood by Western authors—are sure to come to many as a revelation.

On the doctrine of *anatta*, or 'egolessness', i.e., the impersonality and emptiness of all phenomena of existence, the author repeatedly felt the necessity of throwing light from every possible point of view, for it is exactly this doctrine which, together with the doctrine of the conditionality of all phenomena of existence, constitutes the very essence of the whole Teaching of the Buddha without which it will be by no means possible to understand it in its true light. Thus the doctrine of impersonality runs like a red thread right through the whole book.

May this little manual provide an ever-helpful companion and *vade mecum* to all earnest students in their study of the original Buddhist scriptures, and also give to Buddhist authors and lecturers the opportunity of supplementing and deepening their knowledge of the profound teachings of the Buddha!

Should it, for a better understanding, prove necessary to give to certain subjects a more detailed treatment, the carrying out of this task may be reserved for a later edition of this work.

Nyanatiloka
Central Internment Camp
Dehra-Dun, India
28 August 1946

EDITOR'S PREFACE
TO THE THIRD EDITION

The present revised and enlarged Third Edition was intended to be issued in commemoration of the tenth anniversary of the venerable author's passing away on 28 May 1957. But due to unavoidable circumstances the publication had to be delayed.

It was the venerable author's wish to enlarge the first edition of this work, but when a second edition became necessary, he was prevented from expanding it by the illness to which he later succumbed. It rested, therefore, with his pupil, the present editor, to make, within the original scope and character of the work, such additions and revisions as seemed useful.

Over seventy articles have been expanded and partly rewritten; others were slightly revised; more source references were included, and information on literature for further study of the respective subjects was added to some of the articles. But only very few new words have been added (e.g. *anupassanā*, *ānupubbi-kathā*, etc.). This restriction was observed because the venerable author himself thought only of 'a more detailed treatment' of existing articles (see Preface to the first ed.) as he obviously wished to preserve the original form and character of the book. It was also considered that the adding of more words such as those coined in later commentarial and Abhidhammic literature, would be superfluous as in the English language such terms will generally be found only in a few scholarly books and translations which themselves give the explanations needed.

This book is chiefly intended for those who study the Buddhist teachings through the medium of the English language, but wish to familiarise themselves with some of the original Pali terms of doctrinal import. They are in the same position as a student of philosophy or science who has to know the terminology of his field, which for common parlance is mostly not less 'unfamiliar' than are the words of the Pali language found in the Dictionary.

Such acquaintance with the Pali terms of the original texts will also be useful to the student for the purpose of identifying the various renderings of them favoured by different translators. It is deplorable that there is a considerable multiplication of new English coinages for the same doctrinal term. This great variety of renderings has proved to be confusing to those students of Buddhism who are not familiar with the Pali language. Even at this late stage when many translations of Pali texts are in print, it will be desirable if, for the sake of uniformity, translators forgo their preference for their own coining, even if they think them better than others. In any case, doctrinal terms have to be known by definition, just as in the case of philosophical and technical terms in a Western language.

As a small help in the situation described, a number of alternative renderings used by other translators have been included in some articles of this edition. In a very few cases, unacceptable though familiar renderings have been bracketed. Venerable Nyanatiloka's own preferences have been placed within inverted commas. Generally it may be said that his renderings, based on his comprehensive knowledge of texts and doctrine, are very sound and adequate. Only in a very few cases has the editor changed the author's preferred rendering e.g. 'canker' for *āsava* (instead of 'bias'), 'right view' for *sammā-diṭṭhi* (instead of 'right understanding'). The latter change was made for the sake of economising with the few English equivalents for the numerous Pali synonyms for 'knowing', etc.; and also to avoid having to render the opposite term, *micchā-diṭṭhi*, by 'wrong understanding'.

This Dictionary appeared also in the author's own German version (published by Verlag Christiani, Konstanz, Germany) and in a French translation made by the late Mme Suzanne Karpeles (published by Adyar, Paris, 1961).

Nyanaponika
Kandy, Ceylon
February 1970

EDITOR'S PREFACE
TO THE FOURTH EDITION

Only a few minor revisions have been made to the text of the Fourth Edition, which is now issued by the Buddhist Publication Society.

Nyanaponika
Kandy, Sri Lanka
March 1980

EDITOR'S PREFACE
TO THE FIFTH EDITION

In this Fifth Revised Edition the source information from the appendix has been brought into the body of the dictionary. The appendix still contains the list of post-canonical terms, but the citations in the body of the text are listed as "source notes". The citations have received virtually no editing, but the dictionary as a whole has been extensively edited for uniformity in style and usage.

Buddhist Publication Society
Kandy, Sri Lanka
March 1980

ABBREVIATIONS

~	the defined term in the text
A.	Aṅguttara Nikāya (figures refer to number of book (*nipāta*) and sutta)
ABH.	Abhidhamma Piṭaka (Canon)
ABH.S.	Abhidhammattha Saṅgaha
ABH.ST.	*Abhidhamma Studies*, by Nyanaponika Thera (BPS)
ASL.	Atthasālinī (com. to Dhammasaṅgaṇī)
ASL.TR.	Atthasālinī TR. *The Expositor*, tr. by Maung Tin., PTS TR. Series
BOEHTL.	Otto Boehtlingk, *Sanskrit-Wörterbuch*
BPS	Buddhist Publication Society, Kandy
C.NID.	Cūla Niddesa
com.	Commentary
D.	Dīgha Nikāya (figures: number of sutta)
DHP.	Dhammapada
DHS.	Dhammasaṅgaṇī
FUND.	*Fundamentals of Buddhism*, Nyanatiloka (BPS)
GUIDE	*Guide through the Abhidhamma Piṭaka*, Nyanatiloka, 3rd ed. 1971 (BPS)
IT.	Itivuttaka
KATH.	Kathāvatthu
KHP.	Khuddakapāṭha
KHP.TR.	*Minor Readings & Illustrator*, tr. (of KHP. & Com) by Ñāṇamoli Thera. PTS TR. Series
M.	Majjhima Nikāya (figures: number of sutta)
M.NID.	Mahā Niddesa
MIL.	Milindapañha
PATTH.	Paṭṭhāna
P.E.D.	Pali-English Dictionary (PTS)
P. TO D.	*Path to Deliverance*, Nyanatiloka (BPS) (figures: paragraphs)
PTS.M.	Paṭisambhidā Magga
PTS	Pali Text Society's editions
PUG.	Puggala-Paññatti (figures: paragraphs)
R.UND.	*Right Understanding*, tr. (of M. 9 & com.) by Soma Thera (BPS)
S.	Saṃyutta Nikāya (figures: numbers of *saṃyutta* and sutta)
SKR.	Sanskrit

SN.	Sutta Nipāta (figures: numbers of verses)
TAB.	Tables I, II, and III in the Appendix
THERAG.	Theragāthā
Tr.	Translation, translated (by)
UD.	Udāna
VIBH.	Vibhaṅga
VISM.	Visuddhimagga (figures, numbers of chapters, and paragraphing in *Path of Purification*, tr. Ñāṇamoli Thera, third ed., BPS)
WHEEL	*The Wheel*, publ. by BPS
W. OF B.	*The Word of the Buddha*, Nyanatiloka (BPS)
YAM.	Yamaka

BUDDHIST DICTIONARY

A

abandonment, contemplation of: *paṭinissaggānupassanā*, is one of the eighteen chief kinds of insight; see *vipassanā*, further *ānāpāna-sati* (16).

abbhokāsik'aṅga: 'living in the open air', is one of the ascetic means to purification (see *dhutaṅga*).

aberration (in morality and understanding): see *vipatti*.

abhabbāgamana: 'incapable of progressing'. "Those beings who are obstructed by their evil actions (*kamma*, see *karma*), by their defilements (*kilesa*, q.v.), by the result of their evil actions (see *vipāka*), or who are devoid of faith, energy and knowledge, and unable to enter the right path and reach perfection in wholesome things, all those are said to be incapable of progressing" (PUG. 13). According to the com. the 'evil actions' denote the five heinous deeds with immediate result (*ānantarika-kamma*, q.v.), while the 'defilements' refer to the 'evil views with fixed destiny' (*niyata-micchā-diṭṭhi*; see *diṭṭhi*).

Ābhassara: the 'Radiant Ones', are a class of heavenly beings of the fine-material world (*rūpa-loka*); cf. *deva*.

abhibhāyatana: the eight 'stages of mastery', are powers to be obtained by means of the kasina-exercises (see *kasiṇa*). In the com. to M. 77, where *āyatana* is explained by 'means' (*kāraṇa*), it is said: "The *abhibhāyatana* through their counteracting may master (suppress) the adverse states, and by means of higher knowledge they may master the objects of mind." They are means for transcending the sensuous sphere.

The stereotype text often met with in the suttas (e.g. D. 11, 33; M. 77; A. VIII, 65; X, 29) is as follows:

(1) "Perceiving (blue ... red ... yellow ... white) forms on one's own body, one sees forms externally, small ones, beautiful or ugly; and in mastering these one understands: 'I know, I understand.' This is the first stage of mastery.

(2) "Perceiving forms on one's own body, one sees forms externally, large ones. ... This is the second stage of mastery.

(3) "Not perceiving forms on one's own body, one sees forms externally, small ones. ... This is the third stage of mastery.

A

(4) "Not perceiving forms on one's own body, one sees forms externally, large ones. ... This is the fourth stage of mastery.

(5) "Not perceiving forms on one's own body, one sees forms externally, blue forms, forms of blue colour, blue appearance, blue lustre, and mastering these one understands: 'I know, I understand.' This is the fifth stage of mastery."

(6–8) The same is repeated with yellow, red and white forms.

As preparatory kasina-object for the first and second exercise one should choose on one's own body a small or a large spot, beautiful or ugly, and thereon one should concentrate one's full undivided attention, so that this object after a while reappears as mental reflex or image (*nimitta*, q.v.) and, as it were, as something external. Such an exercise, though appearing quite mechanical, if properly carried out will bring about a high degree of mental concentration and entrance into the four absorptions (*jhāna*, q.v.). In the third and fourth exercises the monk by an external kasina-object gains the mental reflexes and absorptions. As objects of the remaining exercises, perfectly clear and radiant colours should be chosen, flowers, cloth, etc.

A kasina-object of small size is said to be suitable for a mentally unsteady nature, one of a large size for a dull nature, a beautiful object for an angry nature, an ugly one for a lustful nature.

In VISM. V it is said: "By means of the earth-kasina one succeeds in reaching the stage of mastery with regard to small and large objects. ... By means of the blue-kasina one succeeds in causing blue forms to appear, in producing darkness, in reaching the stage of mastery with regard to beautiful and ugly colours, in reaching 'deliverance through the beautiful', etc." (cf. *vimokkha* II, 3). The same is also said with regard to the other colour kasinas.

abhijjhā: 'covetousness' is a synonym of *lobha* (see *mūla*) and *taṇhā* (q.v.) and is the eighth link of the unwholesome courses of action (see *kamma-patha*, I).

abhinibbatti: a sutta term for rebirth, see *punabbhava*.

abhiññā: the six 'higher powers', or supernormal knowledges, consist of five mundane (*lokiya*, q.v.) powers attainable through the utmost perfection in mental concentration (*samādhi*, q.v.) and one supermundane (*lokuttara*, q.v.) power attainable through penetrating insight (*vipassanā*, q.v.), i.e., extinction of all cankers (*āsavakkhaya*; see *āóava*), in other words, realisation of arahatship or holiness. They are: (1) magical powers (*iddhi-vidhā*), (2) divine ear (*dibba-sota*), (3) penetration of the minds of others (*ceto-pariya-ñāṇa*), (4) remembrance of former existences (*pubbe-nivāsānussati*), (5) divine eye (*dibba-cakkhu*), (6) extinction of all cankers (*āsavakkhaya*).

The stereotype text met with in all the four sutta collections (e.g. D. 34; M. 4, 6, 77; A. III, 99; V, 23; S. XV, 9 and PUG. 271, 239) is as follows:

(1) "Now, O Bhikkhus, the monk enjoys the various magical powers (*iddhi-vidhā*), such as being one he becomes manifold, and having become manifold he again becomes one. He appears and disappears. Without being obstructed he passes through walls and mountains, just as if through the air. In the earth he dives and rises up again, just as if in the water. He walks on water without sinking, just as if on the earth. Cross-legged he floats through the air, just like a winged bird. With his hand he touches the sun and moon, these so mighty ones, so powerful ones. Even up to the Brahma-world he has mastery over his body.

(2) "With the divine ear (*dibba-sota*) he hears sounds both heavenly and human, far and near.

(3) "He knows the minds of other beings (*parassa ceto-pariya-ñāṇa*), of other persons, by penetrating them with his own mind. He knows the greedy mind as greedy and the non-greedy one as not greedy; knows the hating mind as hating and the non-hating one as not hating; knows the deluded mind as deluded and the non-deluded one as not deluded; knows the shrunken mind and the distracted one, the developed mind and the undeveloped one, the surpassable mind and the unsurpassable one, the concentrated mind and the unconcentrated one, the freed mind and the unfreed one.

(4) "He remembers manifold former existences (*pubbe-nivāsānussati*), such as one birth, two, three, four and five births … hundred thousand births; remembers many formations and dissolutions of worlds: 'There I was, such name I had … and vanishing from there I entered into existence somewhere else … and vanishing from there I again reappeared here.' Thus he remembers, always together with the marks and peculiarities, many a former existence.

(5) "With the divine eye (*dibba-cakkhu* = *yathākammūpaga-ñāṇa* or *cutūpapāta-ñāṇa*) the pure one, he sees beings vanishing and reappearing, low and noble ones, beautiful and ugly ones, sees how beings are reappearing according to their deeds (see *karma*): 'These beings, indeed, followed evil ways in bodily actions, words and thoughts, insulted the noble ones, held evil views,

and according to their evil views they acted. At the dissolution of their body, after death, they have appeared in lower worlds, in painful states of existence, in the world of suffering, in hell. Those other beings, however, are endowed with good action ... have appeared in happy state of existence, in a heavenly world.

(6) "Through the extinction of all cankers (*āsavakkhaya*) even in this very life he enters into the possession of deliverance of mind, deliverance through wisdom, after having himself understood and realised it." 4–6 appear frequently under the name of the 'threefold (higher) knowledge' (*te-vijjā*, q.v.). They are, however, not a necessary condition for the attainment of sainthood (*arahatta*), i.e., of the sixth *abhiññā*. VISM. XI-XIII gives a detailed explanation of the five mundane higher powers, together with the method of attaining them.

In connection with the four kinds of progress (see *paṭipadā*), *abhiññā* means the 'comprehension' achieved on attainment of the paths and fruitions.

abhisamācārika-sīla: 'morality consisting in good behaviour', relates to the external duties of a monk such as towards his superior, etc. "*abhisamācārika-sīla* is a name for those moral rules other than the eight ending with right livelihood (i.e., fourfold right speech, threefold right action and right livelihood, as in the Eightfold Path)" (VISM. I; see *sacca* IV, 3–5). "Impossible is it, O monks, that without having fulfilled the law of good behaviour, a monk could fulfil the law of genuine pure conduct" (A. V, 21). Cf. *ādibrahmacariyakasīla*.

abhisamaya: 'truth-realisation', is the full and direct grasp of the Four Noble Truths by the stream-winner (*sotāpanna*; see *ariya-puggala*). In the com. the term is represented by 'penetration' (*paṭivedha*, q.v.). Frequently occurring as *dhammābhisamaya*, 'realisation of the doctrine' Cf. S. XIII (Abhisamaya Saṃyutta) and PTS.M. (Abhisamaya Kathā).

abhisaṅkhāra: identical with the second link of the *paṭicca-samuppāda* (q.v.), *saṅkhāra* (q.v.; under I, 1) or karma-formations.

ability to acquire insight: cf. *ugghaṭitaññū*, *vipacitaññū*, *neyya*.

abodes: *vihāra* (q.v.). The four Divine ~ : *brahma-vihāra* (q.v.). The nine ~ of beings: *sattāvāsa* (q.v.).

absence: *natthi-paccaya*, one of the twenty-four conditions (*paccaya*, q.v.).

absorption: see *jhāna*.

abstentions, the three: *virati* (q.v.).

access, moment of: see *javana*.

access-concentration: see *samādhi*.

accumulation (of karma): *āyūhana* (q.v.).

āciṇṇaka-kamma: habitual karma, see *karma*.

acinteyya: lit. 'That which cannot or should not be thought, the unthinkable, incomprehensible, impenetrable, that which transcends the limits of thinking and over which therefore one should not ponder. These four unthinkables are: the sphere of a Buddha (*buddhavisaya*), of the meditative absorptions (*jhāna-visaya*), of karma result (*kamma-vipāka*), and brooding over the world (*loka-cintā*), especially over an absolute first beginning of it (see A. IV, 77).

"Therefore, O monks, do not brood over the world as to whether it is eternal or temporal, limited or endless. ... Such brooding, O monks, is senseless, has nothing to do with genuine pure conduct (see *ādibrahmacariyaka-sīla*), does not lead to aversion, detachment, extinction, nor to peace, to full comprehension, enlightenment and Nibbāna, etc." (S. LVI, 41).

acquired image (during concentration): see *nimitta, samādhi, kasiṇa*.

action: karma (q.v.). Right bodily ~ : *sammā-kammanta*, see *sacca* (IV.4).

adaptability (of body, mental factors and consciousness): *kammaññatā* (q.v.); cf. *khandha* (corporeality) and TAB. II.

adaptation-knowledge: *anuloma-ñāṇa* (q.v.).

adherence: *parāmāsa* (q.v.)

adherent: *upāsaka* (q.v.)

adhicitta-sikkhā: 'training in higher mentality', see *sikkhā*.

adhimokkha: 'determination', decision, resolve: is one of the mental concomitants (*cetasika*) and belongs to the group of mental formations (*saṅkhārakkhandha*). In M. 111, it is mentioned together with other mental concomitants. See TAB. II, III.

adhipaññā-dhamma-vipassanā: 'insight into things based on higher wisdom', is one of the eighteen chief kinds of insight (see *vipassanā*).

A

adhipati-paccaya: 'predominance-condition' is one of the twenty-four conditions (*paccaya*, q.v.); if developed, it is considered as the fourfold road to power (*iddhi-pāda*. q.v.).

adhisīla-sikkhā: 'training in higher morality': see *sikkhā*.

adhiṭṭhāna: as a doctrinal term, occurs chiefly in two meanings:

1. 'Foundation': four 'foundations' of an arahat's mentality, mentioned and explained in M. 140: the foundation of wisdom (*paññā*), of truthfulness (*sacca*) of liberality (*cāga*) and of peace (*upasama*). See also D. 33 and com.

2. 'Determination', resolution, in: *adhiṭṭhāna-iddhi*, 'magical power of determination' (see *iddhi*); *adhiṭṭhānapāramī*, 'perfection of resolution' (see *pāramī*).

ādibrahmacariyaka-sīla: 'morality of genuine pure conduct', consists in right speech, right bodily action and right livelihood, forming the third, fourth and fifth links of the Eightfold Path (see *sacca*, IV.3, 4, 5); cf. VISM. I. In A. II, 86 it is said:

"With regard to those moral states connected with and corresponding to the genuine pure conduct, he is morally strong, morally firm and trains himself in the moral rules taken upon himself. After overcoming the three fetters (ego-belief. sceptic doubt and attachment to mere rules and ritual; see *saṃyojana*) he becomes one who will be 'reborn seven times at the utmost' (see *sotāpanna*) and after only seven times more wandering through this round of rebirths amongst men and heavenly beings, he will put an end to suffering."

ādīnavānupassanā-ñāṇa: 'knowledge consisting in contemplation of misery', is one of the eight kinds of insight (*vipassanā*) that form the 'purification of the knowledge and vision of the path-progress (see *visuddhi*, VI. 4). It is further one of the eighteen chief kinds of insight (see *vipassanā*).

adosa: 'hatelessness', is one of the three wholesome roots (*mūla*, q.v.).

adukkha-m-asukhā vedanā: 'feeling which is neither painful nor joyful', i.e., indifferent feeling; see *khandha*, *vedanā*.

advertence (of mind to the object): *āvajjana*, is one of the functions of consciousness (*viññāṇa-kicca*, q.v.). Cf. *manasikāra*.

æon: *kappa*, (q.v.).

agati: the four 'wrong paths' are: the path of greed (*chanda*), of hate (*dosa*), of delusion (*moha*), of cowardice (*bhaya*). "One who is freed from evil impulses is no longer liable to take the wrong path of greed, etc." (A. IV, 17; IX, 7).

age, old: *jarā* (q.v.).

aggregates: *khandha* (q.v.).

agility: *lahutā* (q.v.).

āhāra: 'nutriment', 'food', is used in the concrete sense as material food and as such it belongs to derived corporeality (see *khandha*, Summary I.). In the figurative sense, as 'foundation' or condition, it is one of the twenty-four conditions (*paccaya*, q.v.) and is used to denote four kinds of nutriment, which are material and mental:

1. Material food (*kabaliṅkārāhāra*), which feeds the eightfold corporeality having nutrient essence as its eighth factor (i.e., the solid, liquid, heat, motion, colour, odour, the tastable and nutrient essence; see *rūpa-kalāpa*).

2. Sensorial and mental impression (*phassa*), is a condition for the three kinds of feeling (agreeable, disagreeable and indifferent); see *paṭiccasamuppāda* (6).

3. Mental volition (*manosañcetanā*) (= karma, q.v.) feeds rebirth, see *paṭicca-samuppāda* (2).

4. Consciousness (*viññāṇa*) feeds mind and corporeality; (*nāma-rūpa*; IB., 2) at the moment of conception" (VISM. XI).

LITERATURE (on the four Nutriments): M. 9 & com. (tr. in 'R. UND.'), M. 38; S. XII, 11, 63, 64, *The Four Nutriments of Life*, selected texts & com. (WHEEL 105/106).

āhāra-ja (or **-samuṭṭhāna**) **–rūpa**: 'food-produced corporeality', see *samuṭṭhāna*.

āhāre paṭikkūla-saññā: 'reflection on the loathsomeness of food', fully described in VISM. XI, L.

ahetuka-citta: see *hetu*.

ahetuka-diṭṭhi: 'view of uncausedness' (of existence), see *diṭṭhi*.

ahetu-paṭisandhika: see *paṭisandhi*.

ahiṃsā: see *avihiṃsā*.

ahirika-anottappa: 'lack of moral shame and dread', are two of the four unwholesome factors associated with all karmically unwholesome states

A

of consciousness, the two others being restlessness (*uddhacca*) and delusion (*moha*). Cf. TAB. II.

"There are two sinister things, namely, lack of moral shame and dread, etc." (A. II, 6). "Not to be ashamed of what one should be ashamed of; not to be ashamed of evil, unwholesome things: this is called lack of moral shame" (PUG. 59). "Not to dread what one should dread. ... This is called lack of moral dread" (PUG. 60)

ahosi-kamma: 'ineffective karma', see *karma*.

ājīva: 'livelihood'. About right and wrong livelihood., see *sacca* (IV. 5) and *micchā-magga* (5).

ājīva-pārisuddhi-sīla: 'morality consisting in purification of livelihood', is one of the four kinds of perfect morality, see *sīla*.

Akaniṭṭha: the 'Great Ones', i.e., 'Highest Gods', are the inhabitants of the fifth and highest heaven of the Pure Abodes (*sudd hāvāsa*, q.v.); cf. *avacara*, *deva* (II) *anāgāmī*.

ākāsa: 'space', is, according to com., of two kinds: 1. limited space (*paricchinnākāsa* or *paricchedākāsa*), 2. endless space (*anantākāsa*), i.e., cosmic space.

1. Limited space, under the name of *ākāsa-dhātu* (space element), belongs to derived corporeality (see *khandha*, SUMMARY I; DHS. 638) and to a sixfold classification of elements (see *dhātu*; M. 112, 115, 140). It is also an object of kasina (q.v.) meditation. It is defined as follows: "The space element has the characteristic of delimiting matter. Its function is to indicate the boundaries of matter. It is manifested as the confines of matter; or its manifestation consists in being untouched (by the four great elements), and in holes and apertures. Its proximate cause is the matter delimited. It is on account of the space element that one can say of material things delimited that 'this is above. below, around that'" (VISM. XIV, 63).

2. Endless space is called in ASL.TR. *ajatākāsa*, 'unentangled', i.e., unobstructed or empty space. It is the object of the first immaterial absorption (see *jhāna*), the sphere of boundless space (*ākāsānañcāyatana*). According to Abhidhamma philosophy, endless space has no objective reality (being purely conceptual), which is indicated by the fact that it is not included in the triad of the wholesome (*kusalatika*), which comprises the entire reality. Later Buddhist schools have regarded it as one of several unconditioned or uncreated states (*asaṅkhata dharma*)—a view that is rejected in KATH. (see GUIDE, 70). Theravāda Buddhism

recognises only Nibbāna as an unconditioned element (*asaṅkhatadhātu*: see DHS. 1084).

ākāsa-dhātu: 'space element'; see above and *dhātu*.

ākāsa-kasiṇa: 'space-kasina exercise', see *kasiṇa*.

ākāsānañcāyatana: 'sphere of boundless space', is identical with the first absorption in the immaterial sphere; see *jhāna* (6).

ākiñcañña-ceto-vimutti: see *ceto-vimutti*.

ākiñcaññāyatana: see *jhāna* (7).

akiriya-diṭṭhi: view of the inefficacy of action', see *diṭṭhi*.

akuppā-ceto-vimutti: cf. *ceto-vimutti*.

akuppa-dhamma: 'unshakeable', is one who has attained full mastery over the absorptions (*jhāna*, q.v.). In PUG. 4 it is said:

"What person is unshakeable? If a person gains the meditative attainments of the fine-material and immaterial sphere (*rūpāvacara-arūpāvacara*); and he gains them at his wish, without toil and exertion; and according to his wish, as regards place, object and duration, enters them or arises from them, then it is impossible that in such a person the attainments may become shaken through negligence. This person is unshakeable."

akusala: 'unwholesome', are all those karmic volitions (*kamma-cetanā*; see *cetanā*) and the consciousness and mental concomitants associated therewith, which are accompanied either by greed (*lobha*) or hate (*dosa*) or merely delusion (*moha*); and all these phenomena are causes of unfavourable karma results and contain the seeds of unhappy destiny or rebirth. Cf. *karma*, *paṭiccasamuppāda* (1), TAB. II.

akusala-sādhāraṇa-cetasika: 'general unwholesome mental factors associated with all unwholesome actions' (volitions), are four: (1) lack of moral shame (*ahirika*), (2) lack of moral dread (*anottappa*), (3) restlessness (*uddhacca*), (4) delusion (*moha*). For (1) and (2) see *ahirika-anottappa*, for (3) see *nīvaraṇa*, for (4) *mūla*.

The corresponding term in the field of wholesome consciousness is *sobhana-sādhāraṇa-cetasika* (see *sobhana*).

SOURCE NOTE: this term is probably used for the first time in ABH. S., though already in VISM. XIV the four *cetasika* in question are mentioned amongst the

A

mental factors associated with each of the twelve *akusala-cittas* (TAB. I, 22–33), while in the Abhidhamma Piṭaka (DHS. 365–429) *uddhacca* is found only in the last of the twelve *cittas*, missing in all the remaining eleven *cittas*.

akusala-vitakka: 'unwholesome thoughts' as defined under *akusala* (q.v.). In M. 20, five methods of overcoming them are given: by changing the object, thinking of the evil results, paying no attention, analysing, suppressing.
Tr. in *The Removal of Distracting Thoughts* (WHEEL 21).

alcohol prohibition: see *surāmeraya-majjappamādaṭṭhānā*.

alms, vow of going for; or to do so without omitting any house: see *dhutaṅga*, 3, 4.

alms-bowl eater, the practice of the: see *dhutaṅga*.

alms-giving: *dāna* (q.v.).

alms-goer, the practice of the, see *dhutaṅga*.

alobha: 'greedlessness', is one of the three karmically wholesome roots (*mūla*, q.v.).

āloka-kasiṇa: 'light-kasina-exercise', see *kasiṇa*.

āloka-saññā: 'perception of light'. The recurring canonical passage reads: "Here the monk contemplates the perception of light. He fixes his mind to the perception of the day; as at day-time so at night, and as at night, so in the day. In this way, with a mind clear and unclouded, he develops a stage of mind that is full of brightness." It is one of the methods of overcoming drowsiness, recommended by the Buddha to Mahā-Moggallāna (A. VII, 58). According to D. 33, it is conducive to the development of 'knowledge and vision' (see *visuddhi*), and it is said to be helpful to the attainment of the 'divine eye' (see *abhiññā*).

altruistic joy: *muditā*, is one of the four sublime abodes (*brahma-vihāra*, q.v.).

amata (SKR. *amṛta*; √ *mṛ* to die; = Gr. *ambrosia*): 'deathlessness' according to popular belief also the gods' drink conferring immortality, is a name for Nibbāna (q.v.), the final liberation from the wheel of rebirths, and therefore also from the ever-repeated deaths.

amoha: 'non-delusion', wisdom, is one of the three karmically wholesome roots (*mūla*, q.v.).

anabhijjhā: 'freedom from covetousness', unselfishness, see *kamma-patha* (II. 8).

anabhirati-saññā: see *sabba-loke anabhirati-saññā*.

anāgāmī: the 'non-returner', is a noble disciple (*ariya-puggala*, q.v.) on the third stage of holiness. There are five classes of non-returners, as it is said (e.g. PUG. 42–46):

"A being, through the disappearing of the five lower fetters (*saṃyojana*, q.v.), reappears in a higher world (amongst the devas of the Pure Abodes, *suddhāvāsa*, q.v.), and without returning from that world (into the sensuous sphere) he there reaches Nibbāna.

(1) "He may, immediately after appearing there (in the Pure Abodes) or without having gone beyond half of the lifetime, attain the holy path for the overcoming of the higher fetters. Such a being is called 'one who reaches Nibbāna within the first half of the life' (*antarāparinibbāyī*).

(2) "Or, while living beyond half of the lifetime, or at the moment of death, he attains the holy path for the overcoming of the higher fetters. Such a being is called 'one who reaches Nibbāna after crossing half the lifetime' (*upahacca-parinibbāyī*).

(3) "Or, with exertion he attains the holy path for the overcoming of the higher fetters. Such a being is called 'one who reaches Nibbāna with exertion' (*sasaṅkhāra-parinibbāyī*).

(4) "Or, without exertion he attains the holy path for the overcoming of the higher fetters. Such a being is called 'one who reaches Nibbāna without exertion' (*asaṅkhāra-parinibbāyī*).

(5) "Or, after vanishing from the heaven of the Aviha-gods (see *suddhāvāsa*), he appears in the heaven of the unworried (*Atappa*) gods. After vanishing from there he appears in the heaven of the clearly-visible (*Sudassa*) gods, from there in the heaven of the clear-visioned (*sudassī*) gods, from there in the heaven of the highest (*Akaniṭṭha*) gods. There he attains the holy path for the overcoming of the higher fetters. Such a being is called 'one who passes up-stream to the highest gods' (*uddhamsota-akaniṭṭha-gāmī*)."

analysis of the four elements: *dhātu-vavatthāna* (q.v.).

analytical doctrine: *vibhajja-vāda* (q.v.).

analytical knowledge, the four kinds of: *paṭisambhidā* (q.v.).

A

anaññātañ-ñassāmīt'indriya: is one of the three supermundane senses or faculties, see *indriya* (20).

anantara-paccaya: 'proximity', is one of the twenty-four conditions (*paccaya*, q.v.).

ānantarika-kamma: the five heinous 'actions with immediate destiny' are: parricide, matricide, killing an arahat (saint), wounding a Buddha, creating schism in the monks' order. In A. V., 129 it is said: "There are five irascible and incurable men destined to the lower world and to hell, namely: the parricide," etc. About the fifth see A. X., 35, 38. With regard to the first crime, it is said in D. 2 that if King Ajātasattu had not deprived his father of life, he would have reached entrance into the path of stream-entry.

SOURCE NOTE: this term seems to be used for the first time in KATH. (190) of the ABH. canon; the five crimes mentioned, however, are already enumerated and explained in the old sutta texts (e.g. A. V, 129), as is to be seen from the main part of this work.

ānantariya: the 'Immediacy', is a name for that concentration of mind which is associated with such insight (*vipassanā*, q.v.) as is present in any one of the four kinds of supermundane path consciousness (see *ariya-puggala*), and which therefore is the cause of the immediately following consciousness as its result or 'fruition' (*phala*, q.v.). According to the Abhidhamma, the path (of the *sotāpanna*, etc.) is generated by the insight into the impermanence, misery and impersonality of existence, flashing up at that very moment and transforming and ennobling one's nature forever. It is mentioned under the name of *ānantarikasamādhi* in the Ratana Sutta (SN. V. 22) and in PTS.M. 1, Ñāṇakathā.

ānāpāna-sati: 'mindfulness on in-and-out-breathing', is one of the most important exercises for reaching mental concentration and the four absorptions (*jhāna*, q.v.).

In the Satipaṭṭhāna Sutta (M. 10, D. 22) and elsewhere, four methods of practice are given, which may also serve as basis for insight meditation. The 'Discourse on Mindfulness of Breathing' (Ānāpānasati Sutta, M. 118) and other texts have sixteen methods of practice, which divide into four groups of four. The first three apply to both tranquillity (*samatha*, q.v.) and insight-meditation, while the fourth refers to pure insight practice only. The second and the third group require the attainment of the absorptions.

"With attentive mind he breathes in, with attentive mind he breathes out.

I. (1) "When making a long inhalation he knows: 'I make a long inhalation'; when making a long exhalation he knows: 'I make a long exhalation.'

(2) "When making a short inhalation he knows: 'I make a short inhalation'; when making a short exhalation he knows: 'I make a short exhalation.'

(3) "'Clearly perceiving the entire (breath-) body I will breathe in,' thus he trains himself; 'clearly perceiving the entire (breath-) body I will breathe out,' thus he trains himself.

(4) "'Calming this bodily function I will breathe in,' thus he trains himself; 'calming this bodily function I will breathe out,' thus he trains himself.

II. (5) "'Feeling rapture (*pīti*) I will breathe in,' thus he trains himself; 'feeling rapture I will breathe out,' thus he trains himself.

(6) "'Feeling joy I will breathe in,' thus he trains himself; 'feeling joy I will breathe out,' thus he trains himself.

(7) "'Feeling the mental formation (*citta-saṅkhāra*) I will breathe in,' thus he trains himself, 'feeling the mental formation I will breathe out,' thus he trains himself.

(8) "'Calming the mental formation I will breathe in,' thus he trains himself; 'calming the mental formation I will breathe out,' thus he trains himself.

III. (9) "'Clearly perceiving the mind (*citta*) I will breathe in,' thus he trains himself; 'clearly perceiving the mind I will breathe out,' thus he trains himself.

(10) "'Gladdening the mind I will breathe in,' thus he trains himself; 'gladdening the mind I will breathe out,' thus he trains himself.

(11) "'Concentrating the mind I will breathe in,' thus he trains himself; 'concentrating the mind I will breathe out', thus he trains himself.

(12) "'Freeing the mind I will breathe in,' thus he trains himself; 'freeing the mind I will breathe out,' thus he trains himself.

IV. (13) "'Reflecting on impermanence (*anicca*) I will breathe in,' thus he trains himself; 'reflecting on impermanence I will breathe out,' thus he trains himself.

A

(14) "'Reflecting on detachment (*virāga*) I will breathe in,' thus he trains himself; 'reflecting on detachment I will breathe out,' thus he trains himself.

(15) "'Reflecting on extinction (*nirodha*) I will breathe in,' thus he trains himself; 'reflecting on extinction I will breathe out,' thus he trains himself.

(16) "'Reflecting on abandonment (*paṭinissagga*) I will breathe in, thus he trains himself; 'reflecting on abandonment I will breathe out,' thus he trains himself."

In M. 118 it is further shown how these sixteen exercises bring about the four foundations of mindfulness (*satipaṭṭhāna*, q.v.), namely: 1–4 contemplation of the body, 5–8 contemplation of feeling, 9–12 contemplation of mind (consciousness), 13–16 contemplation of mind objects. Then it is shown how these four foundations of mindfulness bring about the seven factors of enlightenment (*bojjhaṅga*, q.v.); then these again deliverance of mind (*ceto-vimutti*, q.v.) and deliverance through wisdom (*paññā-vimutti*, q.v.).

LITERATURE: Ānāpānasati Saṃyutta (S. LIV). PTS.M. Ānāpānakathā. Full explanation of practice in VISM. VIII, 145ff. For a comprehensive anthology of canonical and commentarial texts, see *Mindfulness of Breathing*, Ñāṇamoli Thera, (BPS, 1964).

anatta: 'non-self', non-ego, egolessness, impersonality, is the last of the three characteristics of existence (*ti-lakkhaṇa*, q.v.). The *anatta* doctrine teaches that neither within the bodily and mental phenomena of existence, nor outside of them, can be found anything that in the ultimate sense could be regarded as a self-existing real ego-entity, soul or any other abiding substance. This is the central doctrine of Buddhism, without understanding which a real knowledge of Buddhism is altogether impossible. It is the only really specific Buddhist doctrine, with which the entire structure of the Buddhist teaching stands or falls. All the remaining Buddhist doctrines may, more or less, be found in other philosophic systems and religions, but the *anatta*-doctrine has been clearly and unreservedly taught only by the Buddha, wherefore the Buddha is known as the *anatta-vādī*, or 'Teacher of Impersonality'. Whosoever has not penetrated this impersonality of all existence, and does not comprehend that in reality there exists only this continually self-consuming process of arising and passing bodily and mental phenomena, and that there is no separate ego-entity within or without this process, he will not be able to understand Buddhism, i.e., the teaching of the Four Noble Truths (*sacca*, q.v.), in the right light. He will think that it is his ego, his personality, that experiences suffering, his personality that performs good and evil actions and will be reborn according to these actions, his personality that will enter into Nibbāna, his personality that walks on the Eightfold Path. Thus it is said in VISM. XVI:

> "Mere suffering exists, no sufferer is found;
> The deeds are, but no doer of the deeds is there;
> Nibbāna is, but not the man that enters it;
> The path is, but no traveller on it is seen."

"Whosoever is not clear with regard to the conditionally arisen phenomena, and does not comprehend that all the actions are conditioned through ignorance, etc., he thinks that it is an ego that understands or does not understand, that acts or causes to act, that comes to existence at rebirth ... that has the sense-impression, that feels, desires, becomes attached, continues and at rebirth again enters a new existence" (VISM. XVII, 117).

While in the case of the first two characteristics it is stated that *all formations* (*sabbe saṅkhārā*) are impermanent and subject to suffering, the corresponding text for the third characteristic states that "*all things* are non-self" (*sabbe dhammā anattā*; M. 35, DHP. 279). This emphasises that the false view of an abiding self or substance is neither applicable to any 'formation' or conditioned phenomenon, nor to Nibbāna, the Unconditioned Element (*asaṅkhata dhātu*).

The Anatta-lakkhaṇa Sutta, the 'Discourse on the Characteristic of Non-self', was the second discourse after Enlightenment, preached by the Buddha to his first five disciples, who after hearing it attained to perfect holiness (*arahatta*).

The contemplation of non-self (*anattānupassanā*) leads to the emptiness liberation (*suññatā-vimokkha*, see *vimokkha*). Herein the faculty of wisdom (*paññindriya*) is outstanding, and one who attains in that way the path of stream-entry is called a Dhamma devotee (*dhammānusārī*; see *ariya-puggala*); at the next two stages of sainthood he becomes a vision-attainer (*diṭṭhippatta*); and at the highest stage, i.e., holiness, he is called 'liberated by wisdom' (*paññā-vimutta*).

For further details, see *paramattha-sacca*, *paṭiccasamuppāda*, *khandha*, *ti-lakkhaṇa*, *nāma-rūpa*, *paṭisandhi*.

LITERATURE: Anatta-lakkhaṇa Sutta, Vinaya I, 13–14; S. XXII, 59; tr. in *Three Cardinal Discourses of the Buddha* (WHEEL 17). Another important text on *anatta* is the *Discourse on the Snake Simile* (Alagaddūpama Sutta, M. 22; tr. in WHEEL 48/49).

A

Other texts in P. TO D. Further: *Anatta and Nibbāna*, by Nyanaponika Thera (WHEEL 11); *The Truth of Anatta*, by Dr. G. P. Malalasekera (WHEEL 94); *The Three Basic Facts of Existence III: Egolessness* (WHEEL 202/204).

anattānupassanā: 'contemplation of non-self' is one of the eighteen chief kinds of insight (see *vipassanā*). See also *anattā*.

anatta-saññā: 'perception of non-self'; see A. VI, 104; A. VII, 48; A. X, 60; UD. IV, 1.

anatta-vāda: the 'doctrine of impersonality', see *anatta*.

āneñja: 'imperturbability', denotes the immaterial sphere (*arūpāvacara; see avacara*); see *saṅkhāra*. cf. M. 106.

anger: see *mūla*.

anicca: 'impermanent' (or, as abstract noun, *aniccatā*, 'impermanence') is the first of the three characteristics of existence (*ti-lakkhaṇa*, q.v.). It is from the fact of impermanence that, in most texts, the other two characteristics, suffering (*dukkha*) and non-self (*anatta*), are derived (S. XXII, 15; UD. IV, I)

"Impermanency of things is the rising, passing and changing of things, or the disappearance of things that have become or arisen. The meaning is that these things never persist in the same way, but that they are vanishing dissolving from moment to moment" (VISM. VII, 3).

Impermanency is a basic feature of all conditioned phenomena, be they material or mental, coarse or subtle, one's own or external: "All formations are impermanent" (*sabbe saṅkhārā aniccā*; M. 35, DHP. 277). That the totality of existence is impermanent is also often stated in terms of the five aggregates (*khandha*, q.v.), the twelve personal and external sense bases (*āyatana* q.v.), etc. Only Nibbāna (q.v.), which is unconditioned and not a formation (*asaṅkhata*), is permanent (*nicca, dhuva*).

The insight leading to the first stage of deliverance, stream-entry (*sotāpatti*; see *ariya-puggala*), is often expressed in terms of impermanence: "Whatever is subject to origination, is subject to cessation" (see Dhammacakkappavattana Sutta, S. XLVI, 11). In his last exhortation, before his *parinibbāna*, the Buddha reminded his monks of the impermanence of existence as a spur to earnest effort: "Behold now, bhikkhus, I exhort you: Formations are bound to vanish. Strive earnestly!" (*vayadhammā saṅkhārā, appamādena sampādetha*; D. 16).

Without the deep insight into the impermanency and insubstantiality of all phenomena of existence there is no attainment of deliverance. Hence comprehension of impermanency gained by direct meditative experience heads two lists of insight knowledge: (a) contemplation of impermanency (*aniccānupassanā*) is the first of the eighteen chief kinds of insight (q.v.); (b) the contemplation of arising and vanishing (*udayabbayānupassanā-ñāṇa*) is the first of nine kinds of knowledge which lead to the 'purification by knowledge and vision of the path-progress' (see *visuddhi*, VI). Contemplation of impermanency leads to the conditionless deliverance (*animitta-vimokkha*; see *vimokkha*). As herein the faculty of confidence (*saddhindriya*) is outstanding, he who attains in that way the path of stream-entry is called a faith-devotee (*saddhānusārī*; see *ariya-puggala*) and at the seven higher stages he is called faith-liberated (*saddhā-vimutta*). See also *anicca-saññā*.

See *The Three Basic Facts of Existence I: Impermanence* (WHEEL 186/187).

aniccānupassanā: 'contemplation of impermanency', is one of the eighteen chief kinds of insight (see *vipassanā*).

anicca-saññā: 'perception of impermanency', is defined in the Girimananda Sutta (A.X. 60) as meditation on the impermanency of the five groups of existence.

"Though, with a faithful heart, one takes refuge in the Buddha, his Teaching and the Community of Monks; or with a faithful heart observes the rules of morality, or develops a mind full of loving kindness, far more meritorious it is if one cultivates the perception of impermanency, be it only for a moment" (A.X. 20).

See A. VI, 102; A. VII, 48; UD. IV, 1; S. XXII, 102.

animitta-ceto-vimutti: see *ceto-vimutti*.

animittānupassanā: see *vipassanā*.

animitta-vimokkha: see *vimokkha*.

añña: 'other', being of the opposite category.

aññā: 'highest knowledge', gnosis, refers to the perfect knowledge of the saint (*arahat*; see *ariya-puggala*). The following passage occurs frequently in the suttas, when a monk indicates his attainment of holiness (*arahatta*): "He makes known highest knowledge (*aññaṃ vyākaroti*), thus: 'Rebirth has ceased, fulfilled is the holy life, the task is accomplished, and there is no more of this to come.'"

The '*faculty* of highest knowledge' (*aññ'indriya* = *aññā-indriya*; see *indriya*), however, is present in six of the eight stages of holiness, that is, beginning with the *fruition* of stream-Winning (*sotāpatti-phala*) up to the path of holiness (*arahatta-magga*). See DHS. (PTS) 362–364, 505, 553; Indriya Vibhaṅga; P. TO D. 162.

aññāmañña-paccaya: 'mutuality-condition,' is one of the twenty-four conditions (*paccaya*, q.v.).

aññātāvindriya: 'the faculty of one who knows', see *indriya*, 22.

aññindriya: 'the faculty of highest knowledge', see *aññā* and *indriya*, 21.

anottappa: see *ahirika*.

answering questions, four ways of: see *pañha-byākaraṇa*.

antarā-parinibbāyī: one of the five kinds of non-returners or *anāgāmī* (q.v.).

antinomies: see *diṭṭhi*.

anuloma-citta: 'adaptation-moment of consciousness', denotes the third of the four moments of impulsion (*javana*, q.v.) flashing up immediately before either reaching the absorptions (*jhāna*, q.v.) or the supermundane paths (see *ariya-puggala*). These four moments of impulsion are: the preparation (*parikamma*), access (*upacāra*), adaptation (*anuloma*) and maturity (*gotrabhū*) moments. For further details, see *javana*, *gotrabhū*.

anuloma-ñāṇa: 'adaptation-knowledge' or conformity-knowledge, is identical with the 'adaptation-to-truth knowledge', the last of nine insight-knowledges (*vipassanā-ñāṇa*) which constitute the purification of knowledge and vision of the path-progress' (see *visuddhi* VI, 9). Cf. VISM. XXI.

anupādisesa-nibbāna: see *Nibbāna*, *upādi*.

anupassanā: 'contemplation'. Fourfold: see *satipaṭṭhāna*. 1. Eightfold: see *vipassanā*. Sevenfold: "The seven contemplations: (1) Contemplating (formations) as impermanent, one abandons the perception of permanency. (2) Contemplating (them) as painful, one abandons the perception of happiness (to be found in them). (3) Contemplating (them) as not self, one abandons the perception of self. (4) Becoming dispassionate, one abandons delighting. (5) Causing fading away, one abandons greed. (6) Causing cessation, one abandons originating. (7) Relinquishing, one abandons grasping" (PTS.M. I, 58). See also VISM. XXI, 43; XXII, 114.

anupubba-nirodha: the nine 'successive extinctions', are the eight extinctions reached through the eight absorptions (*jhāna*, q.v.) and the extinction of feeling and perception (see *nirodha-samāpatti*), as it is said in A. IX, 31 and D. 33:

"In him who has entered the first absorption, the sensuous perceptions (*kāma-saññā*) are extinguished. Having entered the second absorption, thought-conception and discursive thinking (*vitakkavicāra*, q.v.) are extinguished. Having entered the third absorption, rapture (*pīti*, q.v.) is extinguished. Having entered the fourth absorption, in-and-out breathing (*assāsapassāsa*, q.v.) are extinguished. Having entered the sphere of boundless space (*ākāsānañcāyatana*), the corporeality perceptions (*rūpa-saññā*) are extinguished. Having entered the sphere of boundless consciousness (*viññāṇañcāyatana*), the perception of the sphere of boundless space is extinguished. Having entered the sphere of nothingness (*ākiñcaññāyatana*), the perception of the sphere of boundless consciousness is extinguished. Having entered the sphere of neither-perception-nor-non-perception (*neva-saññānāsa ññāyatana*) the perception of the sphere of nothingness is extinguished. Having entered the extinction of perception and feeling (*saññāvedayitanirodha*) perception and feeling are extinguished." For further details, see *jhāna*, *nirodha-samāpatti*.

anupubba-vihāra: the nine 'successive abodes', are identical with the nine *anupubba-nirodha* (see above). In A. IX, 33 they are called successive attainments (*anupubba-samāpatti*).

ānupubbī-kathā: 'gradual instruction', progressive sermon; given by the Buddha when it was necessary to prepare first the listener's mind before speaking to him on the advanced teaching of the Four Noble Truths. The stock passage (e.g. D. 3; D. 14; M. 56) runs as follows:

"Then the Blessed One gave him a gradual instruction—that is to say, he spoke on *liberality* ('giving', *dāna*, q.v.), on *moral conduct* (*sīla*) and on the *heavens* (*sagga*); he explained the peril, the vanity and the depravity of sensual pleasures, and the *advantages of renunciation*. When the Blessed One perceived that the listener's mind was prepared, pliant, free from obstacles, elevated and lucid; then he explained to him that exalted teaching particular to the Buddhas (*Buddhānaṃ sāmukkaṃsikā desanā*), that is: suffering, its cause, its ceasing, and the path."

anurakkhaṇa-padhāna: the 'effort to maintain' wholesome states, see *padhāna*.

anusaya: the seven 'proclivities', inclinations, or tendencies are: sensuous greed (*kāma-rāga*, see *saṃyojana*), grudge (*paṭigha*), speculative opinion (*diṭṭhi*, q.v.), sceptical doubt (*vicikicchā*, q.v.), conceit (*māna*, q.v.), craving for continued existence (*bhavarāga*), ignorance (*avijjā*, q.v.) (D. 33; A. VII, 11, 12).

"These things are called 'proclivities' since, in consequence of their pertinacity, they ever and again tend to become the conditions for the arising of ever new sensuous greed, etc." (VISM. XXII, 60).

YAM. VII, first determines in which beings such and such proclivities exist, and which proclivities, and with regard to what, and in which sphere of existence. Thereafter it gives an explanation concerning their overcoming, their penetration, etc. Cf. GUIDE VI (vii). According to KATH. several ancient Buddhist schools erroneously held the opinion that the *anusayas*, as such, meant merely latent, hence karmically neutral qualities, which however contradicts the Theravāda conception. Cf. GUIDE V, 88, 108, 139.

anussati: 'recollection', meditation, contemplation. The six recollections often described in the suttas (e.g. A. VI, 10, 25; D. 33) are: (1) recollection of the Buddha, (2) his Doctrine, (3) his community of noble disciples, (4) of morality, (5) liberality, (6) heavenly beings (*buddhānussati, dhammānussati, saṅghānussati, sīlānussati, cāgānussati, devatānussati*).

(1) "The noble disciple, Mahānāma, recollects thus: 'This Blessed One is holy, a fully Enlightened One, perfected in wisdom and conduct, faring happily, knower of the worlds, unsurpassed leader of men to be trained, teacher of heavenly beings and men, a Buddha, a Blessed One.'

(2) 'Well proclaimed by the Blessed One is the Doctrine (*dhamma*), directly visible, with immediate fruit, inviting investigation, leading on to Nibbāna, to be comprehended by the wise, each by himself.'

(3) 'Of good conduct is the Community (Saṅgha) of the Blessed One's disciples, of upright conduct, living on the right path, performing their duties, to wit: the four pairs of men or eight individuals (see *ariya-puggala*). This Community of the Blessed One's disciples is worthy of offerings, worthy of hospitality, worthy of gifts, worthy of reverence with raised hands, the unsurpassed field for doing meritorious deeds.'

(4) "The noble disciple further recollects his own morality (*sīla*) which is unbroken, without any breach, undefiled, untarnished, conducive to liberation, praised by the wise, not dependent (on craving or opinions), leading to concentration.

(5) "The noble disciple further recollects his own liberality (*cāga*) thus: 'Blessed truly am I, highly blessed am I who, amongst beings defiled with the filth of stinginess, live with heart free from stinginess, liberal, open-handed, rejoicing in giving, ready to give anything asked for, glad to give and share with others.'

(6) "The noble disciple further recollects the heavenly beings (*devatā*): 'There are the heavenly beings of the retinue of the Four Great Kings, the heavenly beings of the World of the Thirty-Three, the Yāmadevas ... and there are heavenly beings besides (see *deva*). Such faith, such morality, such knowledge, such liberality, such insight, possessed of which those heavenly beings, after vanishing from here, are reborn in those worlds, such things are also found in me.'" (A. III, 70; VI, 10; XI, 12).

"At the time when the noble disciple recollects the Perfect One ... at such a time his mind is neither possessed of greed, nor of hate, nor of delusion. Quite upright at such a time is his mind owing to the Perfect One. ... With upright mind the noble disciple attains understanding of the sense, understanding of the law, attains joy through the law. In the joyous one rapture arises. With heart enraptured, his whole being becomes stilled. Stilled within his being, he feels happiness; and the mind of the happy one becomes firm. Of this noble disciple it is said that amongst those gone astray, he walks on the right path, among those suffering he abides free from suffering. Thus having reached the stream of the law, he develops the recollection of the Enlightened One. ... " (A. VI, 10).

In A. I, 21 (PTS: I, XVI) and A. I, 27 (PTS: XX. 2) another four recollections are added: mindfulness on death (*maraṇa-sati*, q.v.), on the body (*kāyagatāsati*, q.v.), on breathing (*ānāpāna-sati*, q.v.), and the recollection of peace (*upasamānussati*, q.v.).

The first six recollections are fully explained in VISM. VII, the latter four in VISM. VIII.

aparāpariya-vedanīya-kamma: 'karma bearing fruits in later births', see *karma*.

aparihāna-dhamma: 'incapable of relapse', or 'of falling away', namely, with regard to deliverance from some or all fetters of existence (see *saṃyojana*). Thus all noble disciples are called, i.e., all those who have attained any of the four noble paths to holiness (see *ariya-puggala*). With regard to the absorptions (*jhāna*, q.v.), anyone is called 'unrelapsable' who has attained full mastery over the absorptions. See A. VI, 62; PUG. 6. Cf. *akuppa-dhamma*.

aparihāniya-dhamma: 'conditions of welfare' (lit. of non-decline), for a nation. Seven such conditions are mentioned in the Mahā-Parinibbāna Sutta (D. 16). They are followed by five sets of seven, and one set of six conditions, conducive to the welfare of the Community of Monks, the Saṅgha. Identical texts at A. VII, 20–25. To be distinguished from the preceding term.

A

apāya: the four 'lower worlds', i.e., the world of animals, of ghosts, of demons, and hell. See VISM. XIII, 92ff.

āpo-dhātu: 'water-element', see *dhātu*.

appamāda: 'zeal', non-laxity, earnestness, diligence, is considered the foundation of all progress.

Just as all the footprints of living beings are surpassed by the footprint of the elephant, and the footprint of the elephant is considered as the mightiest amongst them, just so have all the meritorious qualities zeal as their foundation, and zeal is considered as the mightiest of these qualities" (A. X, 15).

Cf. the Chapter on Zeal (*Appamāda Vagga*) in DHP., and the Buddha's last exhortation: "Transient are all formations. Strive zealously!" (*appamādena sampādetha*, D. 16). In the commentaries, it is often explained as the presence (lit. 'non-absence') of mindfulness (*satiyā avippavāsa*).

Appamāṇābha: a kind of heavenly being, see *deva*, (II).

appamāṇa-ceto-vimutti: see *ceto-vimutti*.

Appamāṇa-subha: a kind of heavenly being: see *deva* (II).

appamaññā: the four 'boundless states', identical with *brahma-vihāra* (q.v.).

appanā-samādhi: 'attainment concentration' or 'full concentration' (√ *appeti*, to fix), is the concentration existing during absorption (*jhāna*, q.v.), while the neighbourhood or access-concentration (*upacāra-samādhi*) only approaches the first absorption without attaining it; see *samādhi*.

appaṇihita-vimokkha: see *vimokkha*.

appaṇihitānupassanā: see *vipassanā*.

appendants, the three: *kiñcana* (q.v.).

appicchatā: 'having only few wishes', contentedness. One of the indispensable virtues of the monk; cf. A. X. 181–190, and *ariyavaṃsa* (q.v.).

apuññābhisaṅkhāra: see *saṅkhāra*.

arahat and **arahatta-magga**, **-phala**: see *ariya-puggala*.

ārammaṇa: 'object'. There are six: visible object, sound, odour, taste, body-impression, mind-object. The mind-object (*dhammārammaṇa*) may be physical or mental, past, present or future, real or imaginary. The five sense-objects belong to the corporeality-group (*rūpakkhandha*, see *khandha*). They form the external foundations for the sense-perceptions, and without them no sense-perception or sense-consciousness (seeing, hearing, etc.) can arise. Cf. *āyatana*, *paccaya*.

SOURCE NOTE: not found, or not found in this form or meaning, in the oldest parts of the Sutta Piṭaka. see *paccaya* 2.

ārammaṇādhipati, **ārammaṇupanissaya**: see *paccaya*.

āraññikaṅga: the 'exercise of the forest-dweller', is one of the ascetic purification-exercises (*dhutaṅga*, q.v.).

arising and vanishing (of things): the knowledge consisting in the contemplation of, see *visuddhi* (VI. 1.).

ariya-iddhi: see *iddhi*.

ariya-magga: see *ariya-puggala*.

ariya-puggala, or simply **ariya**: 'Noble Ones', 'noble persons'.

(A)

The eight ~ are those who have realised one of the eight stages of holiness, i.e., the four supermundane paths (*magga*) and the four supermundane fruitions (*phala*) of these paths. There are four pairs:

1(a) The one realising the path of stream-winning (*sotāpattimagga*).
1(b) The one realising the fruition of stream-winning (*sotāpattiphala*).

2(a) The one realising the path of once-return (*sakadāgāmimagga*).
2(b) The one realising the fruition of once-return (*sakadāgāmiphala*).

3(a) The one realising the path of non-return (*anāgāmīmagga*).
3(b) The one realising the fruition of non-return (*anāgāmīphala*).

4(a) The one realising the path of holiness (*arahatta-magga*).
4(b) The one realising the fruition of holiness (*arahatta-phala*).

Summed up, there are four noble individuals (*ariya-puggala*): the stream-winner (*sotāpanna*), the once-returner (*sakadāgāmi*), the non-returner (*anāgāmī*), the holy one (*arahat*).

In A. VIII, 10 and A. IX, 16 the *gotrabhū* (q.v.) is listed as the ninth noble individual.

According to the Abhidhamma, 'supermundane path', or simply 'path' (*magga*), is a designation of the moment of entering into one of the four stages of holiness—Nibbāna being the object—produced by intuitional insight (*vipassanā*) into the impermanence, misery and impersonality of existence, flashing forth and forever transforming one's life and nature. By 'fruition' (*phala*) is meant those moments of consciousness which follow immediately thereafter as the result of the path, and which in certain circumstances may repeat for innumerable times during the lifetime.

(I) Through the path of stream-winning (*sotāpattimagga*) one 'becomes' free (whereas in realising the fruition, one 'is' free) from the first three fetters (*saṃyojana*, q.v.) which bind beings to existence in the sensuous sphere, to wit: (1) personality-belief (*sakkāya-diṭṭhi*; see *diṭṭhi*), (2) sceptical doubt (*vicikicchā*, q.v.), (3) attachment to mere rules and rituals (*sīlabbata-parāmāsa*; see *upādāna*).

(II) Through the path of once-return (*sakadāgāmimagga*) one becomes nearly free from the fourth and fifth fetters, to wit: (4) sensuous craving (*kāmacchanda* = *kāma-rāga*; see *rāga*), (5) ill will (*vyāpāda* = *dosa*, see *mūla*).

(III) Through the path of non-return (*anāgāmīmagga*) one becomes fully free from the above-mentioned five lower fetters.

(IV) Through the path of holiness (*arahattamagga*) one further becomes free from the five higher fetters, to wit: (6) craving for fine material existence (*rūpa-rāga*), (7) craving for immaterial existence. (*arūpa-rāga*), (8) conceit (*māna*, q.v.), (9) restlessness (*uddhacca*, q.v.), (10) ignorance (*avijjā*, q.v.).

The stereotype sutta text runs as follows:

(I) "After the disappearance of the three fetters, the monk has won the stream (to Nibbāna) and is no more subject to rebirth in lower worlds, is firmly established, destined for full enlightenment.

(II) "After the disappearance of the three fetters and reduction of greed, hatred and delusion, he will return only once more; and having once more returned to this world, he will put an end to suffering.

(III) "After the disappearance of the five fetters he appears in a higher world, and there he reaches Nibbāna without ever returning from that world (to the sensuous sphere). (IV) "Through the extinction of all cankers (*āsavakkhaya*) he reaches already in this very life the deliverance of mind, the deliverance through wisdom, which is free from cankers, and which he himself has understood and realised." For the various classes of stream-winners and non-returners, see *sotāpanna*, *anāgāmī*.

(B)

The sevenfold grouping of the noble disciples is defined and explained in VISM. XXI, 73 as follows:

(1) the faith-devotee (*saddhānusārī*): "He who is filled with resolution (*adhimokkha*) and, in considering the formations as impermanent (*anicca*), gains the faculty of faith, he, at the moment of the path to stream-winning (A. 1) is called a faith-devotee (*saddhānusārī*)";

(2) the faith-liberated one (*saddhāvimutta*): "At the seven higher stages (A. 2–8) he is called a faith-liberated one";

(3) the body-witness (*kāya-sakkhī*): "He who is filled with tranquillity and, in considering the formations as miserable (*dukkha*), gains the faculty of concentration, he in every respect is considered as a body-witness";

(4) the both-ways-liberated one (*ubhato-bhāga-vimutta*): "He, however, who after reaching the absorptions of the immaterial sphere has attained the highest fruition (of holiness), he is a both-ways-liberated one";

(5) the Dhamma-devotee (*dhammānusārī*), "He who is filled with wisdom and, in considering the formations as non-self (*anatta*), gains the faculty of wisdom, he is at the moment of stream-winning a Dhamma-devotee";

(6) the vision-attainer (*diṭṭhippatta*), "At the later stages (A. 2–7) a vision-attainer";

(7) the wisdom-liberated one (*paññā-vimutta*). "At the highest stage (A. 8) a wisdom-liberated one (*paññāvimutta*)".

Further details about the body-witness, the both-ways-liberated one, and the wisdom-liberated one, see under the three Pali terms. Cf. also M. 70; A. IX, 44; S. XII, 70; PTS.M. II, p. 33, PTS.

ariya-sacca: the Four 'Noble Truths', see *sacca*.

ariya-vaṃsa: the four 'noble usages' of the monk; contentedness with any robe, contentedness with any alms-food, contentedness with any dwelling, and delight in meditation and detachment. In the Ariyavaṃsa Sutta, (A. IV, 28) and similarly in D. 33, it is said:

"Now the monk is contented with any robe, with any alms-food, with any dwelling, finds pleasure and enjoyment in mental training and detachment. But neither is he haughty on that account, nor does he look down upon others. Now, of a monk who herein is fit and indefatigable, who remains clearly conscious and mindful, of such a monk it is said that he is firmly established in the ancient, noble usages known as the most lofty ones." Full tr. of Ariyavaṃsa Sutta in WHEEL 83/84.

ariya-vihāra: see *vihāra*.

arūpa-bhava: see *bhava, loka*.

arūpajjhāna: see *jhāna*.

arūpakkhandha: the four 'immaterial groups' of existence are feeling, perception, mental formations, and consciousness; see *khandha*.

arūpāvacara: see *avacara*.

āruppa: see *jhāna*.

asaṅkhāra-parinibbāyī: the 'one reaching Nibbāna without exertion'; one of the five classes of non-returners (*anāgāmī*, q.v.).

asaṅkhārika-citta: an Abhidhamma term signifying a 'state of consciousness arisen spontaneously', i.e., without previous deliberation, preparation, or prompting by others; hence 'unprepared, unprompted'. This term and its counterpart (*sasaṅkhārikacitta*, q.v.), probably go back to a similar distinction made in the suttas (A. IV, 171; P. TO D. 184). See TAB. I; examples in VISM. XIV, 84ff.

asaṅkhata: the 'unformed, unoriginated, or unconditioned' is a name for Nibbāna, the beyond of all becoming and conditionality.

Asañña-satta: 'unconscious beings', a class of heavenly beings in the fine-material world; see *deva* (II). "There are, O monks, heavenly beings known as the unconscious ones. As soon, however, as in those beings consciousness arises, those beings will vanish from that world. Now, O monks, it may happen that one of those beings after vanishing from that world, may reappear in this world. ... " (D. 24). Further details, see KATH., YAM. (GUIDE, 68, 79, 96ff.).

āsava: (lit: influxes), 'cankers', taints, corruptions, intoxicant biases. There is a list of four (as in D. 16, PTS.M., VIBH.): the canker of sense-desire (*kāmāsava*), of (desiring eternal) existence (*bhavāsava*), of (wrong) views (*diṭṭhāsava*), and of ignorance (*avijjāsava*). A list of *three*, omitting the canker of views, is possibly older and is more frequent in the suttas, e.g. in M. 2, M. 9, D. 33; A. III, 59, 67; A. VI, 63. In VIBH. (Khuddakavatthu VIBH.) both the threefold and fourfold division are mentioned. The fourfold division also occurs under the name of 'floods' (*ogha*) and 'yokes' (*yoga*).

Through the path of stream-entry, the canker of views is destroyed; through the path of non-returning, the canker of sense-desire; through the path of arahatship, the cankers of existence and ignorance. M. 2 shows how to overcome the cankers, namely, through insight, sense-control, avoidance, wise use of the necessities of life, etc. For a commentarial exposition, see ASL.TR. I, 63ff., II, 475ff.

Khīṇāsava, 'one whose cankers are destroyed', or 'one who is canker-free', is a name for the arahat or holy one. The state of arahatship is frequently called *āsavakkhaya*, 'the destruction of the cankers'. Suttas concluding with the attainment of arahatship by the listeners, often end with the words, "During this utterance, the hearts of the Bhikkhus were freed from the cankers through clinging no more" (*anupādāya āsavehi cittāni vimuccimsū'ti*).

āsavakkhaya: see *āsava*.

ascending insight: see *vuṭṭhāna-gāminī-vipassanā*.

ascetic purification practices: see *dhutaṅga*.

asekha: (lit.: 'non-learner'; see *sekha*), a disciple 'perfected in training', one beyond training, an adept. This is a name for the arahat, the holy one (see *ariya-puggala*), since he has reached the perfection in higher moral training, higher mind training and higher wisdom training (see *sikkhā*) and needs no longer to train himself therein.

āsevana-paccaya: 'repetition', is one of the twenty-four conditions (*paccaya*, q.v.).

asmi-māna: (lit.: 'I am'-conceit), 'ego-conceit', may range from the coarsest pride and self-assertion to a subtle feeling of one's distinctiveness or superiority that persists, as the eighth fetter (*saṃyojana*, q.v.), until the attainment of arahatship or holiness. It is based upon the comparison of oneself with others, and may, therefore, manifest itself also as a feeling of inferiority or the claim to be equal (see *māna*). It has to be distinguished from 'ego-belief' (*sakkāya-diṭṭhi*, q.v.) which implies a definite belief or view (*diṭṭhi*) concerning the assumption of a self or soul, and, being the first of the fetters, disappears at attainment of stream-entry (*sotāpatti*; see *ariya-puggala*).

"Even when the five lower fetters have vanished in a noble disciple, there is still in him, with regard to the five groups of clinging, a slight undiscarded measure of the conceit 'I am', of the will 'I am', of the proclivity 'I am'" (S. XXII, 89). see *māna*.

assāsa-passāsa: 'in-and-out-breathing', are corporeal or physical functions or 'formations' (*kāya-saṅkhāra*), while thought-conception and discursive thinking (*vitakka* and *vicāra*) are called verbal functions (*vacīsaṅkhāra*), see *saṅkhāra* (2). In-and-out-breathing forms one of the six aspects of the wind-element (see *dhātu*). Cf. M. 62.

association: *sampayutta-paccaya*, is one of the twenty-four conditions (*paccaya*, q.v.).

asubha: 'impurity', loathsomeness, foulness. In VISM. VI, it is the cemetery contemplations (*sīvathika*, q.v.) that are called 'meditation-subjects of impurity' (*asubha-kammaṭṭhāna*; see *bhāvanā*). In the Girimānanda Sutta (A. X., 50), however, the perception of impurity (*asubha-saññā*) refers to the contemplation of the thirty-two parts of the body (see *kāya-gatā-sati*). The contemplation of the body's impurity is an antidote against the hindrance of sense-desire (see *nīvaraṇa*) and the mental perversion (*vipallāsa*, q.v.) which sees what is truly impure as pure and beautiful. See S. XLVI, 51; A. V. 36, DHP. 7, 8; SN. 193ff., also *The Five Mental Hindrances* (WHEEL 26), 5ff.

asura: 'demons', titans, evil ghosts, inhabiting one of the lower worlds (*apāya*, q.v.).

Atappa: 'the unworried', is the name of a class of deities (see *deva*,) inhabiting the first of the five Pure Abodes (*suddhāvāsa*, q.v.), in which the *anāgāmī* (q.v.) has his last rebirth.

atimāna: 'superiority-conceit', see *māna*.

attā: 'self, ego, personality, is in Buddhism a mere conventional expression (*vohāra-desanā*), and no designation for anything really existing; see *paramattha-desanā*, *anatta*, *puggala*, *satta*, *jīva*.

attachments: see *parāmāsa*.

atta-diṭṭhi (-*vāda*): 'ego-belief', 'personality-belief', see *diṭṭhi*.

attainment-concentration: *appanā-samādhi* (q.v.); see *samādhi*.

attainments, the eight: see *samāpatti*.

atta-kilamatha: 'self-mortification', is one of the two extremes to be avoided, the other extreme being addiction to sensual pleasures (*kāma-sukha*), while the Noble Eightfold Path constitutes the Middle Path (*majjhimā paṭipadā*, q.v.). See the Buddha's first sermon, "The Establishment of the Realm of Dhamma" (Dhammacakkappavattana Sutta).

atta-saññā (~*citta*, ~*diṭṭhi*): 'perception (consciousness, view) of an ego', is one of the four perversions (*vipallāsa*, q.v.).

atta-vādupādāna: 'attachment to the ego-belief', is one of the four kinds of clinging (*upādāna*, q.v.).

attention: see *manasikāra*, *sati*.

attentiveness, attention, mindfulness: see *sati*, *satipaṭṭhāna*.

aṭṭhaṅgika-magga: the 'Eightfold Path', see *magga*.

attha-paṭisambhidā: the 'analytical knowledge of meaning', is one of the four kinds of analytical knowledge (*paṭisambhidā*, q.v.).

atthi-paccaya: 'presence', is one of the twenty-four conditions (*paccaya*, q.v.).

auditory organ: see *āyatana*.

avacara: 'sphere', realm. The three spheres of existence are the sensuous sphere (*kāmāvacara*), the fine material sphere (*rūpāvacara*), and the immaterial sphere (*arūpāvacara*).

"Which things are of the sensuous sphere (*kāmāvacara*)? Whatever things exist within the interval bounded beneath by the *Avīci*-hell and above by the *Paranimmitavasavatti*-heaven (see *deva*), having therein their sphere, and being therein included, to wit: the groups of existence, the elements, bases (see *khandha*, *dhātu*, *āyatana*), corporeality, feeling, perception, mental formations and consciousness, all these things are of the sensuous sphere.

"But which things are of the fine material sphere (*rūpāvacara*)? Whatever things exist within the interval bounded beneath by the Brahma-world and above by the *Akaniṭṭha*-world (see *deva*), having therein their sphere, and being therein included … and also consciousness and mental factors in one who has entered the (fine-material) absorptions, or who has been reborn in that sphere, or who already during his lifetime is living in happiness (of the absorptions), all these things are of the fine-material sphere.

"Which things are of the immaterial sphere (*arūpāvacara*)? Consciousness and mental factors arising within the interval bounded beneath by the beings reborn in the sphere of unbounded space and above by the beings reborn in the sphere of neither-perception-nor-non-perception (see *jhāna* 5–8), and consciousness and mental factors in one who has entered the (immaterial absorptions), or who has been reborn in that sphere, or who already during his lifetime is living in happiness (of the immaterial absorptions), all these things are of the immaterial sphere." (Cf. DHS. 1280, 1282, 1284; VIBH. XVIII).

SOURCE NOTE: *kāmāvacara* is already met with in the oldest sutta texts (e.g. D. 1). *Rūpāvacara* and *arūpāvacara*, however, occur probably for the first time in PTS.M. (I. 83ff.), while in the ABH. canon and the com. all the three terms are frequently mentioned and explained.

āvajjana: 'advertence' of the mind towards the object, forms the first stage in the process of consciousness (see *viññāṇa-kicca*). If an object of the five physical senses is concerned, it is called 'five-door advertence' (*pañca-dvārāvajjana*); in the case of a mental object, 'mind-door advertence' (*mano-dvārāvajjana*).

SOURCE NOTE: not found, or not found in this form or meaning, in the oldest parts of the Sutta Piṭaka, see *citta-vīthi*.

aversion (from existence), contemplation of: see *vipassanā* (VI. 5)

avīci: the name of one of the most frightful hells (*niraya*, q.v.).

avigata-paccaya: 'non-disappearance', is one of the twenty-four conditions (*paccaya*, q.v.).

Aviha: (derivation uncertain; SKR. *avṛha*) is one of the five Pure Abodes (*suddhāvāsa*, q.v.) in the fine-material sphere. For details, see under *anāgāmī*.

avihiṃsā (equivalents: *ahiṃsā*, *avihesā*): 'harmlessness', non-violence, absence of cruelty. The 'thought of harmlessness' (or: 'non-cruelty'; *avihiṃsā-vitakka*) is one of the three constituents of right thought (*sammā-saṅkappa*), i.e., the second factor of the Eightfold Path (see *magga*). In the several lists of 'elements' (*dhātu*) appears also an 'element of harmlessness' (*avihesādhātu*), in the sense of an elementary quality of noble thought. See DHP. 225, 261, 270, 300.

avijjā: 'ignorance,' nescience, unknowing; synonymous with delusion (*moha*, see *mūla*), is the primary root of all evil and suffering in the world, veiling man's mental eyes and preventing him from seeing the true nature of things. It is the delusion tricking beings by making life appear to them as permanent, happy, substantial and beautiful and preventing them from seeing that everything in reality is impermanent, liable to suffering, void of 'I' and 'mine', and basically impure (see *vipallāsa*). Ignorance is defined as 'not knowing the Four Truths, namely, suffering, its origin, its cessation, and the way to its cessation' (S. XII, 4).

As ignorance is the foundation of all life-affirming actions, of all evil and suffering, therefore it stands first in the formula of Dependent Origination (*paṭiccasamuppāda*, q.v.). But for that reason, says VISM. (XVII, 36ff.) ignorance should not be regarded as "the causeless root-cause of the world. … It is not causeless. For a cause of it is stated thus 'With the arising of cankers (*āsava*, q.v.) there is the arising of ignorance' (M. 9). But there is a figurative way in which it can be treated as a root-cause; namely, when it is made to serve as a starting point in an exposition of the Round of Existence. … As it is said: 'No first beginning of ignorance can be perceived, Bhikkhus, before which ignorance was not, and after which it came to be. But it can be perceived that ignorance has its specific condition (*idappaccaya*)" (A. X, 61). The same statement is made (A. X, 62) about the craving for existence (*bhava-taṇhā*; see *taṇhā*). The latter and ignorance are called "the outstanding causes of *kamma* that lead to unhappy and happy destinies" (VISM. XVII, 38).

As ignorance still exists—though in a very refined way until the attainment of arahatship or holiness—it is counted as the last of the ten fetters (*saṃyojana*, q.v.) which bind beings to the cycle of rebirths. As the first two roots of evil, greed and hate (see *mūla*), are on their part rooted in ignorance, consequently all unwholesome states of mind are inseparably bound up with it. Ignorance (or delusion) is the most obstinate of the three roots of evil.

Ignorance is one of the cankers (*āsava*, q.v.) and proclivities (*anusaya*, q.v.). It is often called a hindrance (*nīvaraṇa*; e.g. in S.XV, 3; A.X, 61) but does not appear together with the usual list of five hindrances.

avikkhepa: 'undistractedness', is a synonym of concentration (*samādhi*, q.v.), one-pointedness of mind (*citt'ekaggatā*) and tranquillity (*samatha*, q.v.; further see *samatha-vipassanā*).

avoidance and performance: see *cāritta*, etc. The effort to avoid, see *padhāna*.

avyākata: lit. 'indeterminate'—i.e., neither determined as karmically 'wholesome' nor as 'unwholesome'—are the karmically neutral, i.e., amoral, states of consciousness and mental factors. They are either mere karma results (*vipāka*, q.v.), as e.g. all the sense perceptions and the mental factors associated therewith, or they are karmically independent functions (*kiriya-citta*, q.v.), i.e., neither karmic nor karma resultant. See TAB. I.

SOURCE NOTE: this term in the sense of 'amoral' or 'karmically neutral', does not occur in the old sutta texts, while it is found in PTS.M. (e.g. I, 79ff.). It plays an important role in the ABH. canon (e.g. DHS.) and the philosophical commentaries.

avyāpāda: 'hatelessness', non-ill will, goodness; is one of the three kinds of right thought (see *sacca*, IV. 2), or wholesome thoughts (*vitakka*, q.v.) and is the ninth of the ten wholesome courses of actions (*kamma-patha* II. q.v.). The most frequently used synonyms are *adosa* (see *mūla*) and *mettā* (see *brahma-vihāra*).

awakenment: see *bodhi*.

āyatana: 1. 'spheres', is a name for the four immaterial absorptions; see *jhāna* (5-8).

2. The twelve 'bases' or 'sources' on which depend the mental processes, consist of five physical sense organs and consciousness, being the six personal (*ajjhattika*) bases; and the six objects, the so-called external (*bāhira*) bases, namely:

eye, or visual organ	visible object
ear, or auditory organ	sound, or audible object
nose, or olfactory organ	odour, or olfactive object
tongue, or gustatory organ	taste, or gustative object
body, or tactile organ	body-impression, or tactile object
mind-base, or consciousness (*manāyatana*)	mind-object (*dhammāyatana*)

"By the visual organ (*cakkhāyatana*) is meant the sensitive part of the eye (*cakkhu-pasāda*) built up of the four elements ... responding to sense-stimuli" (*sa-ppaṭigha*). ... (VIBH. II). Similar is the explanation of the four remaining physical sense organs.

Mind-base (*manāyatana* q.v.) is a collective term for all consciousness whatever, and should therefore not be confounded with the mind-element (*mano-dhātu*; see *dhātu* II, 16), which latter performs only the functions of adverting (*āvajjana*) to the sense-object, and of receiving (*sampaṭicchana*) the sense-object. On the functions of the mind, see *viññāṇa-kicca*.

The visible object (*rūpāyatana*) is described in VIBH. II as "that phenomenon which is built up of the four physical elements and appears as colour, etc." What is seen by visual perception, i.e., by eye-consciousness (*cakkhu-*

viññāṇa) are colours and differences of light, but not three-dimensional bodily things.

'Mind-object-base' (*dhammāyatana*) is identical with 'mind-object-element' (*dhamma-dhātu*; see *dhātu* II) and *dhammārammaṇa* (see *ārammaṇa*). It may be physical or mental, past, present or future, real or imaginary.

The five physical sense organs are also called faculties (*indriya*, q.v.), and of these faculties it is said in M. 43: "Each of the five faculties owns a different sphere, and none of them partakes of the sphere of another one; ... they have mind as their support ... are conditioned by vitality, ... but vitality again is conditioned by heat, heat again by vitality, just as the light and flame of a burning lamp are mutually conditioned."

The twelve bases are fully discussed in VISM. XV. In YAM. III (see GUIDE, 98ff.) the twelve terms are subjected to a logical investigation The six personal bases form the fifth link of dependent origination (*paṭicca-samuppāda* 5, q.v.).

āyūhana: (karmic) 'accumulation', is a name used in the commentarial literature for the wholesome and unwholesome volitional activities (karma, q.v.) or karma-formations (*saṅkhāra*; see *paṭicca-samuppāda*), being the bases of future rebirth. "'Accumulation', is a name for the karma-formations, and signifies those volitions (*cetanā*) which arise at the performance of a karma, first while thinking 'I will give alms', and then while actually giving alms (e.g.) for one month or a year. The volition, however, at the time when one is handing the alms over to the recipient; is called karma-process (*kamma-bhava*, see VISM. XVII, IX, X).

Or, the volitions during the first six impulsive-moments (*javana*, q.v.) depending on one and the same state of advertence (*āvajjana*, see *viññāṇa-kicca*), these are called the karma-formations, while the seventh impulsive moment is called the karma-process (*kamma-bhava*). ...

Or, each volition is called 'karma-process' and the accumulation connected with it, 'karma-formation'." (VISM. XVII). Cf. *paṭicca-samuppāda* (2, 10).

SOURCE NOTE: probably met with for the first time in PTS.M. (I, 10ff.).

B

B

bahula-kamma: 'habitual karma', see *karma*.

bala: 'powers'. Among various groups of powers the following five are most frequently met with in the texts: (1) faith (*saddhā*, q.v.), (2) energy (*viriya*, q.v.), (3) mindfulness (*sati*, q.v.), (4) concentration (*samādhi*, q.v.), (5) wisdom (*paññā*, q.v.).

Their particular aspect, distinguishing them from the corresponding five spiritual faculties (*indriya*, q.v.), is that they are unshakeable by their opposites: (1) the power of faith is unshakeable by faithlessness (unbelief); (2) energy, by laziness; (3) mindfulness, by forgetfulness; (4) concentration, by distractedness; (5) wisdom, by ignorance (see PTS.M., Ñāṇa-kathā). They represent, therefore, the aspect of firmness in the spiritual faculties.

According to A.V. 15, the power (1) becomes manifest in the four qualities of the stream-winner (*sotāpannassa aṅgāni*, q.v.), (2) in the four right efforts (see *padhāna*), (3) in the four foundations of mindfulness (*satipaṭṭhāna*, q.v.), (4) in the four absorptions (*jhāna*, q.v.), (5) in the (full comprehension of the) Four Noble Truths (*sacca*, q.v.). Cf. S. XLVIII, 43; S. L. (Bala Saṃyutta).

In A. VII, 3, the powers of moral shame (*hiri*, q.v.) and moral dread (*ottappa*) are added to the aforementioned five. Several other groups of two (see *paṭisaṅkhāna-bala*), four, five and more powers are mentioned in the texts. About the ten powers of a Buddha, see *dasa-bala*.

balance of mental faculties: *indriya samatta* (q.v.).

bases, the twelve of the perceptual process: *āyatana* (q.v.).

beautiful: *sobhana* (q.v.).

beauty, deliverance through the perception of: cf. *vimokkha* (II. 3). To hold for beautiful or pure (*subha*) what is impure (*asubha*), is one of the four perversions (see *vipallāsa*).

behaviour, morality consisting in good: *abhisamācārika-sīla* (q.v.).

being, living: *satta* (q.v.); further see *puggala*. Belief in eternal personality: *bhava-diṭṭhi* (see *diṭṭhi*), *sassata-diṭṭhi* (q.v.).

beings, the nine worlds of: *sattāvāsa* (q.v.).

belief, blind: see *indriya-samatta*.

bhaṅgānupassanā-ñāṇa: 'knowledge consisting in contemplation of dissolution' (of all forms of existence), is one kind of insight; see *visuddhi* (VI, 2).

bhava: 'becoming', 'process of existence', consists of three planes, sensuous existence (*kāma-bhava*), fine-material existence (*rūpa-bhava*), and immaterial existence (*arūpa-bhava*). Cf. *loka*. The whole process of existence may be divided into two aspects:

(1) Karma-process (*kamma-bhava*), i.e., the karmically active side of existence, being the cause of rebirth and consisting in wholesome and unwholesome volitional actions. See *karma*, *paṭicca-samuppāda* (IX).

(2) Karma-produced rebirth, or regenerating process (*uppatti-bhava*), i.e., the karmically passive side of existence consisting in the arising and developing of the karma-produced and therefore morally neutral mental and bodily phenomena of existence. Cf. TAB.

SOURCE NOTE: the twofold division, *kamma* and *uppapatti*, is probably found for the first time in VIBH. of the ABH. canon, but it expresses throughout the genuine teaching of the suttas.

bhāva: (feminine and masculine) 'nature', refers to the sexual characteristics of the body, and belongs to the group of corporeality (see *khandha*). It is a commentarial term for the faculties of femininity and masculinity (see *indriya* 7, 8).

SOURCE NOTE: as an isolated word, signifying the physical nature or faculties of sex, probably occurs only in the com. The expression *itthibhāva* and *purisabhāva*, with the meaning of 'being a man', or 'being a woman', or after *ñatvā*, etc., as for instance *tassā itthibhāvaṃ ñatvā*, 'knowing her to be a woman': such expressions are often found in the oldest sutta texts.

bhava-diṭṭhi: 'belief in being' (eternal personality); see *sassata-diṭṭhi*, *diṭṭhi*.

bhāvanā: 'mental development' (lit. 'calling into existence, producing') is what in English is generally but rather vaguely called 'meditation'. One has to distinguish two kinds: development of tranquillity (*samatha-bhāvanā*), i.e., concentration (*samādhi*), and development of insight (*vipassanā-bhāvanā*), i.e., wisdom (*paññā*).

These two important terms, tranquillity and insight (see *samatha-vipassanā*), are very often met with and explained in the suttas, as well as in the ABH.

Tranquillity (*samatha*) is the concentrated, unshaken, peaceful, and therefore undefiled state of mind, while insight (*vipassanā*) is the intuitive insight into the impermanence, misery and impersonality (*anicca, dukkha, anatta*; see *tilakkhaṇa*) of all bodily and mental phenomena of existence, included in the five groups of existence, namely, corporeality, feeling, perception, mental formations and consciousness; see *khandha*.

Tranquillity, or concentration of mind, according to *Saṅkhepavaṇṇana* (Commentary to *Abhidhammattha Saṅgaha*), bestows a threefold blessing: favourable rebirth, present happy life, and purity of mind which is the condition of insight. Concentration (*samādhi*) is the indispensable foundation and precondition of insight by purifying the mind from the five mental defilements or hindrances (*nīvaraṇa*, q.v.), while insight (*vipassanā*) produces the four supra mundane stages of holiness and deliverance of mind. The Buddha therefore says: "May you develop mental concentration, O monks; for who is mentally concentrated, sees things according to reality" (S. XXII, 5). And in MIL. it is said: "Just as when a lighted lamp is brought into a dark chamber, the lamp-light will destroy the darkness and produce and spread the light, just so will insight, once arisen, destroy the darkness of ignorance and produce the light of knowledge."

VISM. III-XI gives full directions how to attain full concentration and the absorptions (*jhāna*, q.v.) by means of the following forty meditation subjects (*kammaṭṭhāna*):

- Ten kasina-exercises (see *kasiṇa*). These produce the four absorptions.
- Ten loathsome subjects (*asubha*, q.v.). These produce the first absorption.
- Ten recollections (*anussati*, q.v.): of the Buddha (*buddhānussati*), the Doctrine (*dhammānussati*), the Brotherhood of the Noble Ones (*saṅghānussati*), morality, liberality, the heavenly beings, death (*maraṇasati*, q.v.), the body (*kāyagatāsati*, q.v.), in-and-out breathing (*ānāpāna-sati*, q.v.) and peace (*upasamānussati*, q.v.). Among these, the recollection (or mindfulness) of in-and-out breathing may produce all the four absorptions, that of the body the first absorption, the rest only neighbourhood-concentration (*upacāra-samādhi*, see *samādhi*).
- Four sublime abodes (*brahma-vihāra*, q.v.): loving kindness, compassion, altruistic joy, equanimity (*mettā, karuṇā, muditā, upekkhā*). Of these, the first three exercises may produce three absorptions, the last one the fourth absorption only.
- Four immaterial spheres (*arūpāyatana*, see *jhāna*): of unbounded space, unbounded consciousness, nothingness, neither-perception-nor-non-perception. These are based upon the fourth absorption.

- One perception of the loathsomeness of food (*āhāre paṭikkūla-saññā*), which may produce neighbourhood concentration.
- One analysis of the four elements (*catudhātu-vavatthāna*, see *dhātu-vavatthāna*), which may produce neighbourhood-concentration.

Mental development forms one of the three kinds of meritorious action (*puñña-kiriya-vatthu*, q.v.). 'Delight in meditation' (*bhāvanā-rāmatā*) is one of the noble usages (*ariya-vaṃsa*, q.v.).

B

bhāvanā-bala: see *paṭisaṅkhāna-bala*.

bhāvanā-maya-paññā: wisdom based on mental development', see *paññā*.

bhavaṅga-santāna: 'continuity of subconsciousness', see *santāna*.

bhavaṅga-sota and **bhavaṅga-citta**: the first term may tentatively be rendered as the 'undercurrent forming the condition of being, or existence', and the second as 'subconsciousness', though, as will be evident from the following, it differs in several respects from the usage of that term in Western psychology. *Bhavaṅga* (*bhava-aṅga*), which, in the canonical works, is mentioned twice or thrice in the *Paṭṭhāna*, is explained in the Abhidhamma commentaries as the foundation or condition (*kāraṇa*) of existence (*bhava*), as the *sine qua non* of life, having the nature of a process, lit. a flux or stream (*sota*). Herein, since time immemorial, all impressions and experiences are, as it were, stored up, or better said, are functioning, but concealed as such to full consciousness, from where however they occasionally emerge as subconscious phenomena and approach the threshold of full consciousness, or crossing it become fully conscious. This so-called 'subconscious life-stream' or undercurrent of life is that by which might be explained the faculty of memory, paranormal psychic phenomena, mental and physical growth, karma and rebirth. etc. An alternative rendering is 'life-continuum'.

It should be noted that *bhavaṅga-citta* is a karma resultant state of consciousness (*vipāka*, q.v.), and that, in birth as a human or in higher forms of existence, it is always the result of good, or wholesome karma (*kusala-kamma-vipāka*), though in varying degrees of strength (see *paṭisandhi*, end of the article). The same holds true for rebirth-consciousness (*paṭisandhi*) and death consciousness (*cuti*), which are only particular manifestations of subconsciousness. In VISM. XIV it is said:

"As soon as rebirth-consciousness (in the embryo at the time of conception) has ceased, there arises a similar subconsciousness with exactly the same object, following immediately upon rebirth-consciousness and being the result of this or that karma (volitional action done in a former birth and remembered there at the moment before death). And again a further similar state of subconsciousness arises. Now, as long as no other consciousness arises to interrupt the continuity of the life-stream, so long the life-stream, like the flow of a river, rises in the same way again and again, even during dreamless sleep and at other times. In this way one has to understand the continuous arising of those states of consciousness in the life-stream." Cf. *viññāṇa-kicca*. For more details, see FUND. 11.

SOURCE NOTE: these two compound terms belong exclusively to the exegetical literature, while the term *bhavaṅga* is several times, briefly and unexplained, mentioned in the PATTH. of the ABH. canon, as though already known at that time.

bhava-taṇhā: 'craving for (eternal) existence', see *taṇhā*.

bhavāsava: 'canker of existence', see *āsava*.

bhayatupaṭṭhāna-ñāṇa: 'knowledge consisting in the awareness of terror', is one of those kinds of insight-knowledge that form the 'purification by knowledge and vision of the path-progress' (see *visuddhi*, VI.).

bhikkhu: a fully ordained disciple of the Buddha. "Mendicant monk" may be suggested as the closest equivalent for "bhikkhu"; literally it means "he who begs" but bhikkhus do not beg. They silently stand at the door for alms. They live on what is spontaneously given by the supporters. He is not a priest as he is no mediator between God and man. He has no vows for life, but he is bound by his rules which he takes of his own accord. He leads a life of voluntary poverty and celibacy. If he is unable to live the holy life, he can discard the robe at any time.

bhojane mattaññutā: 'knowing the measure in eating'.

"Now, O monks, the monk wisely reflecting partakes of his alms-food, neither for pastime, nor for indulgence, nor to become beautiful or handsome, but only to maintain and support this body, to avoid harm and to assist the holy life, knowing: 'In this way I shall dispel the former pain (of hunger, etc.) and no new pain shall I let arise, and long life, blamelessness and ease will be my share.' This, O monks, is knowing the measure in eating." (A. III. 16). "How O monks, would it be possible for Nanda to lead the absolutely pure life of holiness, if he did not watch over his senses and did not know the measure in eating?" (A. VII, 9).

biases: see *āsava*.

birth process: *upapatti-bhava*, see bhava; Cf. *paṭisandhi*, *jāti*.

bodhi (from verbal root *budhi*, to awaken, to understand): awakenment, enlightenment, supreme knowledge. "[Through *bodhi*] one awakens from the slumber or stupor (inflicted upon the mind) by the defilements (*kilesa*, q.v.) and comprehends the Four Noble Truths (*sacca*, q.v.)" (com. to M. 10).

The enlightenment of a Buddha is called *sammāsambodhi* (q.v.) 'perfect enlightenment'. The faith (*saddhā*, q.v.) of a lay follower of the Buddha is described as "he believes in the enlightenment of the Perfect One" (*saddahati Tathāgatassa bodhiṃ*: M. 53, A. III, 2).

As components of the state of enlightenment and contributory factors to its achievement, are mentioned in the texts: the seven factors of enlightenment (*bojjhaṅga* (q.v.) = *bodhi-aṅga*) and the thirty-seven 'things pertaining to enlightenment' (*bodhipakkhiya-dhammā*, q.v.). In one of the later books of the Sutta-Piṭaka, the Buddhavaṃsa, ten *bodhipācana-dhammā* are mentioned, i.e., qualities that lead to the ripening of perfect enlightenment; these are the ten perfections (*pāramī*, q.v.).

There is a threefold classification of enlightenment: (1) that of a noble disciple (*sāvaka-bodhi*, q.v.). i.e., of an arahat; (2) of an independently enlightened one (*pacceka-bodhi*, q.v.); and (3) of a perfect enlightened one (*sammā-sambodhi*). This threefold division, however, is of later origin, and in this form it neither occurs in the canonical texts nor in the older sutta commentaries. The closest approximation to it is found in a verse sutta which is probably of a comparatively later period, the Treasure Store Sutta (Nidhikkanda Sutta) of the Khuddakapāṭha, where the following three terms are mentioned in stanza 15: *sāvaka-pāramī*, *pacceka-bodhi*, *buddha-bhūmi* (see KHP. TR., 247ff.).

The commentaries (e.g. to M., Buddhavaṃsa, Cariyapiṭaka) generally give a fourfold explanation of the word *bodhi*: (1) the tree of enlightenment, (2) the holy path (*ariya-magga*), (3) Nibbāna, and (4) omniscience (of the Buddha: *sabbaññutā-ñāṇa*). As to (2), the commentaries quote Cula-Nidesa where *bodhi* is defined as the knowledge relating to the four paths (of stream-entry, etc.; *catūsu maggesu ñāṇa*).

Neither in the canonical texts nor in the old commentaries is it stated that a follower of the Buddha may choose between the three kinds of enlightenment and aspire either to become a buddha, a pacceka-buddha, or an arahat-disciple. This conception of a choice between three aspirations is, however, frequently found in present-day Theravāda countries, e.g. in Sri Lanka.

bodhipakkhiya-dhammā: the thirty-seven 'things pertaining to enlightenment', or 'requisites of enlightenment' comprise the entire doctrines of the Buddha. They are:

the four foundations of mindfulness (*satipaṭṭhāna*, q.v.),
the four right efforts (see *padhāna*),
the four roads to power (*iddhi-pāda*, q.v.),
the five spiritual faculties (*indriya*; see *bala*),
the five spiritual powers (*bala*, q.v.),
the seven factors of enlightenment (*bojjhaṅga*, q.v.),
the Noble Eightfold Path (see *magga*).

In M. 77 all the thirty-seven *bodhipakkhiya-dhammā* are enumerated and explained though not called by that name. A detailed explanation of them is given in VISM. XXII. In S.XLVII, 51, 67, only the five spiritual faculties (*indriya*) are called *bodhipakkhiya-dhammā*; and in the Jhāna Vibhaṅga, only the seven factors of enlightenment (*bojjhaṅga*).

See *The Requisites of Enlightenment*, by Ledi Sayadaw (WHEEL 169/172).

Bodhisatta: 'Enlightenment Being', is a being destined to Buddhahood, a future Buddha. According to the traditional belief a Bodhisatta, before reaching his last birth as a Buddha on this earth, is living in the Tusita heaven (see *deva*), the heaven of bliss. Cf. A. IV, 127; VIII, 70.

In the Pali canon and commentaries, the designation 'Bodhisatta' is given only to Prince Siddhattha before his enlightenment and to his former existences. The Buddha himself uses this term when speaking of his life prior to enlightenment (e.g. M. 4, M. 26). Bodhisattahood is neither mentioned nor recommended as an ideal higher than or alternative to arahatship; nor is there any record in the Pali scriptures of a disciple declaring it as his aspiration; see *bodhi*.

bodily action (wholesome or unwholesome): see *karma, karma formations*. Right ~: *sammā-kammanta*; see *magga*.

bodily postures, the four: *iriyā-patha* (q.v.)

body: *kāya* (q.v.) Contemplation on the ~ is one of the four *satipaṭṭhāna* (q.v.).

body-witness: *kāya-sakkhi* (q.v.).

bojjhaṅga: 'the seven factors of enlightenment', consist of mindfulness (*satisam~*; see *sati*), investigation of the law (*dhamma-vicaya-sam~*), energy (*viriyasam~*; see *viriya, padhāna*), rapture (*pītisam~*, q.v.) tranquillity (*passaddhisam~*, q.v.), concentration (*samādhisam~*, q.v.), and equanimity (*upekkhā*, q.v.). "Because they lead to enlightenment, therefore they are called factors of enlightenment" (S. XLVI, 5).

Though in the second factor, *dhamma-vicaya*, the word *dhamma* is taken by most translators to stand for the Buddhist doctrine, it probably refers to the bodily and mental phenomena (*nāma-rūpa-dhammā*) as presented to the investigating mind by mindfulness, the first factor. With that interpretation, the term may be rendered by 'investigation of phenomena'.

In A.X. 102, the seven factors are said to be the means of attaining the threefold wisdom (see *te-vijjā*).

They may be attained by means of the four foundations of mindfulness (*satipaṭṭhāna*, q.v.), as it is said in S. XLVI, 1 and explained in M. 118:

(1) "Whenever, O monks, the monk dwells contemplating the body (*kāya*), feeling (*vedanā*), mind (*citta*) and mind-objects (*dhammā*), strenuous, clearly conscious, mindful, after subduing worldly greed and grief, at such a time his mindfulness is present and undisturbed; and whenever his mindfulness is present and undisturbed, at such a time he has gained and is developing the factor of enlightenment 'mindfulness' (*sati-sambojjhaṅga*), and thus this factor of enlightenment reaches fullest perfection.

(2) "Whenever, while dwelling with mindfulness, he wisely investigates, examines and thinks over the law ... at such a time he has gained and is developing the factor of enlightenment 'investigation of the law' (*dhamma-vicaya~*). ...

(3) "Whenever, while wisely investigating his energy is firm and unshaken ... at such a time he has gained and is developing the factor of enlightenment 'energy' (*viriya~*). ...

(4) "Whenever in him, while firm in energy, arises supersensuous rapture ... at such a time he has gained and is developing the factor of enlightenment 'rapture' (*pīti~*). ...

(5) "Whenever, while enraptured in mind, his body and his mind become composed ... at such a time he has gained and is developing the factor of enlightenment 'tranquillity' (*passaddhi~*).

(6) "Whenever, while being composed in his body and happy, his mind becomes concentrated ... at such a time he has gained and is developing the factor of enlightenment 'concentration' (*samādhi~*).

(7) "Whenever he looks with complete indifference on his mind thus concentrated ... at such a time he has gained and is developing the factor of enlightenment 'equanimity' (*upekkhā*).

LITERATURE: Bojjhaṅga Saṃyutta (S. XLVI); Bojjhaṅga VIBH. For the conditions leading to the arising of each of the factors, see the com. to Satipaṭṭhāna Sutta (*Way of Mindfulness*, by Soma Thera; 3rd ed., 1967, BPS). Further, *The Seven Factors of Enlightenment*, by Piyadassi Thera (WHEEL 1.)

bondages, mental: *cetaso vinibandha* (q.v.).

bonds, the four: *yoga* (q.v.).

both-ways liberated: see *ubhato-bhāga-vimutta, ariya-puggala* B. 4.

boundless consciousness (and ~ space), sphere of: see *jhāna* 5, 6.

brahma-cariya: 'pure (chaste) or holy life', is a term for the life of the monk, and also the life of a lay-devotee who observes the eight moral precepts (*sikkhā-pada*, q.v.), takes as the third precept the vow of chastity, i.e., full abstention from sexual relations. The highest aim and purpose of ~ is, according to M. 29, the 'unshakeable deliverance of mind' (*akuppā ceto-vimutti*).

Brahma-kāyika-deva: the 'heavenly beings of the Brahma-world' inhabit the first three heavens of the fine-material world, (*rūpa-loka*), corresponding to the first absorption (*jhāna*, q.v.). The highest ruler of them is called the Great Brahma (*Mahā-Brahmā*). With caustic humour he is said (D. 11) to pretend: "I am Brahma, the Great Brahmā, the Most High, the Invincible One, the Omniscient One, the Ruler, the Lord, the Creator, the Maker, the Perfect One, the Preserver, the Controller, the Father of all that was and will be." Cf. *deva* (II, 1–3).

brahma-loka: 'Brahma-world', in the widest sense, is a name for the fine-material (*rūpa-loka*) and immaterial world (*arūpa-loka*); in a narrower sense, however, only for the first three heavens of the fine-material world. Cf. *Brahma-kāyika-deva*.

brahma-vihāra: the four 'sublime' or 'divine abodes'—also called the four boundless states (*appamaññā*)—are loving kindness (*mettā*), compassion (*karuṇā*), altruistic (or sympathetic) joy (*muditā*), and equanimity (*upekkhā*). The stereotype text on the development of these four sublime abodes (*brahma-vihāra-bhāvanā*; see *bhāvanā*), often met with in the suttas, is as follows:

"There, O monks, the monk with a mind full of loving kindness pervading first one direction, then a second one, then a third one, then the fourth one, just so above, below and all around; and everywhere identifying himself with all, he is pervading the whole world with mind full of loving kindness, with mind wide, developed, unbounded, free from hate and ill will." Hereafter follows the same theme with compassion, altruistic joy, and equanimity.

LITERATURE: detailed explanation in VISM. IX. For texts see P. TO D., 97ff.; texts on *mettā* in *The Practice of Loving Kindness*, by Ñāṇamoli Thera (WHEEL 7). *The Four Sublime States*, by Nyanaponika Thera (WHEEL 6). *Brahma Vihāra*, by Narada Thera (Vajirarama, Colombo, 1962).

breathing, mindfulness of in-and-out-breathing: *ānāpāna-sati* (q.v.).

Buddha: see *sammā-sambodhi*.

buddhānussati: 'recollection of the Enlightened One', see *anussati*.

Buddha-sāsana: see *sāsana*.

C

cāga: 'liberality', is one of the 'blessings' (see *sampadā*), 'foundations' (see *adhiṭṭhāna*), 'recollections' (see *anussati*), 'treasures' (see *dhana*).

cakka: 'wheel', is one of the seven 'precious possessions' (*ratana*) of a righteous World Emperor (*cakkavatti-rāja*: 'king who owns the wheel,' cf. D. 26), and symbolises conquering progress and expanding sovereignty. From that derives the figurative expression *dhamma-cakkaṃ pavatteti*, 'he sets rolling the Wheel of the Law' and the name of the Buddha's first sermon, Dhammacakkappavattana Sutta (see *dhamma-cakka*). Another figurative meaning of C. is 'blessing'. There are four such 'auspicious wheels' or 'blessings': living in a suitable locality, company of good people, meritorious acts done in the past, right inclinations (A. IV, 31). *Bhava-cakka*, 'wheel of existence', or of life, is a name for 'dependent origination' (see *paṭiccasamuppāda*).

See *The Buddhist Wheel Symbol*, by T.B. Karunaratne (WHEEL 137/138); *The Wheel of Birth* and *Death*, by Bhikkhu Khantipalo (WHEEL 147/149).

cakkh' āyatana: 'the base "visual organ"' (see *āyatana*).

cakkhu: 'eye' see *āyatana*. The following five kinds of 'eyes' are mentioned and explained in C.NID. (PTS, p. 235; the first three also in IT. 52): 1. the physical eye (*maṃsa* ~), 2. the divine eye (*dibba*-~ (*q.v.*); see *abhiññā*), 3. the eye of wisdom (*paññā*-~), 4. the eye of a Buddha (*Buddha*-~), 5. the eye of all-round knowledge (*samanta*-~; a frequent appellation of the Buddha).

cakkhu-dhātu: 'the element "visual organ"' (see *dhātu*).

cakkhu-viññāṇa: 'eye-consciousness' (see *viññāṇa*).

cankers: see *āsava*.

caraṇa: see *vijjā-caraṇa*.

carita: 'nature, character'. In VISM. III there are explained six types of men: the greedy-natured (*rāgacarita*), the hate-natured (*dosa-carita*), the stupid or dull-natured (*moha-carita*), the faithful-natured (*saddhā-carita*), the intelligent-natured (*buddhi-carita*), and the ruminating-natured (*vitakka-carita*).

SOURCE NOTE: *carita*, *rāga*-~, *dosa*-~, *buddhi*-~, etc., are only to be met with in the com. and VISM.

cāritta-sīla and **vāritta-sīla**: 'morality consisting in performance and morality consisting in avoidance,' means "the performance of those moral rules which the Blessed one has ordained to be followed, and the avoidance of those things that the Blessed One has rejected as not to be followed" (VISM. III).

SOURCE NOTE: these terms are only found in the com., as VISM. I, etc., but the teaching indicated by it is frequently mentioned in the old sutta texts as *karaṇīya* and *akaraṇīya* (e.g. A. II, 16).

catu-dhātu-vavatthāna: 'analysis of the four elements', see *dhātu-vavatthāna*.

Catu-mahārājika-deva: a class of heavenly beings of the sensuous sphere, see *deva*.

catu-pārisuddhi-sīla: see *sīla*.

catu-vokāra-bhava: 'four-group existence', is the existence in the immaterial world (*arūpa-loka*; see *loka*), since only the four mental groups (feeling, perception, mental formations, consciousness, see *khandha*) are found there, the corporeality group being absent. Cf. *pañcavokāra-bhava*, *eka-vokāra-bhava*, *vokāra*.

cause: cf. *paccaya* (1). For the five ~ of existence, see *paṭicca-samuppāda* (10).

cemetery, ascetic practice of living in: see *dhutaṅga*.

cemetery-meditations: see *sīvathikā*.

cetanā: 'volition', will, is one of the seven mental factors (*cetasika*, q.v.) inseparably bound up with all consciousness, namely sensorial or mental impression (*phassa*), feeling (*vedanā*), perception (*saññā*), volition (*cetanā*), concentration (*samādhi*), vitality (*jīvita*), advertence (*manasikāra*). Cf. TAB. II, III.

With regard to karmic volition (i.e., wholesome or unwholesome karma) it is said in A. VI, 13: "Volition is action (karma), thus I say, O monks; for as soon as volition arises, one does the action, be it by body, speech or mind." For details, see *paṭicca-samuppāda* (10), *karma*.

cetasika: 'mental things, mental factors', are those mental concomitants which are bound up with the simultaneously arising consciousness (*citta* = *viññāṇa*) and conditioned by its presence. Whereas in the suttas all phenomena of existence are summed up under the aspect of five groups: corporeality, feeling, perception, mental formations, consciousness (see *khandha*), the Abhidhamma as a rule treats them under the more philosophical three aspects:

consciousness, mental factors and corporeality (*citta, cetasika, rūpa*). Thus, of these three aspects, the mental factors (*cetasika*) comprise feeling, perception and the fifty mental formations, altogether fifty-two mental concomitants. Of these, twenty-five are lofty qualities (either karmically wholesome or neutral), fourteen karmically unwholesome, while thirteen are as such karmically neutral, their karmic quality depending on whether they are associated with wholesome, unwholesome or neutral consciousness. For details see TAB. II, III. Cf. *cetanā*.

C

SOURCE NOTE: the term *cetasika* occurs often in the old sutta texts, but only as adj. (e.g. *cetasikaṃ sukhaṃ*, etc.) or, at times, used as a sing. neut. noun (e.g. D. 1; p. 213, PTS). As a designation for mental factors, or concomitants of consciousness (*citta-sampayuttā dhammā*), it is frequently met with in DHS. (§ 1189, 1512) as *cetasika-dhamma*, while in VISM., ABH. S., etc., *cetasika* is used also as a neuter noun, in the sense of mental phenomenon.

cetaso vinibandha: 'mental bondages', are five things which hinder the mind from making right exertion, namely, lust for sensuous objects, for the body, for visible things, for eating and sleeping, and leading the monk's life for the sake of heavenly rebirth. For details, see A.V, 205; X, 14; D. 33; M. 16. Cf. *cetokhila*.

cetokhila: 'mental obduracies', are five things which stiffen and hinder the mind from making right exertion, namely, doubt about the Master, about the Doctrine, about the (holy) Brotherhood, about the training, and anger against one's fellow-monks. For details see A.V, 206, X, 14; D. 33; M. 16. Cf. *cetaso vinibandha*.

ceto-pariya-ñāṇa: 'penetrating knowledge of the mind (of others)', is one of the six higher powers (see *abhiññā* 3).

ceto-vimutti: 'deliverance of mind'. In the highest sense it signifies the fruition of arahatship (see *ariya-puggala*), and in particular, the concentration associated with it. It is often linked with the 'deliverance through wisdom' (*paññā-vimutti*, q.v.), e.g., in the ten powers of a Perfect One (see *dasa-bala*). See *vimokkha* I.

It is also called 'unshakeable deliverance of mind' (*akuppa-~*); further 'boundless deliverance of mind (*appamāṇa-~*); 'deliverance of mind from the conditions of existence, or signless deliverance of mind' (*animittā-~*); 'deliverance of mind from the appendages' (*ākiñgañña-~*), since that state of mind is free from the three bonds, conditions and appendants, i.e., from greed, hatred and ignorance; and since it is void thereof, it is called the 'void deliverance of mind' (*suññatā-~*).

In a more restricted sense, 'boundless deliverance of mind' is a name for the four boundless states, i.e., loving kindness, compassion, altruistic joy, and equanimity (see *brahma-vihāra*); 'd. of m. from the appendages' stands for the 'sphere of nothingness' (*ākiñcaññāyatana*, see *jhāna* 7); 'd. of m. from the conditions of existence', for d. of m. due to non-attention to all conditions of existence; 'void d. of m.' for d. of m. due to contemplating voidness of self. For further details, see M. 43.

C

chaḷ-abhiññā: the six 'higher powers', see *abhiññā*.

chaḷ-abhiñño: an arahat who is a 'possessor of the six higher powers' (see *abhiññā*).

chanda: intention, desire, will.

1. As an *ethically neutral* psychological term, in the sense of 'intention', it is one of those general mental factors (*cetasika*, q.v. TAB. II) taught in the Abhidhamma, the moral quality of which is determined by the character of the volition (*cetanā*, q.v.) associated therewith. The com. explains it as 'a wish to do' (*kattu-kamyatā-chanda*). If intensified, it acts also as a 'predominance condition' (see *paccaya* 3).

2. As an *evil* quality it has the meaning of 'desire', and is frequently coupled with terms for 'sensuality', 'greed', etc., for instance: *kāmacchanda*, 'sensuous desire', one of the five hindrances (see *nīvaraṇa*); *chandarāga*, 'lustful desire' (see *kāma*). It is one of the four wrong paths (see *agati*).

3. As a *good* quality it is a righteous will or zeal (*dhamma-chanda*) and occurs, e.g. in the formula of the four right efforts (see *padhāna*): "The monk rouses his will (*chandaṃ janeti*). ... " If intensified, it is one of the four roads to power (see *iddhipāda*).

change, contemplation of: one of the eighteen chief kinds of insight (*vipassanā*, q.v.).

chaos: cf. *kappa*.

character: on the six kinds of human character, see *carita*.

characteristics of existence, the three: *ti-lakkhaṇa* (q.v.).

chaste life: *brahma-cariya* (q.v.).

chief elements, the four: *mahā-bhūta* (q.v.); *dhātu* (q.v.).

cintāmaya-paññā: 'wisdom (or knowledge) based on thinking', see *paññā*.

citta: 'mind', 'consciousness', 'state of consciousness', is a synonym of *mano* (q.v.) and *viññāṇa* (see *khandha* and TAB. 1). DHS. divides all phenomena into consciousness (*citta*), mental concomitants (*cetasika*, q.v.) and corporeality (*rūpa*).

In *adhicitta*, 'higher mentality', it signifies the concentrated, quietened mind, and is one of the three trainings (see *sikkhā*). The concentration (or intensification) of consciousness is one of the four roads to power (see *iddhipāda*).

citta-ja- (citta-samuṭṭhāna-) rūpa: 'mind-produced corporeality', see *samuṭṭhāna*.

citta-kammaññatā, *~lahutā, ~mudutā, ~paguññatā, ~passaddhi, ~ujukatā*; see TAB. II.

SOURCE NOTE: not found, or not found in this form or meaning, in the oldest parts of the Sutta Piṭaka; see *lahutā*.

cittakkhaṇa: 'consciousness-moment', is the time occupied by one single stage in the perceptual process or cognitive series (*citta-vīthi*; see *viññāṇa-kicca*). This moment again is subdivided into the genetic (*uppāda*), static (*ṭhiti*) and dissolving (*bhaṅga*) moment. One such moment is said in the commentaries to be of inconceivably short duration and to last not longer than the billionth part of the time occupied by a flash of lightning. However that may be, we ourselves know from experience that it is possible within one single second to dream of innumerable things and events. In A. I, 10 it is said, "Nothing, O monks, do I know that changes so rapidly as consciousness. Scarcely anything may be found that could be compared with this so rapidly changing consciousness"; see *khaṇa*.

cittānupassanā: 'contemplation of consciousness', is one of the four foundations of mindfulness (*satipaṭṭhāna*, q.v.)

citta-samuṭṭhāna-rūpa: 'mind-produced corporeality', see *samuṭṭhāna*.

citta-saṅkhāra: see *saṅkhāra*.

citta-santāna: 'consciousness-continuity', see *santāna*.

cittass'ekaggatā: 'one-pointedness of mind', is a synonym of concentration, or *samādhi* (q.v.)

citta-vipallāsa: 'perversion of mind', see *vipallāsa*.

citta-visuddhi: 'purification of mind', is the second of the seven stages of purification (*visuddhi*, II,. q.v.).

citta-vīthi: 'process of consciousness', see *viññāṇa-kicca*.

SOURCE NOTE: this, as well as all terms for the various functions within the processes of consciousness, such as *āvajjanacitta*, *sampaṭicchana*, *santīraṇa*, *votthapana*, *javana*, *tadārammaṇa*, *bhavaṅga*, or *cuti*, are never found in the sutta canon, except *javana*, in PTS.M. Even in the ABH. canon (e.g. PATTH.) only *javana* and *bhavaṅga* are twice or thrice briefly mentioned. The stages, however, must have been more or less known. Cf. e.g. PATTH.: "*Cakkhu-viññāṇaṃ taṃ sampayuttakā ca dhammā* (= *cetasikā*) *mano-dhātuyā* (performing the *sampaṭicchana*-function), *taṃ sampayuttakānañ ca dhammānaṃ* (*cetasikānaṃ*) *anantara-paccayena paccayo. Mano-dhātu … manoviññāṇa-dhātuyā* (performing the *santīraṇa* and *vot thapana* function). … *Purimā purimā kusalā dhammā* (*javanā*) *pacchimānaṃ pacchimānaṃ kusalānaṃ dhammānaṃ* (*javanacittānaṃ*) *anantara-paccayena paccayo … avyākatānaṃ dhammānaṃ* (*tadārammaṇa*- and *bhavaṅga-cittānaṃ …*)."

citt'ekaggatā: *cittass'ekaggatā* (q.v.).

clarity of consciousness: *sampajañña* (q.v.).

clinging, the four kinds of: *upādāna* (q.v.).

cognitive series: see *viññāṇa-kicca*.

companionship: influence of good and bad ~, see *samseva*.

compassion: *karuṇā*, see *brahma-vihāra*.

comprehension, clear: see *sampajañña*. ~ in insight, see *sammasana*. As an alternative tr. for full understanding, see *pariññā*.

co-nascence: *sahajāta-paccaya*, is one of the twenty-four conditions (*paccaya*, q.v.).

conceit: *māna* (q.v.); further see *saṃyojana*.

concentration: *samādhi* (q.v.). Right ~, see *sacca* (IV. 8), *magga* (8). Wrong ~, see *micchā-magga* (8).

conception[1]. thought ~: cf. *vitakka-vicāra*.

conception[2]. (in the mother's womb): *okkanti* (q.v.).

conditions, the twenty-four: *paccaya* (q.v.).

conditions of existence, deliverance from the: see *ceto-vimutti; vimokkha.*

confidence: see *saddhā.*

C

consciousness: *viññāṇa* (see *khandha*), *citta* (q.v.), *mano* (q.v.). Moment of ~: *citta-kkhana* (q.v.). Contemplation of ~: *cittānupassanā*: see *satipaṭṭhāna*. Corporeality produced by ~: *citta-ja-rūpa*, see *samuṭṭhāna*. Abodes or supports of ~: cf. *viññāṇatthiti* (q.v.). Functions of ~: *viññāṇa-kicca* (q.v.).

contemplation: see *anupassanā.*

contentedness (with whatever robe, etc.): see *ariya-vaṃsa.*

contentment: *appicchatā* (q.v.) is one of the ascetic virtues. Cf. A. X, 181–90.

contiguity: *samanantara-paccaya*, is one of the twenty-four conditions (*paccaya*, q.v.).

continuity (of body, subconsciousness, consciousness or groups of existence): *santāna* (q.v.).

control, effort of: see *padhāna.*

conventional (expression or truth): see *desanā.*

corporeality: produced through consciousness, karma, etc.; see *samuṭṭhāna*. Sensitive ~: *pasāda-rūpa*. (q.v.).

corporeality and mind: see *nāma-rūpa.*

corporeality-group: *rūpakkhandha*: see *khandha.*

corporeality-perceptions: *rūpa-saññā*: see *jhāna.*

corruptions: see *upakkilesa.*

cosmogony: cf. *kappa.*

counteractive karma: *upapīḷaka-kamma*, see *karma.*

counter-image (during concentration): see *nimitta, kasiṇa, samādhi.*

course of action (wholesome or unwholesome): *kamma-patha* (q.v.).

covetousness: *abhijjhā* (q.v.); further see *kamma-patha* (1).

cowardice: see *agati.*

craving: *taṇhā* (q.v.), *rāga* (q.v.); further see *mūla.*

created, the: *saṅkhata* (q.v.).

cuti-citta: 'death-consciousness', lit. 'departing consciousness', is one of the fourteen functions of consciousness (*viññāṇa-kicca* q.v.).

SOURCE NOTE: not found, or not found in this form or meaning, in the oldest parts of the Sutta Piṭaka; see *citta-vīthi.*

cutūpapāta-ñāṇa: the 'knowledge of the vanishing and reappearing' (of beings) is identical with the divine eye; see *abhiññā.*

cycle of existence: see *saṃsarā, vaṭṭa.*

D

dāna: 'almsgiving', liberality, offering. "He who gives alms, bestows a fourfold blessing: he helps to long life, good appearance, happiness and strength. Therefore long life, good appearance, happiness and strength will be his share, whether amongst heavenly beings or amongst men" (A. IV, 57).

"Five blessings accrue to the giver of alms: the affection of many, noble association, good reputation, self-confidence, and heavenly rebirth" (see A. V, 34). Seven further blessings are given in A. VII, 54.

Liberality, especially the offering of robes, food, etc., to the monks, is highly praised in all Buddhist countries of Southern Asia as a fundamental virtue and as a means to suppress man's inborn greed and egoism. But, as in any other good or bad action, so also in offering gifts, it is the noble intention and volition that really counts as the action, not the mere outward deed.

Almsgiving or liberality (*dāna*), constitutes the first kind of meritorious activity, the two others being morality (*sīla*, q.v.) and mental development (*bhāvanā*); see *puñña-kiriya-vatthu*. Liberality (*cāga*) forms one of the ten recollections (*anussati*, q.v.) and almsgiving one of the ten perfections (see *pāramī*).

dasa- (Tathāgata-) bala: 'the ten powers (of a Perfect One); or, he who possesses the ten P.', i.e., the Buddha. About him it is said (e.g., M. 12.; A. A X, 21):

"There, O monks, the Perfect One understands according to reality the possible as possible, and the impossible as impossible ... the result of past, present and future actions ... the path leading to the welfare of all ... the world with its many different elements ... the different inclinations in beings ... the lower and higher faculties in beings ... the defilement, purity and rising with regard to the absorptions, deliverances, concentration and attainments ... remembering many former rebirths ... perceiving with the divine eye how beings vanish and reappear again according to their actions (karma) ... gaining, through extinction of all taints, possession of 'deliverance of mind' and 'deliverance through wisdom'. ... "

dasaka-kalāpa: see *rūpa-kalāpa*.

dasa-pāramī: see *pāramī*.

dasa-puñña-kiriya-vatthu: see *puñña-kiriya-vatthu*.

death: *maraṇa* (q.v.). Contemplation of ~: *maraṇānussati* (q.v.). As divine messenger: *devadūta* (q.v.).

death-consciousness: *cuti-citta,* is one of the fourteen functions of consciousness (*viññāṇa-kicca,* q.v.).

deathlessness: *amata* (q.v.).

death-proximate karma: *maraṇāsanna-kamma,* see *karma.*

deciding function (of consciousness): see *viññāṇa-kicca.*

decline (in morality, wisdom, etc.): see *hāna-bhāgiya-sīla.* Liable to ~, *parihāna-dhamma* (q.v.).

defilements: see *kilesa, upakkilesa.* Ten ~ of insight: *vipassanūpakkilesa,* see *visuddhi* VI. Round of ~, see *vaṭṭa* (1).

deliverance: see *vimutti, vimokkha.* The eight kinds of ~ (or liberation), see *vimokkha.* ~ of mind, ~ through voidness, boundless ~ etc., see *ceto-vimutti.* Desire for ~, see *visuddhi* (VI, 6). ~ through wisdom; *paññāvimutti* (q.v.). Three doors of ~ (or gateways of liberation) see *visuddhi* (VI, 8).

deluded consciousness: see TAB. I. 32, 33.

deluded-natured: *moha-carita,* see *carita.*

delusion: see *moha, avijjā.*

demons' realm: *asura-nikāya,* see *apāya.*

departed, the spirits of the: *peta* (q.v.).

dependent origination: *paṭiccasamuppāda* (q.v.).

derived corporeality: *upādā-rūpa* (q.v.); further see *khandha* (I. B.).

desanā: 'exposition' of the doctrine, may be either an exposition true in the highest sense (*paramattha-desanā*); or it may not be true in the highest, but only in the conventional sense (*vohāra-desanā*). See *paramattha, vohāra.*

desire for deliverance: see *visuddhi* (VI, 6).

desireless deliverance: see *vimokkha* (1).

desirelessness, contemplation on: see *vipassanā* (12).

destiny: evil views with fixed ~, *niyata-micchā-diṭṭhi* (q.v.). Men with fixed ~, *niyata-puggala* (q.v.). See *gati*.

destruction: overcoming, or liberation from, evil things through their ~, *samuccheda-pahāna* or *samuccheda-vimutti*; see *pahāna*.

destructive karma: *upaghātaka-kamma*, see *karma*.

detachment: *viveka* (q.v.).

determination: see *adhimokkha*, *adhiṭṭhāna*.

determining: *votthapana* (see *viññāṇa-kicca*).

determining the reality: see *vavatthāna*.

deva (lit: the Radiant Ones; related to Lat. *deus*): heavenly beings, deities, celestials, are beings who live in happy worlds, and who, as a rule, are invisible to the human eye. They are subject, however, just like all human and other beings, to ever-repeated rebirth, old age and death, and thus are not freed from the cycle of existence and from misery. There are many classes of heavenly beings.

I. The six classes of heavenly beings of the sensuous sphere (*kāmāvacara* or *kāma-loka*; see *avacara*, *loka*), are *Cātummahārājika-deva*, *Tāvatiṃsa*, *Yāma*, *Tusita* (see *Bodhisatta*), *Nimmāna-rati*, *Paranimmita-vasavatti*. Cf. *anussati* 6.

II. The heavenly beings of the fine-material sphere (*rūpāvacara* or *rūpa-loka*) are:
1. *Brahma-pārisajja*, *Brahma-purohita*, *Mahābrahmāno* (see *brahma-kāyika-deva*). Amongst these three classes will be reborn those with a weak, medium or full experience of the first absorption (*jhāna*, q.v.).
2. *Parittābha*, *Appamāṇābha*, *Ābhassara*. Here will be reborn those with experience of the second absorption.
3. *Paritta-subha*, *Appamāṇa-subha*, *Subha-kiṇṇa* (or *kiṇha*). Here will be reborn those with experience of the third absorption.
4. *Vehapphala*, *Asañña-satta* (q.v.), *Suddhāvāsa* (q.v.; further see *anāgāmī*). Amongst the first two classes will be reborn those with experience of the fourth absorption, but amongst the third class only *anāgāmīs* (q.v.).

III. The four grades of heavenly beings of the immaterial sphere (*arūpāvacara* or *arūpa-loka*) are: the heavenly beings of the sphere of unbounded space (*ākāsānañcāyatanūpaga-devā*), of unbounded consciousness (*viññāṇañcāyatanūpaga-devā*), of nothingness (*ākiñcaññāyatanūpaga devā*), of neither-perception-nor-non-perception (*nevasaññānāsaññāyatanūpaga-devā*). Here will be reborn those with experience of the four immaterial spheres (*arūpāyatana*; see *jhāna* 5–8).

See *Gods and the Universe* by Francis Story (WHEEL 180/181).

deva-dūta: 'divine messengers', is a symbolic name for old age, disease and death, since these three things remind man of his future and rouse him to earnest striving. In A. III, 35, it is said:

"Did you, O man, never see in the world a man or a woman eighty, ninety or a hundred years old, frail, crooked as a gable-roof, bent down, resting on crutches, with tottering steps, infirm, youth long since fled, with broken teeth, grey and scanty hair, or bald-headed, wrinkled, with blotched limbs? And did it never occur to you that you also are subject to old age, that you also cannot escape it?

"Did you never see in the world a man or a woman, who being sick, afflicted and grievously ill, and wallowing in their own filth, was lifted up by some people, and put down by others? And did it never occur to you that you also are subject to disease, that you also cannot escape it?

"Did you never see in the world the corpse of a man or a woman, one or two or three days after death, swollen up, blue-black in colour, and full of corruption? And did it never occur to you that you also are subject to death, that you also cannot escape it?" See M. 130.

devatānussati: 'recollection of the heavenly beings', see *anussati*.

development (mental): *bhāvanā* (q.v.). Effort to develop, see *padhāna*. Wisdom based on ~, see *paññā*. Gradual ~ of the Eightfold Path, see 'progress of the disciple' (q.v.).

deviation (from morality and understanding): *vipatti* (q.v.).

devotee: *upāsaka* (q.v.).

dhamma: lit. the 'bearer', constitution (or nature of a thing), norm, law (*jus*), doctrine; justice, righteousness; quality; thing, object of mind (see *āyatana*) 'phenomenon'. In all these meanings the word *dhamma* is to be met with in the texts. The com. to D. instances four applications of this term *guṇa* (quality, virtue), *desanā* (instruction), *pariyatti* (text), *nijjīvatā* (soullessness, e.g.

D

"all *dhammā*, phenomena, are impersonal," etc.). The com. to DHS. has *hetu* (condition) instead of *desanā*. Thus, the analytical knowledge of the law (see *paṭisambhidā*) is explained in VISM. XIV. and in VIBH. as *hetumhi-ñāṇa*, knowledge of the conditions.

The Dhamma, as the liberating law discovered and proclaimed by the Buddha, is summed up in the Four Noble Truths (see *sacca*). It forms one of the Three Gems (*ti-ratana*, q.v.) and one of the ten recollections (*anussati* q.v.).

Dhamma, as object of mind (*dhammāyatana*, see *āyatana*) may be anything past, present or future, corporeal or mental, conditioned or not (cf. *saṅkhāra*, 4), real or imaginary.

D

dhamma-cakka: the 'Wheel (realm) of the Law', is a name for the doctrine 'set rolling' (established) by the Buddha, i.e., the Four Noble Truths (*sacca*, q.v.).

"The Perfect One, O monks, the Holy One, Fully Enlightened One, in the Deer Park at Isipatana near Benares, has set rolling (established) the unsurpassed Wheel (realm) of the Law" (M. 141). Cf. *cakka*.

dhamma-desanā: 'exposition of the Doctrine (law)', see *desanā*.

dhamma-dhātu: mind-object-element (see *dhātu*).

dhammānupassanā: 'contemplation of the mind objects' is the last of the four foundations of mindfulness (*satipaṭṭhāna*, q.v.)

dhammānusārī: the 'dhamma-devotee', is one of the seven noble disciples (*ariya-puggala*, q.v.).

dhammānussati: 'recollection of the Law', is one of the ten recollections (*anussati*, q.v.).

dhamma-paṭisambhidā: the 'analytical knowledge of the law, is one of the four kinds of analytical knowledge (*paṭisambhidā*, q.v.).

dhammaṭṭhiti-ñāṇa: 'knowledge of the fixity of law, is a name for that 'insight which is leading up' to the entrance into one of the four supermundane paths (*vuṭṭhāna-gāminī-vipassanā*, q.v.). In the Susima Sutta (S. XII, 70) this (ascending) insight is called the 'knowledge of the fixity of the law': "At first, Susima, there exists the knowledge of the fixity of the law, and later the knowledge of Nibbāna." (See VISM. XXI.)

dhamma-vicaya-sambojjhaṅga: 'investigation of the law as a factor of enlightenment', is one of the seven factors of enlightenment (*bojjhaṅga*, q.v.).

dhammāyatana: 'mind-object as base' (*āyatana*, q.v.).

dhana: 'treasures', a term for the following seven qualities: faith, morality, moral shame, moral dread, learning, liberality, and wisdom. Cf. A. VII, 5, 6. See *Treasures of the Noble*, by Soma Thera (Bodhi Leaves B. 27, BPS).

dhātu: 'elements', are the ultimate constituents of a whole.

(I) The four physical elements (*dhātu* or *mahā-bhūta*), popularly called earth, water, fire and wind, are to be understood as the primary qualities of matter. They are named in Pali: *paṭhavī~*, *āpo~*, *tejo~*, and *vāyo~*. In VISM. XI, 2 the four elements are defined thus: "Whatever is characterised by hardness (*thaddha-lakkkhaṇa*) is the earth or solid-element; by cohesion (*ābandhana*) or fluidity, the water-element; by heating (*paripācana*), the fire or heat-element; by strengthening or supporting (*vitthambhana*), the wind or motion-element. All four are present in every material object, though in varying degrees of strength. If, for instance, the earth element predominates, the material object is called 'solid', etc. For the analysis of the four elements, see *dhātu-vavatthāna*.

(II) The eighteen physical and mental elements that constitute the conditions or foundations of the process of perception, consist of the following:

1. visual organ (eye)
2. auditory organ (ear)
3. olfactory organ (nose)
4. gustatory organ (tongue)
5. tactile organ (body)
6. visible object
7. sound or audible object
8. odour or olfactive object
9. gustative object
10. body-impression element
11. eye-consciousness
12. ear-consciousness
13. nose-consciousness
14. tongue-consciousness
15. body-consciousness
16. mind-element (*mano-dhātu*)
17. mind-object (*dhamma-dhātu*)
18. mind-consciousness (*mano- viññāṇa-dhātu*)

1–10 are physical; 11–16 and 18 are mental; 17 may be either physical or mental. 16 performs the function of advertence (*āvajjana*) towards the object at the inception of a process of sensuous consciousness; it further performs the function of receiving (*sampaṭicchana*) the sensuous object. 18 performs the function of investigation (*santīraṇa*), determining (*votthapana*) and registering (*tadārammaṇa*). For its other functions, see TAB. For the fourteen functions of consciousness, see *viññāṇa-kicca*. Cf. M. 115; S. XIV and especially VIBH. II (GUIDE 28ff.), VISM. XV, 17ff.

Of the many further groupings of elements (enumerated in M. 115), the best known is that of the three world-elements: the sensuous world (*kāma-~*), the fine-material world (*rūpa-~*), the immaterial world (*arūpa-~*); further the sixfold group: the solid, liquid, heat, motion, space, and consciousness (*paṭhavī, āpo, tejo, vāyo, ākāsa, viññāṇa*; see above I), described in M. 140; see also M. 112.

dhātu-vavatthāna: 'analysis (or determining) of the four elements', is described in VISM. XI, 2, as the last of the forty mental exercises (see *bhāvanā*). In a condensed form this exercise is handed down in D. 22 and M. 10 (see *satipaṭṭhāna*), but in detail explained in M. 28, 62, 140. The simile of the butcher in M. 10 ("Just, O monks, as a skilled butcher or butcher's apprentice, after having slaughtered a cow and divided it into separate portions, should sit down at the junction of four highroads; just so does the disciple contemplate this body with regard to the elements") is thus explained in VISM. XI.: "To the butcher, who rears the cow, brings it to the slaughter-house, ties it, puts it there, slaughters it, or looks at the slaughtered and dead cow, the idea 'cow' does not disappear as long as he has not yet cut the body open and taken it to pieces. As soon, however, as he sits down, after having cut it open and taken it to pieces, the idea 'cow' disappears to him, and the idea 'meat' arises. And he does not think: 'A cow do I sell, or 'A cow do they buy.' Just so, when the monk formerly was still an ignorant worldling, layman or a homeless one, the ideas 'living being' or 'man' or 'individual' had not yet disappeared as long as he had not taken this body, whatever position or direction it had, to pieces and analysed it piece by piece. As soon, however, as he analysed this body into its elements, the idea 'living being' disappeared to him, and his mind became established in the contemplation of the elements."

SOURCE NOTE: this term is first used in PTS.M. while the subject in question is often treated in the old sutta texts (e.g. M. 28, 62, 140, etc.). Cf. *sammasana*.

dhutaṅga: (lit. 'means of shaking off (the defilements)'); 'means of purification', ascetic or austere practices. These are strict observances recommended by the Buddha to monks as a help to cultivate contentedness, renunciation, energy and the like. One or more of them may be observed for a shorter or longer period of time.

"The monk training himself in morality should take upon himself the means of purification, in order to gain those virtues through which the purity of morality will become accomplished, to wit: fewness of needs, contentedness, austerity, detachment, energy, moderation, etc." (VISM. II).

VISM. II describes thirteen *dhutaṅgas*, consisting in the following vows:

1. to wear patched-up robes: *paṃsukūlik'aṅga,*
2. to wear only three robes: *tecīvarik'aṅga,*
3. to go for alms: *piṇḍapātik'aṅga,*
4. not to omit any house while going for alms: *sapadānikaṅga,*
5. to eat at one sitting: *ekāsanik'aṅga,*
6. to eat only from the alms-bowl: *pattapiṇḍik'aṅga,*
7. to refuse all further food: *khalu-pacchā-bhattik'aṅga,*
8. to live in the forest: *āraññik'aṅga,*
9. to live under a tree: *rukkha-mūlik'aṅga,*
10. to live in the open air: *abbhokāsik'aṅga,*
11. to live in a cemetery: *susānik'aṅga,*
12. to be satisfied with whatever dwelling: *yathā-santhatik'aṅga,*
13. to sleep in the sitting position (and never lying down): *nesajjik'aṅga.*

These thirteen exercises are all, without exception, mentioned in the old sutta texts (e.g. M. 5, 113; A. V., 181–90), but never together in one and the same place.

"Without doubt, O monks, it is a great advantage to live in the forest as a hermit, to collect one's alms, to make one's robes from picked-up rags, to be satisfied with three robes" (A.I, 30).

The vow of no. 1, for example, is taken in the words: "I reject robes offered to me by householders," or "I take upon myself the vow of wearing only robes made from picked-up rags." Some of the exercises may also be observed by the lay-adherent.

Here it may be mentioned that each newly ordained monk, immediately after his being admitted to the Order, is advised to be satisfied with whatever robes, alms-food, dwelling and medicine he gets: "The life of the monks depends on the collected alms as food … on the root of a tree as dwelling … on robes made from patched-up rags … on stale cow's urine as medicine. May you train yourself therein all your life."

Since the moral quality of any action depends entirely upon the accompanying intention and volition, this is also the case with these ascetic practices, as is expressly stated in VISM. Thus the mere external performance is not the real exercise, as it is said (PUG. 275–84): "Some one might be going for alms; etc. out of stupidity and foolishness—or with evil intention and filled with desires—or out of insanity and mental derangement—or because such practice had been praised by the Noble Ones. … " These exercises are, however properly observed "if they are taken up only for the sake of frugality, of contentedness, of purity, etc."

On *dhutaṅga* practice in modern Thailand, see *With Robes and Bowl*, by Bhikkhu Khantipalo (WHEEL 82/83).

SOURCE NOTE: this compound term is used only in the com. The only place in the suttas where the first part, *dhuta*, is used in the above sense, is found in S. XIV. The names of the performers of these thirteen ascetic exercises, however, are all mentioned in the suttas, but scattered here and there, for instance: *paṃsukūlika, āraññika, piṇḍapātika, ekāsanika, tecīvarika, sapādānacārī, sosānika, abhhokāsika, nesajjika, yathāsanthatika*, in M. 5, 113; A. V, 181–190, etc.; *rukkhamūlika, khalupacchābhattika* and *pattapiṇḍika* in A. V, 189ff. etc.

D

dibba-cakkhu: the 'divine eye', is one of the six higher powers (*abhiññā*, q.v.), and one of the three kinds of knowledge (*te-vijjā*, q.v.).

dibba-loka: heavenly world, see *deva*.

dibba-sota: the 'divine ear', is one of the six higher powers (*abhiññā*, q.v.).

dibba-vihāra: see *vihāra*.

disappearance: *vigata-paccaya*, is one of the twenty-four conditions (*paccaya*, q.v.).

disciplinary code: see *pātimokkha*.

discursive thinking: *vicāra*, see *vitakka-vicāra*.

disease: one of the 'divine messengers' (*devadūta*, q.v.).

disinterestedness (regarding the whole world): see *sabbaloke anabhirati-saññā*.

dispensation: see *sāsana*.

dissociation: *vippayutta-paccaya*, is one of the twenty-four conditions (*paccaya*, q.v.).

dissolution, contemplation of: *khayānupassanā*, is one of the eighteen chief kinds of insight (*vipassanā*, q.v.).

diṭṭha-dhamma-vedanīya-kamma: karma bearing fruit in this present life, see *karma*.

diṭṭhi: (lit. 'sight'; √ *dis*, to see): view, belief, speculative opinion, insight. If not qualified by *sammā*, 'right', it mostly refers to wrong and evil view or opinion, and only in a few instances to right view, understanding or insight (e.g. *~ppatta*, q.v.; *~-visuddhi*, purification of insight; *~-sampanna*, possessed of insight).

Wrong or evil views (*diṭṭhi* or *micchā-~*) *are* declared as utterly rejectable for being a source of wrong and evil aspirations and conduct, and liable at times to lead man to the deepest abysses of depravity, as it is said in A. I, 22:

"No other thing than evil views do I know, O monks, whereby to such an extent the unwholesome things not yet arisen arise, and the unwholesome things already arisen are brought to growth and fullness. No other thing than evil views do I know, whereby to such an extent the wholesome things not yet arisen are hindered in their arising, and the wholesome things already arisen disappear. No other thing than evil views do I know, whereby to such an extent human beings at the dissolution of the body, at death, are passing to a way of suffering, into a world of woe, into hell." Further in A. I, 23: "Whatever a man filled with evil views performs or undertakes, or whatever he possesses of will, aspiration, longing and tendencies, all these things lead him to an undesirable, unpleasant and disagreeable state, to woe and suffering."

From the Abhidhamma (DHS.) it may be inferred that evil views, whenever they arise, are associated with greed (see TAB. I. 22, 23, 26, 27).

Numerous speculative opinions and theories, which at all times have influenced and still are influencing mankind, are quoted in the sutta-texts. Amongst them, however, the wrong view which everywhere, and at all times, has most misled and deluded mankind is the personality-belief, the ego-illusion. This personality-belief (*sakkāya-diṭṭhi*), or ego-illusion (*atta-diṭṭhi*), is of two kinds: eternity-belief and annihilation-belief.

Eternity-belief (*sassata-diṭṭhi*) is the belief in the existence of a persisting ego-entity, soul or personality, existing independently of those physical and mental processes that constitute life and continuing even after death.

Annihilation-belief (*uccheda-diṭṭhi*), on the other hand, is the belief in the existence of an ego-entity or personality as being more or less identical with those physical and mental processes, and which therefore, at the dissolution at death, will come to be annihilated. For the twenty kinds of personality-belief, see *sakkāya-diṭṭhi*.

Now, the Buddha neither teaches a personality which will continue after death, nor does he teach a personality which will be annihilated at death, but he shows us that 'personality', 'ego', 'individual', 'man', etc., are nothing but mere conventional designations (*vohāra-vacana*) and that in the ultimate sense (see *paramattha-sacca*) there is only this self-consuming process of physical and mental phenomena that continually arise and again disappear immediately. For further details, see *anatta, khandha, paṭiccasamuppāda.*

"The Perfect One is free from any theory (*diṭṭhigata*), for the Perfect One has seen what corporeality is, and how it arises and passes away. He has seen what feeling ... perception ... mental formations ... consciousness are, and how they arise and pass away. Therefore I say that the Perfect One has won complete deliverance through the extinction, fading away, disappearance, rejection and casting out of all imaginings and conjectures, of all inclination to the 'vain-glory of 'I' and 'mine'." (M. 72).

D

The rejection of speculative views and theories is a prominent feature in a chapter of the Sutta-Nipāta, the Aṭṭhaka-Vagga.

The so-called 'evil views with fixed destiny' (*niyata-micchā-diṭṭhi*) constituting the last of the ten unwholesome courses of action (*kamma-patha*, q.v.), are the following three:

(1) the fatalistic 'view of the uncausedness' of existence (*ahetukadiṭṭhi*), taught by Makkhali-Gosāla, a contemporary of the Buddha who denied every cause for the corruptness and purity of beings, and asserted that everything is minutely predestined by fate.

(2) the 'view of the inefficacy of action' (*akiriya-diṭṭhi*), taught by Pūraṇa-Kassapa, another contemporary of the Buddha who denied every karmic effect of good and bad actions: "To him who kills, steals, robs, etc., nothing bad will happen. For generosity, self-restraint and truthfulness, etc. no reward is to be expected."

(3) nihilism (*natthika-diṭṭhi*), taught by Ajita-Kesakambali, a third contemporary of the Buddha who asserted that any belief in good action and its reward is a mere delusion, that after death no further life would follow, that man at death would become dissolved into the elements, etc.

For further details about these three views, see D. 2, M. 60; commentarial exposition in WHEEL 98/99, p. 23.

Frequently mentioned are also the ten antinomies (*antagāhikā micchā-diṭṭhi*): 'Finite is the world' or 'infinite is the world' ... 'body and soul are identical' or 'body and soul are different' (e.g. M. 63).

In the Brahmājala Sutta (D. 1), sixty-two false views are classified and described, comprising all conceivable wrong views and speculations about man and world. See *The All-Embracing Net of Views* (Brahmājala Sutta), tr. with com. by Bhikkhu Bodhi (BPS). Further see D. 15, 23, 24, 28; M. 11, 12, 25, 60, 63, 72, 76, 101, 102, 110; A. II, 16; X, 93; S. XXI, XXIV; PTS.M. Ditthikathā, etc.

Wrong views (*diṭṭhi*) are one of the proclivities (see *anusaya*), cankers (see *āsava*), clingings (see *upādāna*), one of the three modes of perversions (see *vipallāsa*). Unwholesome consciousness (*akusala-citta*), rooted in greed, may be either with or without wrong views (*~gata-sampayutta* or *vippayutta*); see DHS.; TAB. I.

On right view (*sammā-~*), see *magga* and M. 9 (tr. with com. in 'R.UND.').

D

diṭṭhi-nissita-sīla: 'morality based on wrong views', see *nissaya*.

diṭṭhippatta: the 'vision attainer', is one of the seven Noble Persons (*ariya-puggala*, q.v.).

diṭṭhi-vipallāsa: 'perversion of views', see *vipallāsa*.

diṭṭhi-visuddhi: 'purification of view' is the third of the seven stages of purification (*visuddhi* III, q.v.).

diṭṭh'upādāna: 'clinging to views', is one of the four kinds of clinging (*upādāna*, q.v.).

divine abode: see *vihāra*.

divine ear and eye: see *abhiññā*.

divine messengers, the three: *deva-dūta* (q.v.).

doctrine of the Buddha: see *dhamma*, *sāsana*.

dogmatic articles, the three: *titthāyatana* (q.v.).

domanassa: lit. 'sad-mindedness', grief, i.e., mentally painful feeling (*cetasika-vedanā*), is one of the five feelings (*vedanā*, q.v.) and one of the twenty-two faculties (*indriya*, q.v.). According to the Abhidhamma, grief is always associated with antipathy and grudge, and therefore karmically unwholesome (*akusala*, q.v.) Cf. TAB. I. 30, 31.

domanassupavicāra: 'indulging in grief', see *manopavicāra*.

doors of deliverance, the three: *vimokkha-dvāra*; see *vimokkha* I; *visuddhi* VI, 8.

dosa: 'hatred', anger, is one of the three unwholesome roots (*mūla*, q.v.). *~citta*: hate consciousness; see TAB. I (30, 31).

dosa-carita: 'angry-or hate-natured', see *carita*.

doubt, sceptical: *vicikicchā* (q.v.), *kaṅkhā* (q.v.).

dread, moral: *ottappa* see *hiri-ottappa*.

drinking intoxicants: see *surāmeraya*.

dry-visioned: see *sukkha-vipassaka*.

duccarita: 'evil conduct', is threefold—in deeds, words, and thoughts. See *kamma-patha* (I).

D

duggati: 'woeful course' (of existence), see *gati*.

dukkha: (1) 'pain', painful feeling, which may be bodily and mental (see *vedanā*).

(2) 'Suffering', 'ill'. As the first of the Four Noble Truths (see *sacca*) and the second of the three characteristics of existence (see *ti-lakkhaṇa*), the term *dukkha* is not limited to painful experience as under (1), but refers to the unsatisfactory nature and the general insecurity of all conditioned phenomena which, on account of their impermanence, are all liable to suffering, and this includes also pleasurable experience. Hence 'unsatisfactoriness' or 'liability to suffering' would be more adequate renderings, if not for stylistic reasons. Hence the first truth does not deny the existence of pleasurable experience, as is sometimes wrongly assumed. This is illustrated by the following texts:

"Seeking satisfaction in the world, monks, I had pursued my way. That satisfaction in the world I found. In so far as satisfaction existed in the world, I have well perceived it by wisdom. Seeking for misery in the world, monks, I had pursued my way. That misery in the world I found. In so far as misery existed in the world, I have well perceived it by wisdom. Seeking for the escape from the world, monks, I had pursued my way. That escape from the world I found. In so far as an escape from the world existed, I have well perceived it by wisdom" (A. III, 101).

"If there were no satisfaction to be found in the world, beings would not be attached to the world. ... If there were no misery to be found in the world, beings would not be repelled by the world. ... If there were no escape from the world, beings could not escape therefrom" (A. III, 102).

See *dukkhatā*. For texts on the Truth of Suffering, see W. OF B. and 'Path'. See also *The Three Basic Facts of Existence*, II. *Suffering* (WHEEL 191/193).

dukkhānupassanā: see *vipassanā*.

dukkhatā (abstr. noun fr. *dukkha*): 'the state of suffering', painfulness, unpleasantness, the unsatisfactoriness of existence. "There are three kinds of suffering: (1) suffering as pain (*dukkha-dukkhatā*), (2) the suffering inherent in the formations (*saṅkhāradukkhatā*), (3) the suffering in change (*vipariṇāmadukkhatā*)" (S. XLV, 165; D. 33).

(1) is the bodily or mental feeling of pain as actually felt. (2) refers to the oppressive nature of all formations of existence (i.e., all conditioned phenomena), due to their continual arising and passing away; this includes also experiences associated with neutral feeling. (3) refers to bodily and mental pleasant feelings, "because they are the cause for the arising of pain when they change" (VISM. XIV, 34ff.).

dukkha-paṭipadā: 'painful progress', see *paṭipadā*.

dvi-hetuka-paṭisandhi: see *paṭisandhi*.

dwellings: suitable ~ for monks, see *senāsana*. Satisfied with whatever ~, see *dhutaṅga*.

E

earnestness: *appamāda* (q.v.).

earth-element: see *dhātu* (I).

eating, knowing the measure in: *bhojane mattaññutā* (q.v.).

effort: the four right ~, *samma-ppadhāna*, see *padhāna*. Right ~, see *sacca* (IV 6), *magga* (6). Five elements of ~: *padhāniyaṅga* (q.v.).

ego-entity: *attā* (q.v.).

E

ego-belief: see *diṭṭhi*, *sakkāya-diṭṭhi*, *vipallāsa*.

ego-idea, **ego-perception**: see *vipallāsa*.

egolessness: *anatta* (q.v.).

eightfold path: see *magga*.

eka-bījī: 'germinating only once more', is the name for one of the three kinds of stream-winners: see *sotāpanna*.

ekāsanik'aṅga: the exercise of eating at one sitting, is one of the ascetic practices; see *dhutaṅga*.

eka-vokāra-bhava: one-group existence, is the existence of the unconscious beings (*asañña-satta*, q.v.) as they possess only the corporeality-group. Cf. *catuvokāra-bhava*, *pañca-vokāra-bhava*.

elasticity (of corporeality, mental factors or consciousness): *mudutā*, see *khandha* (Corporeality I.B.) and TAB. II.

elders, the teaching of the: Theravāda (q.v.).

elements: *dhātu* (q.v.). Analysis of the four ~: *dhātuvavatthāna* (q.v.).

emotion: eight sources of ~: *saṃvega-vatthu* (q.v.). The four places rousing ~; *saṃvejanīya-ṭhāna* (q.v.).

emptiness: *suññatā* (q.v.). Contemplation of ~: *suññatānupassanā*. For emptiness of self, pertaining to the four truths, see *sacca*.

ends: 'attaining two ends simultaneously', *sama-sīsī* (q.v.).

energy: *viriya* (q.v.); further see *bojjhaṅga, bala, pāramī.*

enlightened one, the: *Buddha*, see *sammā-sambuddha.*

enlightenment: *bodhi* (q.v.). The seven elements of ~: *bojjhaṅga* (q.v.). A being destined for ~: *Bodhisatta* (q.v.).

enthusiasm: *pīti* (q.v.).

envy: *issā* (q.v.).

equality-conceit: see *māna.*

equanimity: *upekkhā* (q.v.) = *tatra-majjhattatā* (q.v.). Knowledge consisting in ~ with regard to all formations, see *visuddhi* (VI, 8). Indulging in ~, see *manopavicāra.*

equilibrium of mental faculties: *indriyasamatta* (q.v.).

escape: *nissaraṇa* (see *pahāna*).

eternity: cf. *kappa.*

eternity-belief: *sassata-diṭṭhi*, see *diṭṭhi.*

exertion: see *padhāna, viriya, magga* (6). Reaching Nibbāna with or without ~, see *anāgāmī.*

existence: *bhava* (q.v.). The five groups of ~: *khandha* (q.v.). The four substrata of ~: *upadhi* (q.v.). Courses of ~: *gati* (q.v.). Wheel of ~: *saṃsāra* (q.v.). Craving for ~: *bhava-taṇhā;* see *taṇhā*. The three characteristics of ~: *ti-lakkhaṇa* (q.v.).

expression (bodily and verbal): see *viññatti.*

extinction: see *nirodha;* ~ of craving: *taṇhakkhaya* (q.v.).

extremes: the two ~ and the middle path, see *majjhimapaṭipadā.*

eye: five kinds, see *cakkhu*. Visual organ, see *āyatana.*

eye-consciousness: *cakkhu-viññāṇa*, see *dhātu, khandha.*

eye-organ: see *āyatana.*

E

F

factors: mental ~, see *cetasika*. ~ of absorption, see *jhāna*. ~ of enlightenment, see *bojjhaṅga*.

faculties: *indriya* (q.v.); see also *paccaya* 16.

fading away: see *virāga*.

faith: *saddhā* (q.v.).

faith-devotee and **faith-liberated one**: see *ariya-puggala* (B).

faithful-natured: *saddhā-carita*, see *carita*.

fatalism: see *diṭṭhi*.

favour, four ways of showing: see *saṅgaha-vatthu*.

feeling: *vedanā* (q.v.); further see *khandha*. Contemplation of ~: *vedanānupassanā*, see *satipaṭṭhāna*.

femininity: see *bhāva*, *indriya*.

fetters: the ten ~ binding to existence, see *saṃyojana*.

few wishes: see *appicchatā*.

fine-material sphere or world: see *avacara*, *loka*. Absorptions of the: *rūpajjhāna*, see *jhāna*.

fire-element: see *dhātu* (I).

fivefold sense-door, advertence to the: *pañcadvārāvajjana*, see *viññāṇa-kicca*.

five-group existence: *pañca-vokāra-bhava* (q.v.).

fixed destiny: see *niyata-micchā-diṭṭhi*, *niyata-puggala*.

fixity: see *niyama*, *tathatā*, *dhammaṭṭhiti-ñāṇa*.

floods, the four: *ogha* (q.v.); identical with the four cankers (*āsava*, q.v.).

food, material: is one of the four nutriments (*āhāra*, q.v.). Food-produced corporeality, see *samuṭṭhāna*. Refusing all further ~, see *dhutaṅga*. Loathsomeness of ~ see *āhāre paṭikkūla-saññā*.

foolish babble: *sampha-ppalāpa*, see *karma, kamma-patha* (I); cf. *tiracchāna-kathā.*

forbearance: *khanti* (q.v.).

forest-dweller, ascetic practice for the: see *dhutaṅga.*

formation: *saṅkhāra* (q.v.).

foundation: *nissaya*, one of the twenty-four conditions (*paccaya*, q.v.). Wrong ~ of morality, see *nissaya.* ~ of sympathy: *saṅgaha-vatthu* (q.v.) ~-forming absorptions: *pādakajjhāna* (q.v.); ~ of an arahat's mentality: see *adhiṭṭhāna.*

foundations of mindfulness, the four: *satipaṭṭhāna* (q.v.).

four-group existence: *catu-vokāra-bhava* (q.v.).

freedom of will, problem of the: cf. *paṭiccasamuppāda* (X).

friend, noble: *kalyāṇa-mitta* (q.v.).

frivolous talk: cf. *tiracchāna-kathā, kamma-patha* (I, 7), *karma, micchā-vācā.*

fruition (result of supermundane path): *phala*, see *ariya-puggala* (A).

fruits of monk-life: *sāmañña-phala* (q.v.)

full comprehension: *pariññā* (q.v.).

functional consciousness, or consciousness functioning independently of karma: *kiriya-citta* (q.v.); see *viññāṇa-kicca.*

functions of consciousness: *viññāṇa-kicca* (q.v.).

G

gantha: 'tie'. "There are four ties: the bodily tie (*kāya-gantha*) of covetousness (*abhijjhā*), of ill will (*vyāpāda*), of clinging to rule and ritual (*sīla-bbata-parāmāsa*), of dogmatical fanaticism (*idaṃsaccābhinivesa*)" (D. 33). "These things are ties, since they tie this mental and material body" (VISM. XXII, 54).

garuka-kamma: weighty karma, see *karma*.

gati (lit. 'going'): 'course of existence', destiny, destination. "There are five courses of existence: hell, animal kingdom, ghost realm, human world, heavenly world" (D. 33; A. XI, 68). Of these, the first three count as woeful courses (*duggati*, see *apāya*), the latter two as happy courses (*sugati*).

gems, the three: *ti-ratana* (q.v.).

generation, the four modes of: *yoni* (q.v.).

G

germinating once more: *eka-bījī*, is the name of one of the three kinds of *sotāpanna* (q.v.).

ghosts: cf. *peta*, *yakkha*, see *loka*.

giving: *dāna* (q.v.).

gladness: *somanassa* (q.v.). Indulging in ~, see *manopavicāra*.

gnosis: see *indriya* (21).

gotrabhū: lit. 'who has entered the lineage (of the Noble Ones)', i.e., the Matured One.

(I) 'Maturity-Moment' (*gotrabhū-citta*) is the last of the four impulsive moments (*javana*, q.v.; cf. *viññāṇa-kicca*) immediately preceding the entering into an absorption (*jhāna*, q.v.) or into one of the supermundane paths (see *ariya-puggala*, A.). Cf. *visuddhi* VII.

(II) The 'Matured One'. "He who is endowed with those things, immediately upon which follows the entrance into the noble path (*ariya-magga*), this person is called a 'Matured One'." (PUG. 10). In the com. to this passage it is said: "He who through perceiving Nibbāna, leaves behind the whole multitude of worldlings (*puthujjana*, q.v.), the family of worldlings, the circle of worldlings, the designation of a worldling and enters into the multitude of the Noble Ones, the family of the Noble Ones, the circle of the Noble Ones, and obtains the designation of a Noble One, such a being is called a Matured One." By this state of consciousness is meant the lightning-like transitional stage between the state of a worldling and that of a *sotāpanna*; see *ariya-puggala*. *Gotrabhū* is mentioned in this sense, i.e., as the ninth *ariya-puggala* (q.v.), in A. IX, 10; X, 16.

SOURCE NOTE: not found, or not found in this form or meaning, in the oldest parts of the Sutta Piṭaka; see *javana*.

gotrabhū-ñāṇa: 'maturity-knowledge'; see *gotrabhū*, *visuddhi* (VII)

gradual instruction: *ānupubbī-kathā* (q.v.).

grasping: cf. *parāmāsa*, *upādāna*.

great man, the eight thoughts of a: *mahāpurisavitakka* (q.v.).

greed: *lobha* (q.v.).

greedy consciousness: see Tab, I, III, (22–29).

greedy-natured: *rāga-carita*, see *carita*.

grief: *domanassa* (q.v.). Indulging in ~, see *manopavicāra*.

groups: of existence, see *khandha*; corporeal groups, see *rūpa-kalāpa*; corporeality-group, see *rūpa-kāya*; mind-group, see *nāma-kāya*.

growth, bodily: *rūpassa upacaya*: see *khandha* I.

grudge: see *paṭigha*.

gustatory organ: see *āyatana*.

H

habitual karma: *bahula-kamma*, see *karma*.

hadaya-vatthu: 'heart as physical base' of mental life. The heart, according to the commentaries as well as to the general Buddhist tradition, forms the physical base (*vatthu*) of consciousness. In the canonical texts, however, even in the Abhidhamma Piṭaka, no such base is ever localised, a fact which seems to have first been discovered by Shwe Zan Aung (*Compendium of Philosophy*, 277ff.). In the PATTH. we find repeatedly only the passage: "That material thing based on which mind-element and mind-consciousness element function" (*yaṃ rūpaṃ nissāya manodhātu ca manoviññāṇa-dhātu ca vattanti, taṃ rūpaṃ*).

hāna-bhāgiya-sīla, *~-samādhi*, *~-paññā*: morality, concentration or wisdom connected with decline. The other three stages are: *ṭhiti-bhāgiya-sīla*, etc. morality, etc. connected with a standstill; *visesa-bhāgiya-sīla*, etc.: morality, etc. connected with progress; *nibbedha-bhāgiya-sīla*, etc.: morality, etc. connected with penetration. Cf. A. IV, 179; VI, X, 71.

"'Decline' (*hāna*) is to be understood with regard to the arising of opposing qualities, 'standstill' (*ṭhiti*) with regard to the standstill of the corresponding attentiveness, 'progress' (*visesa*) with regard to higher excellency, 'penetration' (*nibbedha*) with regard to the arising of perception and reflection connected with the turning away (from existence)" (VISM. III). Cf. *vodāna* (2).

happiness: feeling of, see *sukha*; the idea of ~ (of the world), see *vipallāsa*.

happy courses of existence: see *gati*.

harmlessness: see *avihiṃsā*.

hasituppāda-citta: lit. 'consciousness producing mirth' (smile), is found in the Abhidhammattha Saṅgaha as a name for the joyful mind-consciousness element (*manoviññāṇa-dhātu*, TAB. I, 72) arising as functional consciousness independent of karma (*kiriya-citta*), only in the arahat.

SOURCE NOTE: this term is used in ABH. S. for the *citta*, TAB. I, 72. This type of consciousness (the Buddha's smile) is often implied in the suttas.

hate and **hatelessness**: (*dosa*, *adosa*) are two of the six karmic roots (*mūla*, q.v.) or root-conditions (*hetu*; *paccaya* 1).

hate-rooted consciousness: see TAB. I, (30, 31).

hate-natured: *dosa-carita*, see *carita*.

health-infatuation: see *mada*.

hearer (disciple): *sāvaka* (q.v.).

heat-element: *tejo-dhātu*, see *dhātu*.

hell: *niraya* (q.v.).

hetu: 'cause', condition, reason; (Abhidhamma) root-condition. In sutta usage it is almost synonymous with *paccaya*, 'condition', and often occurs together with it ('What is the cause, what is the condition', *ko hetu ko paccayo?*).

In Abhidhamma, it denotes the wholesome and unwholesome roots (*mūla*, q.v.). In that sense, as 'root-condition' (*hetu-paccaya*; see *paccaya*), it is the first of the twenty-four conditions given in the introduction to the Paṭṭhāna (see GUIDE, p. 117). The DHS. (1052–1082) and Paṭṭhāna (Duka-paṭṭh; GUIDE, p. 144) have sections on roots (*hetu*). The term is also used (a) for the classification of consciousness, as *sa-hetuka* and *a-hetuka*, with and without concomitant root-conditions; (b) for a division of rebirth-consciousness into *ahetuka*, *dvihetuka* and *tihetuka*, without, with two, or with three root-conditions (see *paṭisandhi*).

For *ahetuka-diṭṭhi*, the false view of the uncausedness of existence, see *diṭṭhi*.

higher wisdom: clear insight based on ~: see *vipassanā*. Training in ~, see *sikkhā*.

highest knowledge: see *aññā*.

hindrances, the five: *nīvaraṇa* (q.v.).

hiri-ottappa: 'moral shame and moral dread', are associated with all karmically wholesome consciousness (see TAB. II).

"To be ashamed of what one ought to be ashamed of, to be ashamed of performing evil and unwholesome things: this is called moral shame. To be in dread of what one ought to be in dread of, to be in dread of performing evil and unwholesome things: this is called moral dread" (Pug, 79, 80).

"Two lucid things, O monks, protect the world: moral shame and moral dread. If these two things were not to protect the world, then one would respect neither one's mother, nor one's mother's sister, nor one's brother's wife, nor one's teacher's wife. ... " (A. II, 7). Cf. *ahirika*. See ASL.TR. I, 164ff.

homelessness, going into: *pabbajjā* (q.v.). Cf. Progress of the disciple.

human world: cf. *loka*, *gati*.

I

iddhi: 'power', 'magical power'. The magical powers constitute one of the six kinds of higher spiritual powers (*abhiññā*, q.v.). One distinguishes many kinds of magical powers: the power of determination (*adhiṭṭhān'iddhi*), i.e., the power of becoming oneself manifold; the power of transformation (*vikubbana-iddhi*), i.e., the power of adopting another form; the power of spiritual creation (*manomaya-iddhi*), i.e., the power of letting issue from this body another mentally produced body; the power of penetrating knowledge (*ñāṇa-vipphara-iddhi*), i.e., the power of inherent insight to remain unhurt in danger; the power of penetrating concentration (*samādhivipphāra-iddhi*) producing the same result. The magical powers are treated in detail in VISM. XII; PTS.M., VIBH, They are not a necessary condition for final deliverance.

'Noble power' (*ariya-iddhi*) is the power of controlling one's ideas in such a way that one may consider something not repulsive as repulsive and something repulsive as not repulsive, and remain all the time imperturbable and full of equanimity. This training of mind is frequently mentioned in the suttas (e.g. M. 152, A. V. 144), but only once the name of *ariya-iddhi* is applied to it (D. 28). See further PTS.M., Iddhi-kathā, VISM. XII.

SOURCE NOTE: most, or perhaps all, of the ten terms listed at VISM. XII, as *adhiṭṭhāna*, etc., are absent in the older sutta texts. In PTS.M. (II, 205–214), however, they are enumerated in due order and minutely explained. The magical powers indicated by these terms are, nevertheless, for the most part explicitly described already in the oldest sutta texts. Cf. D. 34; M. 3; A. III, 99, etc.

iddhi-pāda: 'roads to power' (or success) consist of the following four qualities:

"For as guides, they indicate the road to power connected therewith; and because they form, by way of preparation, the roads to the power constituting the fruition of the path" (VISM. XII), namely: "concentration of intention (*chanda-samādhi*) accompanied by effort of will (*padhāna-saṅkhāra samannā-gata*), concentration of energy (*viriyasamādhi*) ... concentration of consciousness (*cittasamādhi*) ... and concentration of investigation (*vīmaṃsa-samādhi*) accompanied by effort of will."

As such, they are supermundane (*lokuttara*, i.e., connected with the path or the fruition of the path; see *ariya-puggala*). But they are mundane (*lokiya*, q.v.)

as predominant factors (*adhipati*; see *paccaya* 3), for it is said: "Because the monk, through making intention a predominant factor, reaches concentration, it is called the concentration of intention (*chanda-samādhi*), etc." (VISM. XII).

"These four roads of power lead to the attaining and acquiring of magical power, to the power of magical transformation, to the generation of magical power, and to mastery and skill therein" (PTS.M. II, 205, PTS). For a detailed explanation, see VISM. XII.

"Once the monk has thus developed and often practised the four roads to power, he enjoys various magical powers ... hears with the divine ear heavenly and human sounds ... perceives with his mind the mind of other beings ... remembers many a former existence ... perceives with the divine eye beings passing away and reappearing ... attains, after the extinction of cankers, deliverance of mind and deliverance through wisdom, free from cankers. ... (S. LI, 2). For a detailed explanation of these six higher powers, see *abhiññā*.

"Whosoever, O monks, has missed the four roads to power, he has missed the right path leading to the extinction of suffering; but whosoever, O monks, has reached the four roads to power, he has reached the right path leading to the extinction of suffering" (S. LI, 2).

See the chapter on *Iddhipāda* in *The Requisites of Enlightenment* by Ledi Sayadaw (WHEEL 169/172).

ignorance: *avijjā* (q.v.); further see *paṭiccasamuppāda* (1).

ill-humour, heavenly beings who come to grief through: *mano-padosika-deva* (q.v.).

ill will: *vyāpāda*, is a synonym of *dosa* (see *mūla*) and *paṭigha* and is one of the ten fetters (*saṃyojana*, q.v.), five hindrances (*nīvaraṇa*, q.v.) and ten unwholesome courses of action (see *kamma-patha*, I).

image, mental: see *nimitta*, *samādhi*, *kasiṇa*.

immaterial sphere: *arūpāvacara*: cf. *avacara*, *jhāna* (5–8); TAB. I.

immaterial world: *arūpa-loka*, see *loka*.

immediacy: an alternative rendering for contiguity-condition, *samanatara-paccaya*, which is one of the twenty-four conditions (*paccaya*, q.v.)

immediate, the: *ānantariya* (q.v.).

immortality: see *amata*.

imperfections: see *upakkilesa*.

impermanence: *anicca* (q.v.). Contemplation of ~, cf. *vipassanā* (1).

impersonality of existence: see *anatta*. Contemplation of: see *vipassanā* (3).

imperturbable karma-formations: *āneñjābhisaṅkhāra*, see *saṅkhāra*.

impression, sensorial or mental: *phassa* (q.v.).

impulsion: *javana* (q.v.).

impurities: see *upakkilesa*.

impurity of the body, contemplation of the: see *asubha*, *sīvathikā*.

inclinations: see *anusaya*.

independently enlightened: *pacceka-buddha* (q.v.).

indifferent feeling: see *vedanā*, *upekkhā*.

individual: *puggala* (q.v.).

indriya: 'faculties', is a name for twenty-two partly physical, partly mental, phenomena often treated in the suttas as well as in the Abhidhamma. They are:

1. eye: *cakkhu* 2. ear: *sota* 3. nose: *ghāna* 4. tongue: *jivhā* 5. body: *kāya* 6. mind: *mano*	six Bases (*āyatana*, q.v.)
7. femininity: *itthi* 8. masculinity: *purisa* 9. vitality: *jīvita*	Sex (*bhāva*, q.v.)
10. bodily pleasant feeling: *sukha* 11. bodily pain: *dukkha* 12. gladness: *somanassa* 13. sadness: *domanassa* 14. indifference: *upekkhā*	five Feelings (*vedanā*, q. v.)

I

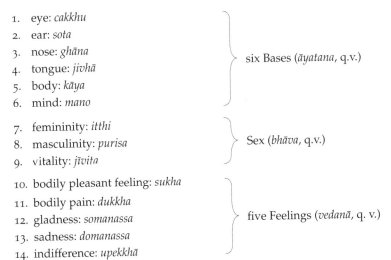

15. faith: *saddhā* 16. energy: *viriya* 17. mindfulness: *sati* 18. concentration: *samādhi* 19. wisdom: *paññā*	Five Spiritual Faculties (see *bala*)
20. the assurance: 'I shall know what I did not yet know!': *aññātañ-ñassāmīt'indriya* 21. the faculty of highest knowledge: *aññindriya* 22. the faculty of him who knows: *aññātāvindriya*.	three Supermundane Faculties

(1–5, 7–8) are physical; (9) is either physical or mental. All the rest are mental. (14) (see *upekkhā*) is here merely indifferent feeling (= *adukkha-m-asukhā vedanā*, i.e., 'neither pleasant nor unpleasant feeling') and not identical with that highly ethical state of equanimity (= *tatramajjhattatā*, i.e., 'keeping everywhere the middle', the equipoise of mind), also called *upekkhā* which belongs to the group of mental formations (*saṅkhārakkhandha*; see Tab II). (20) arises at the moment of entering the sotāpatti-path (*sotāpatti-magga*), (21) on reaching the sotāpatti-fruition (*sotāpatti-phala*), (22) at attaining the arahat-fruition (*arahatta-phala*). For the three last, see *ariya-puggala*.

The faculties, excepting (7) and (8), form one of the twenty-four conditions (*paccaya* 16, q.v.).

In VIBH. V all these faculties are treated in the above order, whereas S. XLVIII enumerates and explains them by way of the above indicated groups, leaving only 20–22 unexplained. See VISM. XVI; P. TO D. 138ff. For the five spiritual faculties (15–19), see *The Way of Wisdom* (WHEEL 65/66).

indriya-paccaya: see *paccaya* 16.

indriya-samatta: 'equilibrium, balance, or harmony of faculties', relates to the five spiritual faculties: faith, energy, mindfulness, concentration and wisdom (see *indriya* 15–19). Of these there are two pairs of faculties, in each of which both faculties should well counter-balance each other, namely: faith and wisdom (*saddhā, paññā*, q.v.) on the one hand and energy and concentration (*viriya, samādhi*, q.v.) on the other. For excessive faith with deficient wisdom leads to blind belief, while excessive wisdom with deficient faith leads to cunning. In the same way, great energy with weak concentration leads to restlessness, while strong concentration with deficient energy leads to indolence. Though for both faculties in each of the two pairs a balanced degree of intensity is desirable, mindfulness should be allowed to develop to the highest degree of strength. Cf. VISM. III.

SOURCE NOTE: this term is probably found for the first time in the com., esp. VISM. IV. The rudiments of this doctrine, however, are already found in the old sutta texts, e.g. A. III, 100.

indriya-saṃvara-sīla: 'morality consisting of purity of restraint of the senses', see *sīla*.

indriyesu gutta-dvāratā: 'guarding the sense-doors' is identical with sense-control (*indriya-saṃvara*, see *sīla*).

in-and-out-breathing, watching over: *ānāpāna-sati* (q.v.).

inducement: an alternative rendering for decisive-support condition, *upanissaya*, is one of the twenty-four conditions (*paccaya*; q.v.).

indulging (in joy, sadness etc.): see *manopavicāra*.

ineffective karma: see *karma*.

infatuation: cf. *mada*, *moha* (see *mūla*), *avijjā*.

inference of meaning: an 'expression the meaning of which is to be inferred': *neyyattha-dhamma* (q.v.). Antonym: 'expression with an established meaning': *nītattha-dhamma* (see *neyyattha-dhamma*).

inferiority-conceit: see *māna*.

influxes (cankers), the four: *āsava* (q.v.).

inoperative consciousness, karmically: see *kiriya-citta*.

inseparable mental factors, the seven ~ in all consciousness: see *cetanā*, *phassa*, *nāma*.

insight: cf. *paññā*, *vipassanā*, *ñāṇa*.

intelligent-natured: see *carita*.

intention: *chanda* (q.v.).

interest: *pīti* (q.v.); cf. TAB. II.

intimation: cf. *viññatti*.

intoxicants: see *āsava*.

intoxicating drinks, the evil effect of taking: see *surāmeraya*.

investigating function (of consciousness): *santīraṇa*, see *viññāṇa-kicca*.

investigation, full understanding through: *tīraṇapariññā*, see *pariññā*. 'Investigation' (*vīmaṃsā*) is one of the four roads to power (*iddhipāda*, q.v.) and one of the four predominants (*adhipati*; see *paccaya* 3). ~ of truth: *dhamma-vicaya*, is one of the seven factors of enlightenment (*bojjhaṅga*, q.v.).

iriyā-patha (lit. 'ways of movement'): 'bodily postures', i.e., going, standing, sitting, lying. In the Satipaṭṭhāna Sutta (see *satipaṭṭhāna*), they form the subject of a contemplation and an exercise in mindfulness.

"While going, standing, sitting or lying down, the monk knows 'I go', 'I stand', 'I sit', 'I lie down'; he understands any position of the body." "The disciple understands that there is no living being, no real ego, that goes, stands, etc., but that it is by a mere figure of speech that one says: 'I go', 'I stand', and so forth." (com.).

issā: 'envy', is a karmically unwholesome (*akusala*) mental factor, which is occasionally associated with hate-rooted consciousness (see TAB. I, 30, 31,). Explained in PUG. 55.

itthindriya: 'femininity', see *bhāva*.

J

janaka-kamma: 'regenerative karma', see *karma*.

jarā: 'old age, decay', is one of the three divine messengers (see *deva-dūta*, q.v.). For its conditioning by birth, see *paṭiccasamuppāda* (11).

jāti: 'birth', comprises the entire embryonic process beginning with conception and ending with parturition.

"The birth of beings belonging to this or that order of beings, their being born, their conception (*okkanti*) and springing into existence, the manifestation of the groups (corporeality, feeling, perception, mental formations, consciousness; see *khandha*), the acquiring of their sensitive organs: this is called birth" (D. 22). For its conditioning by the prenatal karma-process (*kamma-bhava*; see *bhava*), see *paṭiccasamuppāda* (9, 10), *paṭisandhi*.

javana (fr. *javati*, to impel): 'impulsion', is the phase of full cognition in the cognitive series, or perceptual process (*citta-vīthi*; see *viññāṇa-kicca*) occurring at its climax, if the respective object is large or distinct. It is at this phase that karma is produced, i.e., wholesome or unwholesome volition concerning the perception that was the object of the previous stages of the respective process of consciousness. There are normally seven impulsive moments. In mundane consciousness (*lokiya*, q.v.), any of the seventeen karmically wholesome classes of consciousness (TAB. I, 1–17) or of the twelve unwholesome ones (TAB. I, 22–23) may arise at the phase of impulsion. For the arahat, however, impulsion has no longer a karmic, i.e., rebirth-producing character, but is a karmically independent function (*kiriya*, q.v.; TAB. I, 72–89). There are further eight supermundane classes of impulsion (TAB. I, 18–21, 66–69).

The four impulsive moments immediately before entering an absorption (*jhāna*, q.v.) or one of the supermundane paths (*magga*; see *ariya-puggala*) are: the preparatory (*parikamma*), approach (*upacāra*), adaptation (*anuloma*), and maturity-moment (*gotrabhū*, q.v.). In connection with entering the earth-kasina absorption (see *kasiṇa*), they are explained as follows, in VISM. IV:

"After the breaking off of the subconscious stream of being (*bhavaṅga-sota*, q.v.), there arises the 'advertence at the mind-door' (*manodvārāvajjana*, see *viññāṇa-kicca*), taking as object the earth-kasina (while thinking), 'Earth! Earth!' Thereupon, four or five impulsive moments flash forth, amongst which the last one (maturity-moment) belongs to the fine-material sphere (*rūpāvacara*), whereas the rest belong to the sense-sphere (*kāmāvacara*; see *avacara*), though the last one is more powerful in thought conception, discursive thinking, interest (rapture), joy and concentration (cf. *jhāna*) than the states of consciousness belonging to the sense-sphere. They are called 'preparatory' (*parikamma-samādhi*), as they are preparing for the attainment-concentration (*appanā-samādhi*); 'approaching' (*upacāra-samādhi*), as they are close to the attainment-concentration and are moving in its neighbourhood; 'adaptive' (*anuloma*), as they adapt themselves to the preceding preparatory states and to the succeeding attainment concentration. The last one of the four is called 'matured' (*gotrabhū*). In a similar way, the impulsive moments before reaching the divine ear are described in VISM. XIII, 1. Cf. *Karma*.

SOURCE NOTE: the only reference in the Sutta Piṭaka is PTS.M. II, 73: *kusala-kammassa javana-khaṇe*, "in the impulsion-moment of a wholesome karma." In the Abhidhamma Piṭaka it is briefly mentioned in the Paṭṭhāna, but without explanation, as if already known. The teaching of the flashing forth of four *javanas* immediately before entering the *jhāna* or *lokuttara-magga*, i.e., *parikamma, upacāra, anuloma, gotrabhū* is, as such, without doubt a later development in the commentarial literature.

jewels, the three: *ti-ratana* (q.v.).

jhāna: 'absorption' (meditation) refers chiefly to the four meditative absorptions of the fine-material sphere (*rūpajjhāna* or *rūpāvacara-jjhāna*; see *avacara*). They are achieved through the attainment of full (or attainment-, or ecstatic) concentration (*appanā*, see *samādhi*), during which there is a complete, though temporary, suspension of fivefold sense-activity and of the five hindrances (see *nīvaraṇa*). The state of consciousness, however, is one of full alertness and lucidity. This high degree of concentration is generally developed by the practice of one of the forty subjects of tranquillity meditation (*samatha-kammaṭṭhāna*; see *bhāvanā*). Often also the four immaterial spheres (*arūpāyatana*) are called absorptions of the immaterial sphere (*arūpajjhāna* or *arūpāvacara-jjhāna*). The stereotype text, often met with in the suttas, runs as follows:

(1) "Detached from sensual objects, O monks, detached from unwholesome consciousness, attached with thought-conception (*vitakka*) and discursive thinking (*vicāra*), born of detachment (*vivekaja*) and filled with rapture (*pīti*) and joy (*sukha*) he enters the first absorption.

(2) "After the subsiding of thought-conception and discursive thinking, and

by gaining inner tranquillity and oneness of mind, he enters into a state free from thought-conception and discursive thinking, the second absorption, which is born of concentration (*samādhi*), and filled with rapture (*pīti*) and joy (*sukha*).

(3) "After the fading away of rapture he dwells in equanimity, mindful, clearly conscious; and he experiences in his person that feeling of which the Noble Ones say, 'Happy lives the man of equanimity and attentive mind'; thus he enters the third absorption.

(4) "After having given up pleasure and pain, and through the disappearance of previous joy and grief, he enters into a state beyond pleasure and pain, into the fourth absorption, which is purified by equanimity (*upekkhā*) and mindfulness.

(5) "Through the total overcoming of the perceptions of matter, however, and through the vanishing of sense-reactions and the non-attention to the perceptions of variety, with the idea, 'Boundless is space', he reaches the sphere of boundless space (*ākāsānañcāyatana*) and abides therein.

"By 'perceptions of matter' (*rūpa-saññā*) are meant the absorptions of the fine-material sphere, as well as those objects themselves ... "(VISM. X, 1).

"By 'perceptions of sense-reactions' (*paṭigha-saññā*) *are* meant those perceptions that have arisen due to the impact of sense organs (eye, etc.) and the sense-objects (visible objects, etc.). They are a name for the perception of visible objects, as it is said (Jhāna-VIBH.): 'What are here the perceptions of sense-reactions? They are the perceptions of visible objects, sounds, etc.' Surely, they do no longer exist even for one who has entered the first absorption, etc., for at such a time the five-sense consciousness is no longer functioning. Nevertheless, this is to be understood as having been said in praise of this immaterial absorption, in order to incite the striving for it" (VISM. X, 16).

"Perceptions of variety (*nānatta-saññā*) are the perceptions that arise in various fields, or the various perceptions" (ib.). Hereby, according to VISM. X, 20, are meant the multiform perceptions outside the absorptions.

(6) "Through the total overcoming of the sphere of boundless space, and with the idea 'Boundless is consciousness', he reaches the sphere of boundless consciousness (*viññāṇañcāyatana*) and abides therein.

(7) "Through the total overcoming of the sphere of boundless consciousness, and with the idea 'Nothing is there', he reaches the sphere of nothingness (*ākiñcaññāyatana*) and abides therein.

(8) "Through the total overcoming of the sphere of nothingness he reaches the sphere of neither-perception-nor-non-perception (*nevasaññā-n'āsaññā-yatana*) and abides therein."

"Thus the first absorption is free from five things (i.e., the hindrances, *nīvaraṇa*, q.v.), and five things are present (i.e., the factors of absorption; *jhānaṅga*). Whenever the monk enters the first absorption, there have vanished sensuous desire, ill will, sloth and torpor, restlessness and scruples, doubts; and there are present: thought-conception (*vitakka*), discursive thinking (*vicāra*) rapture (*pīti*), joy (*sukha*), and concentration (*samādhi*). In the second absorption there are present: rapture, joy and concentration; in the third: joy and concentration; in the fourth: equanimity (*upekkhā*) and concentration" (VISM. IV).

The four absorptions of the immaterial sphere (see above 5–8) still belong, properly speaking, to the fourth absorption as they possess the same two constituents. The fourth fine-material absorption is also the base or starting point (*pādaka-jhāna*, q.v.) for the attaining of the higher spiritual powers (*abhiññā*, q.v.).

In the Abhidhamma, generally a fivefold instead of a fourfold division of the fine-material absorptions is used: the second absorption has still the constituent 'discursive thinking' (but without thought-conception), while the third, fourth and fifth correspond to the second, third, and fourth, respectively, of the fourfold division (see TAB. I, 9–13). This fivefold division is based on such sutta texts as A. VIII, 63.

For the eight absorptions as objects for the development of insight (*vipassanā*), see *samatha-vipassanā*; full details are given in VISM. IV-X.

Jhāna in its widest sense (e.g. as one of the twenty-four conditions; see *paccaya* 17), denotes any—even momentary or weak—absorption of mind, when directed on a single object.

jhānaṅga: 'constituents (or factors) of absorption', see *jhāna*.

jhāna-paccaya: one of the twenty-four conditions (*paccaya*, q.v.).

jīva: life, vital principle, individual soul. 'Soul (life) and body are identical' and 'soul and body are different', these two frequently quoted wrong views fall under the two kinds of personality-belief (*sakkāya-diṭṭhi*; see *diṭṭhi*), i.e., the first one under the annihilation-belief (*uccheda-diṭṭhi*) and the second under the eternity-belief (*sassata-diṭṭhi*).

"Verily, if one holds the view that the soul (life) is identical with the body, in that case a holy life is not possible; or if one holds the view that the soul (life) is something quite different, also in that case a holy life is impossible. Both these extremes the Perfect One has avoided and shown the Middle Doctrine, which says: 'On ignorance depend the karma-formations, on the karma-formations depends consciousness', etc." (S. XII, 35).

jīvita and **jīvitindriya**: 'life, vitality', may be either physical (*rūpa-jīvitindriya*) or mental (*nāma-jīvitindriya*). The latter is one of the mental factors inseparably associated with all consciousness; cf. *nāma, cetanā, phassa*.

jīvita-navaka-kalāpa: ninefold vital group, see *rūpakalāpa*.

joy: *somanassa* (q.v.). Altruistic ~: *muditā* (see *brahma-vihāra*).

K

kabaliṅkārāhāra: lit. 'food formed into balls', i.e., food formed into mouthfuls for eating (according to Indian custom); it denotes 'material food' and belongs, together with the three mental nutriments, to the group of four nutriments (see *āhāra*).

kalāpa, 'group', 'unit': 1. 'corporeal unit' (see *rūpakalāpa*).

2. It has the meaning of 'group of existence' (*khandha*) in *kalāpasamma-sana* (see *sammasana*), i.e., 'comprehension by groups', which is the application of 'methodical (or inductive) insight' (*naya-vipassanā*) to the comprehension of the five aggregates (*khandha*) as impermanent, painful and non-self. It is a process of methodical summarisation, or generalisation, from one's own meditative experience that is applied to each of the five aggregates, viewed as past, present, future, as internal and external, etc. In VISM. XX, where the 'comprehension by groups' is treated in detail, it is said to constitute 'the beginning of insight' as it leads to the 'knowledge of rise and fall', being the first of the eight insight-knowledges (see *visuddhi* VI). It is necessary for accomplishing the fifth purification (see *visuddhi* V; VISM. XX, 2, 6ff.).

SOURCE NOTE: this doctrinal term, as well as the doctrine of the different corporeal units or groups, such as the *suddhaṭṭhaka-~*, *jīvitanavaka-~*, *cakkhudasaka-~*, etc. (see VISM. XVIII), belong only to the later developments of exegetical literature, as VISM. etc.

kalpa (SKR.): *kappa* (q.v.).

kalyāṇa-mitta: 'noble (or good) friend', is called a senior monk who is the mentor and friend of his pupil, "wishing for his welfare and concerned with his progress", guiding his meditation; in particular, the meditation teacher (*kammaṭṭhānacariya*) is so called. For details see VISM. III, 28, 57ff. The Buddha said that "noble friendship is the entire holy life" (S. III, 18; XLV, 2), and he himself is the good friend par excellence: "Ananda, it is owing to my being a good friend to them that living beings subject to birth are freed from birth" (S. III, 18).

kāma: may denote, 1. subjective sensuality, 'sense desire'; 2. objective sensuality, the five sense-objects.

1. Subjective sensuality, or sense-desire, is directed to all five sense-objects, and is synonymous with *kāmacchanda*, 'sensuous desire', one of the five hindrances (*nīvaraṇa*, q.v.); *kāma-rāga*, sensuous lust', one of the ten fetters (*saṃyojana*, q.v.); *kāma-taṇhā*, 'sensuous craving', one of the three cravings (*taṇhā*, q.v.); *kāmavitakka*, 'sensuous thought', one of the three wrong thoughts (*micchā-saṅkappa*; see *vitakka*). Sense-desire is also one of the cankers (*āsava*, q.v.) and clingings (*upādāna*, q.v.).

2. Objective sensuality is, in the canonical texts, mostly called *kāma-guṇa*, 'cords (or strands) of sensuality'.

"There are five cords of sensuality: the visible objects, cognisable by eye-consciousness, that are desirable, cherished, pleasant, lovely, sensuous and alluring; the sounds ... smells ... tastes ... bodily impressions cognisable by body-consciousness, that are desirable. ... " (D. 33; M. 13, 26, 59, 66).

These two kinds of *kāma* are called 1. *kilesa-kāma*, i.e., *kāma* as a mental defilement, 2. *vatthu-kāma*, i.e., *kāma* as the object-base of sensuality; first in M.NID. I, 1, and frequently in the commentaries.

Sense-desire is finally eliminated at the stage of the non-returner (*anāgāmī*; see *ariya-puggala*, *saṃyojana*).

The peril and misery of sense-desire is often described in the texts, e.g. in stirring similes at M. 22, 54, and in the 'gradual instruction' (see *ānupubbī-kathā*). See further M. 13, 45, 75; SN. V. 766ff.; DHP. 186, 215.

The texts often stress the fact that what binds man to the world of the senses are not the sense organs nor the sense-objects but lustful desire (*chandarāga*). On this see A. VI, 63; S. XXXV, 122, 191.

SOURCE NOTE: *vatthu-~* and *kilesa-~* are probably found for the first time in M.NID. 1. They correspond to the *pañca kāmaguṇā* (*cakkhu-viññeyyā rūpā, etc.*) and *kāma-rāga* in the older sutta texts (e.g. A. VI, 68).

kāma-bhava: 'sensuous existence', see *bhava*.

kāmacchanda: 'sensuous desire', see *nīvaraṇa*, *chanda*.

kāma-guna: see *kāma*.

kāma-loka: 'sensuous world', see *loka*.

kāma-rāga: 'sensuous lust', is one of the ten fetters (*saṃyojana*, q.v.).

kāmāsava: see *āsava*.

kāma-sukh'allikānuyoga: 'being addicted to sensual pleasures', is one of the two extremes to be avoided by the monk; see *majjhimā paṭipadā*.

kāma-taṇhā: 'sensuous craving', see *taṇhā*.

kāmāvacara: 'sensuous sphere', see *avacara*.

kāmesumicchācāra: lit. 'wrong or evil conduct with regard to sensual things'; 'sexual misconduct' refers to adultery, and to such behaviour with minors or other persons under guardianship. The abstaining from such unlawful behaviours is one of the five moral rules (see *sikkhā-pada*) binding upon all Buddhists. Through any other sexual act one does not become guilty of the above transgression, which is considered a great crime. The monk, however, has to observe perfect chastity.

In many suttas (e.g. A.X., 176) we find the following explanation: "He avoids sexual misconduct, abstains from it. He has no intercourse with girls who are still under the protection of father or mother, brother, sister or relatives, nor with married women, nor female convicts, nor, lastly, with betrothed girls."

kamma: (wholesome or unwholesome) action, see *karma*.

SOURCE NOTE: *ahosi-, janaka-, garuka-, bahula-, upatthambhaka-, upaghātaka-, upapīḷaka-, maraṇāsanna-, upacchedaka-*~ None of these terms is found in the sutta or ABH. canon. They have been introduced by the commentators (e.g. in ABH. S. and VISM.) for the purpose of a systematic grouping of the various aspects and functions of karma. The term *kaṭattā*, however, occurs repeatedly in the ABH. canon in such expressions as: '*Yasmiṃ samaye … kusalassa kammassa kaṭattā … cakkhuviññāṇaṃ hoti. …*' (DHS. § 431); or: '*Yaṃ atthi rūpaṃ kammassa kaṭattā. …*' (DHS. § 653); or '*katattā ca rūpānaṃ*' (PATTH.), etc.

kamma-bhava: see *bhava, paṭiccasamuppāda*.

kammaja-rūpa: 'karma-produced corporeality', see *samuṭṭhāna*.

kammaññatā: 'adaptability', i.e., of corporeality (*rūpassa*; see *khandha*, summary I), mental factors (*kāya*), and of consciousness (*citta*); cf. TAB. II.

SOURCE NOTE: not found, or not found in this form or meaning, in the oldest parts of the Sutta Piṭaka; see *lahutā*.

kammanta, sammā~: 'right action', see *magga*.

kamma-paccaya: 'karma as condition', see *paccaya* (13).

kamma-patha: 'course of action', is a name for the group of ten kinds of either unwholesome or wholesome actions, viz.

I. The tenfold unwholesome courses of action (*akusala-kamma-patha*):
- three bodily actions: killing, stealing, sexual misconduct;
- four verbal actions: lying, slandering, rude speech, foolish babble;
- three mental actions: covetousness, ill will, evil views.

Unwholesome mental courses of action comprise only extreme forms of defiled thought: the greedy wish to appropriate others' property, the hateful thought of harming others, and pernicious views. Milder forms of mental defilement are also unwholesome, but do not constitute 'courses of action'.

II. The tenfold wholesome course of action (*kusalakamma-patha*):
- three bodily actions: avoidance of killing, stealing, sexual misconduct;
- four verbal actions: avoidance of lying, slandering, rude speech, foolish babble; i.e., true, conciliatory, mild, and wise speech;
- three mental actions: unselfishness, good-will, right views.

Both lists occur repeatedly, e.g. in A. X, 28, 176; M. 9; they are explained in detail in M. 114, and in com. to M. 9 (R.UND., p. 14), ASL.TR. I, 126ff.

kamma-samuṭṭhāna-rūpa: 'corporeality produced through karma', see *samuṭṭhāna*.

kammaṭṭhāna: lit. 'working-ground' (i.e., for meditation), is the term in the com. for 'subjects of meditation'; see *bhāvanā*.

SOURCE NOTE: this term, as a designation for the meditation exercises (*bhāvanā*), is found only in the com. In the suttas the word is only used in a concrete sense for 'field of activity or occupation', as agriculture, trade, etc.

kamma-vaṭṭa: 'karma-round', see *vaṭṭa*.

kammāyūhana: see *āyūhana*.

kāmupādāna: 'sensuous clinging', is one of the four kinds of clinging (*upādāna*, q.v.).

kaṅkhā: 'doubt'; either an intellectual, critical doubt or an ethically and psycho-logically detrimental doubt. The latter may either be a persistent negative scepticism or wavering indecision. Only the detrimental doubt (identical with *vicikicchā*, q.v.) is to be rejected as karmically unwholesome, as it paralyses thinking and hinders the inner development of man. Reasoned, critical doubt in dubious matters is thereby not discouraged.

The sixteen doubts enumerated in the suttas (e.g. M. 2) are the following:

"Have I been in the past? Or, have I not been in the past? What have I been in the past? How have I been in the past? From what state into what state did I change in the past? Shall I be in the future? Or, shall I not be in the future? What shall I be in the future? How shall I be in the future? From what state into what state shall I change in the future? Am I? Or, am I not? What am I? How am I? Whence has this being come? Whither will it go?"

kaṅkhā-vitaraṇa-visuddhi: 'purification by overcoming doubt', is the fourth of the seven stages of purification (*visuddhi*, q.v.).

kappa (SKR. *kalpa*): 'world-period', an inconceivably long space of time, an aeon. This again is subdivided into four sections: world-dissolution (*samvaṭṭakappa*) dissolving world), continuation of the chaos (*samvaṭṭa-ṭṭhāyī*), world-formation (*vivaṭṭa-kappa*), continuation of the formed world (*vivaṭṭaṭṭhāyī*).

"How long a world-dissolution will continue, how long the chaos, how long the formation, how long the continuation of the formed world, of these things; O monks, one hardly can say that it will be so many years, or so many centuries, or so many millennia, or so many hundred thousands of years" (A. IV, 156). A detailed description of the four world-periods is given in that stirring discourse on the all-embracing impermanence in A. VII, 62.

The beautiful simile in S. XV, 5 may be mentioned here:

"Suppose, O monks, there was a huge rock of one solid mass, one mile long, one mile wide, one mile high, without split or flaw. And at the end of every hundred years a man should come and rub against it once with a silken cloth. Then that huge rock would wear off and disappear quicker than a world-period. But of such world-periods, O monks, many have passed away, many hundreds, many thousands, many hundred thousands. And how is this possible? Inconceivable, O monks, is this *saṃsāra* (q.v.), not to be discovered is any first beginning of beings, who obstructed by ignorance and ensnared by craving, are hurrying and hastening through this round of rebirths."

Compare here Grimm's German fairy-tale of the little shepherd boy: 'In Farther Pommerania there is the diamond-mountain, one hour high, one hour wide, one hour deep. There every hundred years a little bird comes and whets its little beak on it. And when the whole mountain is ground off, then the first second of eternity has passed."

karma (SKR.), Pali: *kamma*: 'action', correctly speaking denotes the wholesome and unwholesome volitions (*kusala-* and *akusala-cetanā*) and their concomitant mental factors, causing rebirth and shaping the destiny of beings. These karmic volitions (*kamma cetanā*) become manifest as wholesome or unwholesome actions by body (*kāya-kamma*), speech (*vacīkamma*) and mind (*mano-kamma*). Thus the Buddhist term *karma* by no means signifies the result of actions, and quite certainly not the fate of man, or perhaps even of whole nations (the so-called wholesale or mass-karma), misconceptions which, through the influence of theosophy, have become widely spread in the West.

"Volition (*cetanā*), O monks, is what I call action (*cetanāhaṃ bhikkhave kammaṃ vadāmi*), for through volition one performs the action by body, speech, or mind. ... There is karma (action), O monks, that ripens in hell. ... Karma that ripens in the animal world. ... Karma that ripens in the world of men. ... Karma that ripens in the heavenly world. ... Threefold, however, is the fruit of karma: ripening during the lifetime (*diṭṭha-dhammavedanīya-kamma*), ripening in the next birth (*upapajjavedanīya-kamma*), ripening in later births (*aparāpariya-vedanīya-kamma*). ... " (A.VI, 63).

The three conditions or roots (*mūla*, q.v.) of unwholesome karma (actions) are greed, hatred, delusion (*lobha*, *dosa*, *moha*); those of wholesome karma are: unselfishness (*alobha*), hatelessness (*adosa* = *mettā*, good-will), undeludedness (*amoha* = *paññā*, knowledge).

"Greed, O monks, is a condition for the arising of karma; hatred is a condition for the arising of karma; delusion is a condition for the arising of karma." (A. III, 109).

"The unwholesome actions are of three kinds, conditioned by greed, or hate, or delusion.

"Killing ... stealing ... sexual misconduct ... lying ... slandering ... rude speech ... foolish babble, if practised, carried on, and frequently cultivated, leads to rebirth in hell, or amongst the animals, or amongst the ghosts" (A. III, 40). "He who kills and is cruel goes either to hell or, if reborn as man, will be short-lived. He who torments others will be afflicted with disease. The angry one will look ugly, the envious one will be without influence, the stingy one will be poor, the stubborn one will be of low descent, the indolent one will be without knowledge. In the contrary case, man will be reborn in heaven or reborn as man, he will be long-lived, possessed of beauty, influence, noble descent and knowledge" (cf. M. 135).

For the above tenfold wholesome and unwholesome course of action, see *kamma-patha*. For the five heinous crimes with immediate result, see *ānantarika-kamma*.

"Owners of their karma are the beings, heirs of their karma, their karma is their womb from which they are born, their karma is their friend, their refuge. Whatever karma they perform, good or bad, thereof they will be the heirs" (M. 135).

With regard to the time of the taking place of the karma result (*vipāka*), one distinguishes, as mentioned above, three kinds of karma:

1. karma ripening during the lifetime (*diṭṭhadhamma-vedanīya-kamma*);
2. karma ripening in the next birth (*upapajjavedanīya-kamma*);
3. karma ripening in later births (*aparāpariyavedanīya-kamma*).

The first two kinds of karma may be without karma result (*vipāka*), if the circumstances required for the taking place of the karma result are missing, or if, through the preponderance of counteractive karma and their being too weak, they are unable to produce any result. In this case they are called *ahosi-kamma*, lit. 'karma that has been', in other words, ineffectual karma.

The third type of karma, however, which bears fruit in later lives, will, whenever and wherever there is an opportunity, be productive of karma result. Before its result has ripened, it will never become ineffective as long as the life-process is kept going by craving and ignorance.

According to the com., e.g. VISM. XIX, the first of the seven karmic impulsive-moments (*kamma javana*; see *javana*) is considered as 'karma ripening during the lifetime', the seventh moment as 'karma ripening in the next birth', the remaining five moments as 'karma ripening in later births'.

With regard to their functions one distinguishes types of *kamma*:

1. Regenerative (or productive) karma (*janaka-kamma*) produces the five groups of existence (corporeality, feeling, perception, mental formations, consciousness) at rebirth as well as during life-continuity.
2. Supportive (or consolidating) karma (*upatthambhaka-kamma*) does not produce karma results but is only able to maintain the already produced karma results.
3. Counteractive (suppressive or frustrating) karma (*upapīḷaka-kamma*) counteracts or suppresses the karma results.
4. Destructive (or supplanting) karma (*upaghātaka*-or *upacchedaka-kamma*) destroys the influence of a weaker karma and effects only its own result.

With regard to the priority of their result one distinguishes:

1. weighty karma (*garuka-kamma*),
2. habitual karma (*āciṇṇaka-* or *bahula-kamma*),
3. death-proximate karma (*maraṇāsanna-kamma*),
4. stored-up karma (*kaṭattā-kamma*).

(1, 2) The weighty (*garuka*) and the habitual (*bahula*) wholesome or unwholesome karma are ripening earlier than the light and rarely performed karma. (3) The death-proximate (*maraṇāsanna*) karma—i.e., the wholesome or unwholesome volition present immediately before death, which often may be the reflex of some previously performed good or evil action (*kamma*), or of a sign of it (*kamma-nimitta*), or of a sign of the future existence (*gati-nimitta*)—produces rebirth. (4) In the absence of any of these three actions at the moment before death, the stored-up (*kaṭattā*) karma will produce rebirth.

A real, and in the ultimate sense true, understanding of Buddhist karma doctrine is possible only through a deep insight into the impersonality (see *anatta*) and conditionality (see *paṭiccasamuppāda, paccaya*) of all phenomena of existence. "Everywhere, in all the forms of existence ... such a one is beholding merely mental and physical phenomena kept going by their being bound up through causes and effects.

"No doer does he see behind the deeds, no recipient apart from the karma-fruit. And with full insight he clearly understands that the wise ones are using merely conventional terms when, with regard to the taking place of any action, they speak of a doer, or when they speak of a receiver of the karma results at their arising."

Therefore the ancient masters have said:

'No doer of the deeds is found,
No one who ever reaps their fruits;
Empty phenomena roll on:
This view alone is right and true.

'And while the deeds and their results
Roll on, based on conditions all,
There no beginning can be seen,
Just as it is with seed and tree.'" (VISM. XIX)

Karma (*kamma-paccaya*) is one of the twenty-four conditions (*paccaya*, q.v.); see *kamma*, source note.

LITERATURE: *Karma and Rebirth*, by Nyanatiloka (WHEEL 9); *Survival and Karma*

K

in Buddhist Perspective, by K.N. Jayatilleke (WHEEL 141/143); *Kamma and its Fruit* (WHEEL 221/224).

karma-accumulation: *āyūhana* (q.v.).

karma-formations: *saṅkhāra*, i.e., wholesome or unwholesome volitions (*cetanā*) manifested as actions of body, speech or mind, form the second link of the formula of dependent origination (*paṭicca-samuppāda*, q.v.).

karma-process: see *bhava, paṭiccasamuppāda.*

karma-produced corporeality: see *samuṭṭhāna.*

karma result: *vipāka* (q.v.).

karma-round: *kamma-vaṭṭa* (see *vaṭṭa*).

karmically acquired corporeality: *upādiṇṇarūpa* (q.v.).

karmically wholesome, unwholesome, neutral: *kusala* (q.v.), *akusala* (q.v.), *avyākata* (q.v.); cf. TAB. I.

karuṇā: 'compassion', is one of the four sublime abodes (*brahma-vihāra*, q.v.).

kasiṇa: (perhaps related to SKR. *krtsna*, 'all, complete, whole'), is the name for a purely external device to produce and develop concentration of mind and attain the four absorptions (*jhāna* q.v.). It consists in concentrating one's full and undivided attention on one visible object as preparatory image (*parikamma-nimitta*), e.g. a coloured spot or disc, or a piece of earth, or a pond at some distance, etc., until at last one perceives, even with the eyes closed, a mental reflex, the acquired image (*uggaha-nimitta*). Now, while continuing to direct one's attention to this image, there may arise the spotless and immovable counter-image (*paṭibhāga-nimitta*), and together with it the neighbourhood-concentration (*upacāra-samādhi*) will have been reached. While still persevering in the concentration on the object, one finally will reach a state of mind where all sense-activity is suspended, where there is no more seeing and hearing, no more perception of bodily impression and feeling, i.e., the state of the first mental absorption (*jhāna*, q.v.).

The ten kasinas mentioned in the suttas are: earth-kasina, water, fire, wind, blue, yellow, red, white, space, and consciousness. "There are ten kasina-spheres: someone sees the earth kasina, above, below, on all sides, undivided, unbounded … someone sees the water-kasina, above, below, etc." (M. 77; D. 33) Cf. *abhibhāyatan, bhāvanā*; further see FUND. IV.

For space and consciousness-kasina we find in VISM. V the names limited space-kasina (*paricchinnākāsa-kasiṇa*) and light-kasina (*āloka-kasiṇa*).

For full description see VISM. IV-V; also ASL.TR. I, 248.

kaṭattā-kamma: 'stored-up karma', see *karma*.

SOURCE NOTE: not found, or not found in this form or meaning, in the oldest parts of the Sutta Piṭaka; see *kamma*.

kāya (lit: accumulation): 'group', 'body', may either refer to the physical body (*rūpa-kāya*) or to the mental body (*nāma-kāya*). In the latter case it is either a collective name for the mental groups (feeling, perception, mental formations, consciousness; see *khandha*), or merely for feeling, perception and a few of the mental formations (see *nāma*), e.g. in *kāya-lahutā*, etc. (cf. TAB. II). *Kāya* has this same meaning in the standard description of the third absorption (*jhāna*, q.v.) "and he feels joy in his mind or his mental constitution (*kāya*)", and (e.g. PUG. 1–8) of the attainment of the eight deliverances (*vimokkha*, q.v.); "having attained the eight deliverances in his mind, or his person (*kāya*)." *Kāya* is also the fifth sense organ, the body-organ; see *āyatana*, *dhātu*, *indriya*.

kāya-gatā-sati: 'mindfulness with regard to the body', refers sometimes (e.g. VISM. VIII, 2) only to the contemplation on the thirty-two parts of the body, some-times (e.g. M. 119) to all the various meditations comprised under the 'contemplation of the body' (*kāyānupassanā*), the first of the four 'foundations of mindfulness' (*satipaṭṭhāna*, q.v.), consisting partly in concentration (*samādhi*) exercises, partly in insight (*vipassanā*) exercises. On the other hand, the cemetery meditations (*sīvathika*, q.v.) mentioned in the Satipaṭṭhāna Sutta (M. 10) are nearly the same as the ten contemplations of loathsomeness (*asubha-bhāvanā*, q.v.). of VISM. VI, whereas elsewhere the contemplation on the thirty-two parts of the body is called the 'reflection on impurity' (*paṭikkūla-saññā*).

In such texts as: 'One thing, O monks, developed and repeatedly practised, leads to the attainment of wisdom. It is the contemplation on the body' (A. I), the reference is to all exercises mentioned in the first Satipaṭṭhāna.

VISM. VIII, 2 gives a detailed description and explanation of the method of developing the contemplation on the thirty-two parts of the body. This exercise can produce the first absorption only (*jhāna*, q.v.). The stereotype text given in the Satipaṭṭhāna Sutta and elsewhere—but leaving out the brain—runs as follows: "And further, O monks, the monk contemplates this body from the soles of the feet upward, and from the tops of the hairs downward, with skin stretched over it, and filled with manifold impurities: 'This body has hairs of the head, hairs of the body, nails, teeth, skin, flesh, sinews, bones, marrow, kidneys, heart, liver, diaphragm, spleen, lungs, intestines, bowels, stomach, excrement, bile, phlegm, pus, blood, sweat, fat, tears, skin grease, spittle, nasal mucus, oil of the joints, and urine. … "

VISM. VIII, 2 says "By repeating the words of this exercise one will become well acquainted with the wording, the mind will not rush here and there, the different parts will become distinct and appear like a row of fingers, or a row of hedge-poles. Now, just as one repeats the exercise in words, one should do it also in mind. The repeating in mind forms the condition for the penetration of the characteristic marks. … He who thus has examined the parts of the body as to colour, shape, region, locality and limits, and considers them one by one, and not too hurriedly, as something loathsome, to such a one, while contemplating the body, all these things at the same time are appearing distinctly clear. But also when keeping one's attention fixed outwardly (i.e., to the bodies of other beings), and when all the parts appear distinctly, then all men and animals moving about lose the appearance of living beings and appear like heaps of many different things. And it looks as if those foods and drinks, being swallowed by them, were being inserted into this heap of things. Now, while again and again one is conceiving the idea 'Disgusting! Disgusting!'—omitting in due course several parts—gradually the attainment-concentration (*appanāsamādhi*, i.e., the concentration of the *jhāna*) will be reached. In this connection, the appearing of forms … is called the acquired image (*uggaha-nimitta*), the arising of loathsomeness, however, the counter-image (*paṭibhāga-nimitta*)."

kāya-kamma: 'bodily action', see *karma, kamma-patha*.

kāya-kammaññatā, *~-lahutā, ~-mudutā, ~-pāguññatā, ~-passaddhi, ~-ujukatā*; see TAB. II. For *~-passaddhi*, see further *bojjhaṅga*.

kāya-lahutā: agility or lightness of mental factors (see *lahutā*).

K

SOURCE NOTE: not found, or not found in this form or meaning, in the oldest parts of the Sutta Piṭaka; *-mudutā, -kammaññatā, -pāguññatā, -ujukatā*, see *lahutā*.

kāyānupassanā: 'contemplation of the body', is one of the four foundations of mindfulness; see *satipaṭṭhāna*.

kāya-passaddhi: 'serenity or quietude of the sense' (P.E.D.), see *bojjhaṅga*.

kāya-sakkhi: 'body-witness', is one of the seven noble disciples (see *ariya-puggala*, B.). He is one who "in his own person (lit. body) has attained the eight deliverances (*vimokkha*, q.v.), and after wisely understanding the phenomena, the cankers have partly come to extinction" (PUG. 32). In A. IX, 44 it is said: "A monk, O brother, attains the first absorption (*jhāna*, q.v.), and as far as this domain reaches, so far he has realised it in his own person. Thus the Blessed One calls such a person a body-witness in certain respects. (The same is then repeated with regard to the seven higher absorptions). Further again, O brother, the monk attains the extinction of perception and feeling (see *nirodha-samāpatti*), and after wisely understanding the phenomena, all the cankers come to extinction. Thus, O brother, the Blessed One calls such a person a body-witness in all respects."

kāya-viññatti: see *viññatti*.

khalu-pacchā-bhattik'aṅga: see *dhutaṅga*.

khaṇa: 'moment', see *cittakkhaṇa*.

SOURCE NOTE: the three phases in a moment of consciousness, i.e., *uppāda*, *ṭhiti*, *bhaṅga*, are probably mentioned for the first time in the commentaries; but there is a close parallel in two sutta texts which may have been the source for that teaching of a three-phased moment of consciousness:

"There are three characteristics of what is conditioned (*saṅkhatassa lakkhaṇā*): an arising (*uppādo*) is apparent, a passing away (*vayo*) is apparent, a change in the existing (*ṭhitassa aññathattaṃ*: com. = ageing) is apparent" (A. III, 47). The same three phases are mentioned in S. XXII, 37, where they are applied to each of the five *khandha*.

khandha: the five 'groups (of existence)' or 'groups of clinging' (*upādānakkhandha*); alternative renderings: aggregates, categories of clinging's objects. These are the five aspects in which the Buddha has summed up all the physical and mental phenomena of existence, and which appear to the ignorant man as his ego, or personality, to wit:

(1) the corporeality group (*rūpakkhandha*),
(2) the feeling group (*vedanākkhandha*),
(3) the perception group (*saññā-kkhandha*),
(4) the mental-formation group (*saṅkhārakkhandha*),
(5) the consciousness-group (*viññāṇa-kkhandha*).

"Whatever there exists of corporeal things, whether past, present or future, one's own or external, gross or subtle, lofty or low, far or near, all that belongs to the corporeality group. Whatever there exists of feeling ... of perception ...

of mental formations ... of consciousness ... all that belongs to the consciousness-group" (S. XXII, 48). Another division is that into the two groups: mind (2–5) and corporeality (1) (*nāma-rūpa*), while in Dhamma Saṅganī, the first book of the Abhidhamma, all the phenomena are treated by way of three groups: consciousness (5), mental factors (2–4), corporeality (1), in Pali *citta, cetasika, rūpa*. Cf. GUIDE I.

What is called individual existence is in reality nothing but a mere process of those mental and physical phenomena, a process that since time immemorial has been going on, and that also after death will still continue for unthinkably long periods of time. These five groups, however, neither singly nor collectively constitute any self-dependent real ego-entity, or personality (*attā*), nor is there to be found any such entity apart from them. Hence the belief in such an ego-entity or personality, as real in the ultimate sense, proves a mere illusion.

> "When all constituent parts are there,
> The designation 'cart' is used;
> Just so, where the five groups exist,
> Of 'living being' do we speak." (S. V. 10).

The fact ought to be emphasised here that these five groups, correctly speaking, merely form an abstract classification by the Buddha, but that they as such, i.e., as just these five complete groups, have no real existence, since only single representatives of these groups, mostly variable, can arise with any state of consciousness. For example, with one and the same unit of consciousness only one single kind of feeling, say joy or sorrow, can be associated and never more than one. Similarly, two different perceptions cannot arise at the same moment. Also, of the various kinds of sense-cognition or consciousness, only one can be present at a time, for example, seeing, hearing or inner consciousness, etc. Of the fifty mental formations, however, a smaller or larger number are always associated with every state of consciousness, as we shall see later on.

Some writers on Buddhism who have not understood that the five *khandha* are just classificatory groupings, have conceived them as compact entities ('heaps', 'bundles'), while actually, as stated above, the groups never exist as such, i.e., they never occur in a simultaneous totality of all their constituents. Also those single constituents of a group which are present in any given body-and-mind process, are of an evanescent nature, and so also their varying combinations. Feeling, perception and mental formations are only different aspects and functions of a single unit of consciousness. They are to consciousness what redness, softness, sweetness, etc. are to an apple and have as little separate existence as those qualities.

In S. XXII, 56, there is the following short definition of these five groups:

"What, O monks, is the corporeality-group? The four primary elements (*mahā-bhūta* or *dhātu*) and corporeality depending thereon, this is called the corporeality-group.

"What, O monks, is the feeling-group? There are six classes of feeling: due to visual impression, to sound impression, to odour impression, to taste impression, to bodily impression, and to mind impression. ...

"What, O monks, is the perception-group? There are six classes of perception: perception of visual objects, of sounds, of odours, of tastes, of bodily impressions, and of mental impressions. ...

"What, O monks, is the group of mental formations? There are six classes of volitional states (*cetanā*): with regard to visual objects, to sounds, to odours, to tastes, to bodily impressions and to mind objects. ...

"What, O monks, is the consciousness-group? There are six classes of consciousness: eye-consciousness, ear-consciousness, nose-consciousness, tongue-consciousness, body-consciousness, and mind-consciousness."

About the inseparability of the groups it is said: "Whatever, O brother, there exists of feeling, of perception and of mental formations, these things are associated, not dissociated, and it is impossible to separate one from the other and show their difference. For whatever one feels, one perceives; and whatever one perceives, of this one is conscious" (M. 43).

Further: "Impossible is it for anyone to explain the passing out of one existence and the entering into a new existence, or the growth, increase and development of consciousness independent of corporeality, feeling, perception and mental formations" (S. XII, 53).

For the inseparability and mutual conditionality of the four mental groups see *paccaya* (6, 7).

Regarding the impersonality (*anatta*) and emptiness (*suññatā*) of the five groups, it is said in S. XXII, 49:

"Whatever there is of corporeality, feeling, perception, mental formations and consciousness, whether past, present or future, one's own or external, gross or subtle, lofty or low, far or near, this one should understand according to reality and true wisdom: 'This does not belong to me, this am I not, this is not my Ego.'" Further in S. XXII, 95: "Suppose that a man who is not blind were to behold the many bubbles on the Ganges as they are driving along; and he should watch them and carefully examine them. After carefully examining them, however, they will appear to him empty, unreal and unsubstantial. In exactly the same way does the monk behold all the corporeal phenomena … feelings … perceptions … mental formations … states of consciousness, whether they be of the past, present or future … far or near. And he watches them and examines them carefully; and after carefully examining them, they appear to him empty, unreal and unsubstantial."

The five groups are compared, respectively, to a lump of froth, a bubble, a mirage, a coreless plantain stem, and a conjuring trick (S. XXII, 95). See the Khandha Saṃyutta (S. XXII); VISM. XIV.

SUMMARY OF THE FIVE GROUPS

I. CORPOREALITY GROUP (*rūpakkhandha*)

A. Underived (*no-upādā*): four elements

the solid, or earth-element	(*paṭhavī-dhātu*)
the liquid, or water-element	(*āpo-dhātu*)
heat, or fire-element`	(*tejo-dhātu*)
motion, or wind-element	(*vāyo-dhātu*)

B. Derived (*upādā*): twenty-four secondary phenomena

Physical sense organs of: seeing, hearing, smelling, tasting, body
Physical sense-objects: form, sound, odour, taste, (bodily impacts)

'Bodily impacts' (*photthabba*) are generally omitted in this list, because these physical objects of body-sensitivity are identical with the aforementioned solid element, heat and motion element. Hence their inclusion under 'derived corporeality' would be a duplication.

femininity	(*itthindriya*)
virility	(*purisindriya*)
physical base of mind	(*hadaya-vatthu*, q.v.)
bodily expression	(*kāya-viññatti*; see *viññatti*)
verbal expression	(*vacī-viññatti*)
physical life	(*rūpa-jīvita*; see *jīvita*)
space element	(*ākāsa-dhātu*, q.v.)
physical agility	(*rūpassa lahutā*)
physical elasticity	(*rūpassa mudutā*)
physical adaptability	(*rūpassa kammaññatā*)
physical growth	(*rūpassa upacaya*)

physical continuity	(*rūpassa santati*; see *santāna*)
decay	(*jarā*, q.v.)
impermanence	(*aniccatā*)
nutriment	(*āhāra*, q.v.)

II. FEELING GROUP (*vedanākkhandha*)
All feelings may, according to their nature, be classified as five kinds:

bodily agreeable feeling:	*sukha = kāyikā sukhā vedanā*
bodily painful feeling:	*dukkha = kāyikā dukkhā vedanā*
mentally agreeable feeling:	*somanassa = cetasikā sukhā vedanā*
mentally painful feeling:	*domanassa = cetasikā dukkhā vedanā*
indifferent feeling:	*upekkhā = adukkha-m-asukhā vedanā*

III. PERCEPTION GROUP (*saññā-kkhandha*)
All perceptions are divided into six classes: perception of form, sound, odour, taste, bodily impression, and mental impression.

IV. GROUP OF MENTAL FORMATIONS (*saṅkhārakkhandha*)
This group comprises fifty mental phenomena, of which eleven are general psychological elements, twenty-five lofty (*sobhana*) qualities, fourteen karmically unwholesome qualities. Cf. TAB. II.

V. CONSCIOUSNESS GROUP (*viññāṇa-kkhandha*)
The suttas divide consciousness, according to the se nses, into six classes: eye-, ear-, nose-, tongue-, body-, mind-consciousness.

The Abhidhamma and commentaries, however, distinguish, from the karmic or moral viewpoint, eighty-nine classes of consciousness. Cf. *viññāṇa* and TAB. I. The moral quality of feeling, perception and consciousness is determined by the mental formations.

khandha-parinibbāna: see *Nibbāna*.

khandha-santāna: see *santāna*.

khanti: 'patience', forbearance', is one of the ten perfections (*pāramī*, q.v.).

khayānupassanā: 'contemplation of dissolution', is one of the eighteen chief kinds of insight (see *vipassanā*).

Khiḍḍa-padosikā devā: 'the celestial beings corruptible by pleasures', are a class of devas (q.v.) of the sensuous sphere. They waste their time in merriment, play and enjoyment, and thereby become thoughtless, and in their thoughtlessness they fall from that world (D. 1; 24).

khīṇāsava: 'the one in whom all cankers are destroyed' is a name for the arahat, or holy one; see *āsava*.

kicca: 'function'. Regarding the fourteen functions of consciousness, see *viññāṇa-kicca*.

kilesa: 'defilements', are mind-defiling, unwholesome qualities. VISM. XXII, 49, 65: "There are ten defilements, thus called because they are themselves defiled, and because they defile the mental factors associated with them. They are: (1) greed (*lobha*), (2) hate (*dosa*), (3) delusion (*moha*), (4) conceit (*māna*), (5) speculative views (*diṭṭhi*), (6) sceptical doubt (*vicikicchā*), (7) mental torpor (*thīna*), (8) restlessness (*uddhacca*); (9) shamelessness (*ahirika*), (10) lack of moral dread or unconscientiousness (*anottappa*)." For 1–3, see *mūla*; 4, see *māna*; 5, see *diṭṭhi*; 6–8, see *nīvaraṇa*; 9 and 10, see *ahirika-anottappa*.

The ten are explained in DHS. 1229ff. and enumerated in VIBH. XII. No classification of the ~ is found in the suttas, though the term occurs quite often in them. For the related term, *upakkilesa* (q.v.; 'impurities') different lists are given.

SOURCE NOTE: the ten *kilesa* are probably for the first time enumerated and explained in DHS. (§§ 1229–1239). There they are, however, called *kilesa-vatthu*, which name (*dasa-kilesa-vatthu*) is already mentioned in PTS. I, 130, though there they are neither enumerated nor explained.

kilesa-kāma: 'sensuality considered as defilement' (see *kilesa*) might well be called 'subjective sensuality', in contradistinction to 'objective sensuality' (*vatthu-kāma*), i.e., the sensuous objects (*kāma-guṇa*). Cf. *kāma*.

kilesa-parinibbāna: see *Nibbāna* (1).

killing: see *karma*, *kamma-patha*, *sikkhā-pada*.

kiñcana: 'something', i.e., something evil that sticks or adheres to character. 'Evil appendant', is a name for the three unwholesome roots (*mūla*). "There are three appendants: greed (*lobha*) is an appendant, hate (*dosa*) is an appendant, delusion (*moha*) is an appendant" (D. 33). 'Freed from appendants' (*akiñcana*) is a term for the perfectly holy one (*arahat*).

kiriya- (or **kriya-**) **citta**: 'functional consciousness' or 'karmically inoperative consciousness', is a name for such states of consciousness as are neither karmically wholesome (*kusala*), nor unwholesome (*akusala*), nor karma results (*vipāka*); that is, they function independently of karma. Thus are also called all those worldly mental states in the arahat which are accompanied by two or three noble roots (greedlessness, hatelessness, undeludedness), being in the arahat karmically neutral and corresponding to the karmically wholesome states of a non-arahat (see TAB. 1–8 and 73–89), as well as the rootless mirth-producing (*hasituppāda*) mind-consciousness-element of the arahat (TAB. 72); further, that mind-element (*mano-dhātu*) which performs the function of advertence (*āvajjana*) to the sense object (TAB. 70), and that mind-consciousness-element (*manoviññāṇa-dhātu*) which performs the functions of deciding (*votthapana*) and advertence to the mental object (TAB. 71). The last-named two elements, of course, occur in all beings.

Together with karma resultant consciousness (*vipāka*) it belongs to the group of 'karmically neutral consciousness' (*avyākata*). See TAB. I (last column).

SOURCE NOTE: this is a term first used in the ABH. canon (e.g. DHS. 566–582). It has an important place in post-canonical ABH. literature, e.g. VISM. XIV.

knowledge: cf. *paññā, ñāṇa, vijjā, vipassanā, abhiññā.*

kolaṅkola: 'passing from one noble family to another', is the name for one of the three kinds of *sotāpanna* (q.v.).

kriya-citta: *kiriya* (q.v.).

kukkucca: lit. 'wrongly-performed-ness' (*ku* + *kṛta* + *ya*), i.e., scruples, remorse, uneasiness of conscience, worry, is one of the karmically unwholesome (*akusala*) mental faculties (TAB. II) which, whenever it arises, is associated with hateful (discontented) consciousness (TAB. I and III, 30, 31). It is the 'repentance over wrong things done, and right things neglected' (com. To A. I). Restlessness and scruples (*uddhacca-kukkucca*), combined, are counted as one of the five mental hindrances (*nīvaraṇa*, q.v.).

kuppa-dhamma: 'liable to perturbation', is one who has not yet attained full mastery over the absorptions. In PUG. 3 it is said: "What person is liable to perturbation? Such a person gains the attainments of the fine-material and immaterial sphere (see *avacara*). But he does not gain them at his wish, nor without toil and exertion; and not at his wish as regards place, object and duration, does he enter them or arise from them. Thus it is well possible that in case of such a person, through negligence, the attainments will become perturbed. This person is liable to perturbation."

kusala: 'karmically wholesome' or 'profitable', salutary, morally good, (skilful). Conotations of the term, according to ASL., are: of good health, blameless, productive of favourable karma result, skilful. It should be noted that com. excludes the meaning 'skilful', when the term is applied to states of consciousness.

It is defined in M. 9 as the ten wholesome courses of action (see *kamma-patha*). In psychological terms, 'karmically wholesome' are all those karmic volitions (*kamma-cetanā*) and the consciousness and mental factors associated therewith, which are accompanied by two or three wholesome roots (see *mūla*), i.e., by greedlessness (*alobha*) and hatelessness (*adosa*), and in some cases also by non-delusion (*amoha*: wisdom, understanding). Such states of consciousness are regarded as '*karmically* wholesome' as they are causes of favourable karma results and contain the seeds of a happy destiny or rebirth. From this explanation, two facts should be noted: (1) it is volition that makes a state of consciousness, or an act, 'good' or 'bad'; (2) the moral criterion in Buddhism is the presence or absence of the three wholesome or moral roots (see *mūla*).

The above explanations refer to *mundane* (*lokiya*, q.v.) wholesome consciousness. *Supermundane* wholesome (*lokuttara-kusala*) states, i.e., the four paths of sanctity (see *ariya-puggala*), have as results only the corresponding four fruitions; they do not constitute karma, nor do they lead to rebirth, and this applies also to the good actions of an arahat (TAB. I, 73–80) and his meditative states (TAB. 1, 81–89), which are all karmically inoperative (functional; see *kiriya*).

Kusala belongs to a threefold division of all consciousness, as found in the Abhidhamma (DHS.), into wholesome (*kusala*), unwholesome (*akusala*) and karmically neutral (*avyākata*), which is the first of the triads (*tika*) in the Abhidhamma schedule (*mātikā*); see GUIDE, 4ff., 12ff.; VISM. XIV, 83ff.

kusala-kamma-patha: 'wholesome course of action', see *kamma-patha*.

kusala-mūla: the 'wholesome roots' or 'roots of wholesome action', are greedlessness (*alobha*), hatelessness (*adosa*), and non-delusion (*amoha*; see *mūla*). They are identical with *kusala-hetu* (see *paccaya*, 1).

K

kusala-vipāka: the (mental) 'karma result of wholesome karma' (see *karma*).

L

lahutā: 'lightness', or 'agility', may be of three kinds: of corporeality (*rūpassa lahutā*; see *khandha*, I), of mental factors (*kāya-lahutā*), and of consciousness (*cittalahutā*). Cf. TAB. II.

SOURCE NOTE: as *rūpassa-*, *kāya-*, or *citta-*, are for the first time found in the ABH. canon, esp. DHS. All, however, perhaps with the sole exception of *paguññatā*, are implied in the sutta canon, e.g. *'citte mudu-bhūte kammanīye'* (M. 4); *'lahu-saññañ ca kāye okkamitvā'* (S. LI, 22); *'cittaṃ ujukaṃ akaṃsu'* (S. I, 26; PTS). *Kāya-passaddhi* and *citta-passaddhi*, however, are well known in the old sutta texts in this connection.

lakkhaṇa: 'characteristics'. For the three ~ of existence, see *ti-lakkhaṇa*.

law: *dhamma* (q.v.).

learning, wisdom based on: see *paññā*.

liberality: *dāna* (q.v.), *cāga* (q.v.).

liberation: see *vimokkha*.

life-infatuation: see *mada*.

light, perception of: see *āloka-saññā*.

light-kasina: see *kasiṇa*.

lightness (of corporeality, mental factors and consciousness): *lahutā* (q.v.).

loathsomeness (of the body): see *asubha*, *sivathikā*, *kāyagatāsati*.

lobha: 'greed', is one of the three unwholesome roots (*mūla*, q.v.) and a synonym of *rāga* (q.v.) and *taṇhā* (q.v.).

lobha-carita: 'greedy-natured', see *carita*.

lofty consciousness: see *sobhana*.

lohita-kasiṇa: 'red-kasina', see *kasiṇa*.

loka: 'world', denotes the three spheres of existence comprising the whole universe, i.e., (1) the sensuous world (*kāma-loka*), or the world of the five senses; (2) the fine-material world (*rūpa-loka*), corresponding to the four fine-material absorptions (see *jhāna* 1–4); (3) the immaterial world (*arūpa-loka*), corresponding to the four immaterial absorptions (see *jhāna*, 5–8).

The sensuous world comprises the hells (*niraya*), the animal kingdom (*tirac-chāna-yoni*), the ghost realm (*peta-loka*), the demon world (*asura-nikāya*), the human world (*manussa-loka*) and the six lower celestial worlds (see *deva* I). In the fine-material world (see *deva* II) still exist the faculties of seeing and hearing, which, together with the other sense faculties, are temporarily suspended in the four absorptions. In the immaterial world (see *deva* III) there is no corporeality whatsoever, only the four mental groups (see *khandha*) exist there.

Though the term *loka* is not applied in the suttas to those three worlds, but only the term *bhava*, 'existence' (e.g. M. 43), there is no doubt that the teaching about the three worlds belongs to the earliest, i.e., sutta-period, of the Buddhist scriptures, as many relevant passages show.

loka-dhamma: 'worldly conditions'. "Eight things are called worldly conditions, since they arise in connection with worldly life, namely: gain and loss, honour and dishonour, happiness and misery, praise and blame" (VISM. XXII). Cf. also A. VIII, 5.

lokiya: 'mundane', are all those states of consciousness and mental factors—arising in the worldling, as well as in the Noble One—which are not associated with the supermundane (*lokuttara*) paths and fruitions of *sotāpatti*, etc. See *ariya-puggala*, A.

lokuttara: 'supermundane', is a term for the four paths and four fruitions of *sotāpatti*, etc. (see *ariya-puggala*), with Nibbāna as ninth. Hence one speaks of 'nine supermundane things' (*nava-lokuttara-dhamma*). Cf. *lokiya*.

loving kindness: *mettā*, see *brahma-vihāra*.

lower fetters, the five: see *saṃyojana*.

lower worlds, the four: *apāya* (q.v.).

low speech: *tiracchāna-kathā* (q.v.).

lust: see *rāga*.

M

macchariya: 'stinginess', avarice. "There are five kinds of stinginess, O monks; regarding the dwelling place, regarding families, regarding gain, regarding recognition, regarding mental things' (A. IX, 49; PUG. 56).

mada: 'infatuation'. "Infatuation is of three kinds: youth-infatuation, health-infatuation, life-infatuation" (D. 33). "Infatuated by youth-infatuation, by health-infatuation and by life-infatuation, the ignorant worldling pursues an evil course in bodily actions, speech and thought, and thereby, at the dissolution of the body, after death, passes to a lower world, to a woeful course of existence, to a state of suffering and hell" (A. III, 39).

magga: 'path'. 1. For the four supermundane paths (*lokuttara-magga*), see *ariya-puggala* 2. The Eightfold Path (*aṭṭhaṅgika-magga*) is the path leading to the extinction of suffering, i.e., the last of the Four Noble Truths (*sacca*, q.v.), namely:

1. Right view	(*sammā-diṭṭhi*)	III. Wisdom (*paññā*)
2. Right thought	(*sammā-saṅkappa*)	
3. Right speech	(*sammā-vācā*)	I. Morality (*sīla*)
4. Right bodily action	(*sammā-kammanta*)	
5. Right livelihood	(*sammā-ājīva*)	
6. Right effort	(*sammā-vāyāma*)	II. Concentration (*samādhi*)
7. Right mindfulness	(*sammā-sati*)	
8. Right concentration	(*sammā-samādhi*)	

1. Right view or right understanding (*sammā-diṭṭhi*) is the understanding of the Four Noble Truths about the universality of suffering (unsatisfactoriness), of its origin, its cessation, and the path leading to that cessation. See the Discourse on 'Right Understanding' (M. 9, tr. and com. in 'R.UND.').

2. Right thought (*sammā-saṅkappa*): thoughts free from sensuous desire, from ill will, and cruelty.

3. Right speech (*sammā-vācā*): abstaining from lying, tale-bearing, harsh language, and foolish babble.

4. Right bodily action (*sammā-kammanta*): abstaining from killing, stealing, and sexual misconduct.

5. Right livelihood (*sammā-ājīva*): abstaining from a livelihood that brings harm to other beings, such as trading in arms, in living beings, intoxicating drinks, poison; slaughtering, fishing, soldiering, deceit, treachery soothsaying, trickery, usury, etc.

6. Right effort (*sammā-vāyāma*): the effort of avoiding or overcoming evil and unwholesome things, and of developing and maintaining wholesome things (see *padhāna*).

7. Right mindfulness (*sammā-sati*): mindfulness and awareness in contemplating body, feelings, mind, and mind-objects (see *sati*, *satipaṭṭhāna*).

8. Right concentration (*sammā-samādhi*): concentration of mind associated with wholesome (*kusala*) consciousness, which eventually may reach the absorptions (*jhāna*, q.v.). Cf. *samādhi*.

There are to be distinguished two kinds of concentration, mundane (*lokiya*) and supermundane (*lokuttara*) concentration. The latter is associated with those states of consciousness known as the four supermundane paths and fruitions (see *ariya-puggala*). As it is said in M. 117:

"I tell you, O monks, there are two kinds of right view: the understanding that it is good to give alms and offerings, that both good and evil actions will bear fruit and will be followed by results. ... This, O monks, is a view which, though still subject to the cankers, is meritorious, yields worldly fruits, and brings good results. But whatever there is of wisdom, of penetration, of right view conjoined with the path—the holy path being pursued, this is called the supermundane right view (*lokuttara-sammā-diṭṭhi*), which is not of the world, but which is supermundane and conjoined with the path."

In a similar way the remaining links of the path are to be understood.

As many of those who have written about the Eightfold Path have misunderstood its true nature, it is therefore appropriate to add here a few elucidating remarks about it, as this path is fundamental for the understanding and practice of the Buddha's teaching.

First of all, the figurative expression 'path' should not be interpreted to mean that one has to advance step by step in the sequence of the enumeration until, after successively passing through all the eight stages, one finally may reach one's destination, Nibbāna. If this really were the case, one should have realised, first of all, right view and penetration of the truth, even before one could hope to proceed to the next steps, right thought and right speech; and each preceding stage would be the indispensable foundation and condition for each succeeding stage. In reality, however, the links

3–5 constituting moral training (*sīla*), are the first three links to be cultivated, then the links 6–8 constituting mental training (*samādhi*), and at last right view, etc. constituting wisdom (*paññā*).

It is, however, true that a really unshakeable and safe foundation to the path is provided only by right view which, starting from the tiniest germ of faith and knowledge, gradually, step by step, develops into penetrating insight (*vipassanā*) and thus forms the immediate condition for the entrance into the four supermundane paths and fruits of holiness, and for the realisation of Nibbāna. Only with regard to this highest form of supermundane insight, may we indeed say that all the remaining links of the path are nothing but the outcome and the accompaniments of right view.

Regarding the mundane (*lokiya*) eightfold path, however, its links may arise without the first link, right view.

Here it must also be emphasised that the links of the path not only do not arise one after the other, as already indicated, but also that they, at least in part, arise simultaneously as inseparably associated mental factors in one and the same state of consciousness. Thus, for instance, under all circumstances at least four links are inseparably bound up with any karmically wholesome consciousness, namely 2, 6, 7 and 8, i.e., right thought, right effort, right mindfulness and right concentration (M. 117), so that as soon as any one of these links arises, the three others also do so. On the other hand, right view is not necessarily present in every wholesome state of consciousness.

Magga is one of the twenty-four conditions (see *paccaya* 18).

LITERATURE: *The Noble Eightfold Path and its Factors Explained*, by Ledi Sayadaw (WHEEL 245/247). *The Buddha's Ancient Path*, by Piyadassi Thera (BPS). *The Noble Eightfold Path*, by Bhikkhu Bodhi (WHEEL 308/311).

maggāmagga-ñāṇadassana-visuddhi: 'purification by knowledge of what is path and non-path', is one of the seven stages of purification (*visuddhi* V, q.v.).

magga-paccaya: 'path as a condition', is one of the twenty-four conditions (*paccaya*, q.v.).

magical powers: see *iddhi*; *abhiññā* (1).

mahā-bhūta: the four 'primary elements', is another name for the four elements (*dhātu*) underlying all corporeality; see *dhātu*.

Mahā-brahmāno: 'great gods'; a class of heavenly beings in the fine-material world; see *deva*, II.

M

mahaggata: lit., 'grown great', i.e., 'developed', exalted, supernormal. As *mahaggata-citta*, it is the state of 'developed consciousness', attained in the fine-material and immaterial absorptions (see *jhāna*); it is mentioned in the mind-contemplation of the Satipaṭṭhāna Sutta (M. 10). As *mahaggatārammaṇa*, it is the 'developed mental object' of those absorptions and is mentioned in the 'object triad' of the Abhidhamma schedule and DHS. (see GUIDE, p. 6).

mahāpurisa-vitakka: the eight 'thoughts of a great man', are described in A. VIII, 30, and D. 34.

mahā-vipassanā: the eighteen 'chief kinds of insight', see *vipassanā*.

maintain: effort to maintain wholesome things, see *padhāna*.

majjhimā paṭipadā: 'Middle Path', is the Noble Eightfold Path which, by avoiding the two extremes of sensual lust and self-torment, leads to enlightenment and deliverance from suffering.

To give oneself up to indulgence in sensual pleasure (*kāma-sukha*), the base, common, vulgar, unholy, unprofitable; and also to give oneself up to self-torment (*atta-kilamatha*), the painful, unholy, unprofitable, both these two extremes the Perfect One has avoided and has found the Middle Path (see *magga*), which causes one both to see and to know, and which leads to peace, to discernment, to enlightenment, to Nibbāna. It is the Noble Eightfold Path, the way that leads to the extinction of suffering, namely: right understanding, right thought, right speech, right bodily action, right livelihood, right effort, right mindfulness, and right concentration" (S. LVI, 11).

mala: 'stain', is a name for the three karmically unwholesome roots (*akusala-mūla*); greed, hate and delusion (*lobha, dosa, moha*).

māna: 'conceit', pride, is one of the ten fetters binding to existence (see *saṃyojana*). It vanishes completely only at the entrance to arahatship, or holiness (cf. *asmimāna*). It is further one of the proclivities (see *anusaya*) and defilements (see *kilesa*).

"The (equality-) conceit (*māna*), the inferiority-conceit (*omāna*) and the superiority-conceit (*atimāna*): this threefold conceit should be overcome. For, after overcoming this threefold conceit, the monk, through the full penetration of conceit, is said to have put an end suffering" (A. VI, 49).

"Those ascetics and Brahman priests who, relying on this impermanent, miserable and transitory nature of corporeality, feelings, perceptions, mental formations and consciousness, fancy: 'Better am I', or 'Equal am I', or

'Worse am I', all these imagine thus through not understanding reality" (S. XXII, 49).

In reality no ego-entity is to be found. Cf. *anatta*.

manasikāra: 'attention', 'mental advertence', 'reflection'.

1. As a psychological term, attention belongs to the formation-group (*saṅkhārakkhandha*; see TAB. II) and is one of the seven mental factors (*cetasika*) that are inseparably associated with all states of consciousness (see *cetanā*). In M. 9, it is given as one of the factors representative of mind (*nāma*) It is the mind's first 'confrontation with an object' and 'binds the associated mental factors to the object.' It is, therefore, the prominent factor in two specific classes of consciousness: i.e., 'advertence (*āvajjana*, q.v.) at the five sense-doors' (TAB. I, 70) and at the mind-door (TAB. I, 71). These two states of consciousness, breaking through the subconscious life-continuum (*bhavaṅga*), form the first stage in the perceptual process (*citta-vīthi*; see *viññāṇa-kicca*). See VISM. XIV, 152.

2. In a more general sense, the term appears frequently in the suttas as *yoniso-manasikāra*, 'wise (or reasoned, methodical) attention' or 'wise reflection'. It is said, in M. 2, to counteract the cankers (*āsava*, q.v.); it is a condition for the arising of right view (see M. 43), of stream-entry (see *sotāpattiyaṅga*), and of the factors of enlightenment (see S. XLVI, 2.49, 51). 'Unwise attention' (*ayoniso-manasikāra*) leads to the arising of the cankers (see M. 2) and of the five hindrances (see S. XLVI, 2.51).

manāyatana: 'mind-base', is a collective term for all the different states of consciousness; see *āyatana*.

maṅgala: means, in general usage, anything regarded as 'auspicious', 'lucky', or a 'good omen'. Against the contemporary superstitious notions about it, the Buddha, in the Mahāmaṅgala Sutta (SN., VV. 258ff.), set forth thirty-six'blessings' that are truly auspicious, i.e., conducive to happiness, beginning with the 'avoidance of bad company' and ending with a 'serene mind'. It is one of the most popular suttas in Buddhist countries, and a fundamental text on Buddhist lay ethics.

Tr. in *Everyman's Ethics* (WHEEL 14). See *Life's Highest Blessings*, by Dr. R.L. Soni. (WHEEL 254/256).

mano: 'mind', is in the Abhidhamma used as synonym of *viññāṇa* (consciousness) and *citta* (state of consciousness, mind). According to the com. to VISM., it sometimes means subconsciousness (see *bhavaṅga-sota*).

mano-dhātu: 'mind-element', is one of the eighteen elements (see *dhātu* II). This term, unlike *manāyatana* (q.v.), does not apply to the whole of consciousness, but designates only that special element of consciousness which first, at the beginning of the process of sense-perception, performs the function of advertence (*āvajjana*; TAB. I, 70) to the sense-object and, then after twice having become conscious of it performs the function of reception (*sampaticchana*; TAB. I, 39, 55) into mind-consciousness. See *viññāṇa-kicca*.

manodvārāvajjana: see *citta-vīthi*.

SOURCE NOTE: not found, or not found in this form or meaning, in the oldest parts of the Sutta Piṭaka.

mano-kamma: 'mental action', see *karma, kamma-patha*.

manomayā iddhi: see *iddhi*.

Manopadosika-deva: 'the celestial beings corruptible by temper', are a class of *devas* (q.v.) of the sensuous sphere. "They spend their time in becoming annoyed with one another, and getting into a temper, and thus by being bodily and mentally exhausted, they pass from that world" (D. 1; 24).

manopavicāra: 'mental indulging'. There are mentioned eighteen ways of indulging: six in gladness (*somanassūpavicāra*), six in sorrow (*domanassa*), six in indifference (*upekkhā*). "Perceiving with the eye a visible form ... hearing with the ear a sound ... being in mind conscious of an object, one indulges in the joy-producing object, the sorrow-producing object, the indifference-producing object ... " (M. 137; A. III, 61). In the com. to A., *upavicāra* is said to be identical with *vitakka-vicāra* (q.v.).

mano-sañcetanā: 'mental volition', see *āhāra*.

manovinññāṇa-dhātu: 'mind-consciousness element', one of the eighteen 'elements' (see *dhātu* II). This term is generally used as a name for that consciousness-element which performs the functions of investigation (*santīraṇa*), determining (*votthapana*), registering (*tadārammaṇa*), *etc*. See TAB. I, 40, 41, 56, 71, 72.

Māra: (lit. 'the killer'), is the Buddhist 'tempter-figure." He is often called 'Māra the Evil One' (*pāpimā māro*) or *Namuci* (lit. 'the non-liberator', i.e., the opponent of liberation). He appears in the texts both as a real person (i.e., as a deity) and as personification of evil and passions, of the totality of worldly existence, and of

M

death. Later Pali literature often speaks of a 'fivefold Māra' (*pañca*-~): 1. ~ as a deity (*devaputta*-~), 2. the ~ of defilements (*kilesa*-~), 3. the ~ of the aggregates (*khandha* -~), 4. the ~ of the karma-formations (*kamma*-~), and 5. ~ as death (*maccu*-~).

As a real person, ~ is regarded as the deity ruling over the highest heaven of the sensuous sphere (*kāmāvacara*), that of the *paranimmitavasavatti-devas*, the 'deities wielding power over the creations of others' (com. to M. 1). According to tradition, when the Bodhisatta was seated under the Bodhi tree, ~ tried in vain to obstruct his attainment of Enlightenment, first by frightening him through his hosts of demons, etc., and then by his three daughters' allurements. This episode is called 'Māra's war' (~-*yuddha*). For seven years ~ had followed the Buddha, looking for any weakness in him; that is, six years before the Enlightenment and one year after it (SN. V. 446). He also tried to induce the Buddha to pass away into Parinibbāna without proclaiming the Dhamma, and also when the time for the Buddha's Parinibbāna had come, he urged him on. But the Buddha acted on his own insight in both cases. See D. 16.

For (3) ~ as the aggregates, see S. XXIII, 1, 11, 12, 23. See Padhāna Sutta (SN. V. 425 ff.); Māra Saṃyutta (S. IV).

maraṇa: 'death', in ordinary usage, means the disappearance of the vital faculty confined to a single lifetime, and therewith of the psycho-physical life-process conventionally called 'man, animal, personality, ego', etc. Strictly speaking, however, death is the continually repeated dissolution and vanishing of each momentary physical-mental combination, and thus it takes place every moment. About this momentaneity of existence, it is said in VISM. VIII:

"In the absolute sense, beings have only a very short moment to live, life lasting as long as a single moment of consciousness lasts. Just as a cart-wheel, whether rolling or whether at a standstill, at all times only rests on a single point of its periphery, even so the life of a living being lasts only for the duration of a single moment of consciousness. As soon as that moment ceases, the being also ceases. For it is said: 'The being of the past moment of consciousness has lived, but does not live now, nor will it live in future. The being of the future moment has not yet lived, nor does it live now, but it will live in the future. The being of the present moment has not lived, it does live just now, but it will not live in the future.'"

In another sense, the coming to an end of the psycho-physical life-process of the arahat, or perfectly holy one, at the moment of his passing away may be called the final and ultimate death, as up to that moment the psycho-physical life-process was still going on from life to life.

Death, in the ordinary sense, combined with old age, forms the twelvth link in the formula of dependent origination (*paṭicca-samuppāda* q.v.).

For death as a subject of meditation, see *maraṇānussati;* as a function of consciousness, see *viññāṇa-kicca*.

maraṇāsanna-kamma: see *karma*.

maraṇānussati: 'recollection of death', is one of the ten recollections treated in detail in VISM. VIII:

"Recollection of death, developed and frequently practised, yields great reward, great blessing, has Deathlessness as its goal and object. But how may such recollection be developed?

"As soon as the day declines, or as the night vanishes and the day is breaking, the monk thus reflects: 'Truly, there are many possibilities for me to die: I may be bitten by a serpent, or be stung by a scorpion or a centipede, and thereby I may lose my life. But this would be an obstacle for me. Or I may stumble and fall to the ground, or the food eaten by me may not agree with my health; or bile, phlegm and piercing body gases may become disturbing, or men or ghosts may attack me, and thus I may lose my life. But this would be an obstacle for me.' Then the monk has to consider thus: 'Are there still to be found in me unsubdued evil, unwholesome things which, if I should die today or tonight, might lead me to suffering?' Now, if he understands that this is the case, he should use his utmost resolution, energy, effort, endeavour, steadfastness, attentiveness and clear-mindedness in order to overcome these evil, unwholesome things" (A. VIII, 74).

In VISM. VIII it is said: 'He who wishes to develop this meditation, should retreat to solitude, and while living secluded he should thus wisely reflect: 'Death will come to me! The vital energy will be cut off!' Or: 'Death! Death!' To him, namely, who does not wisely reflect, sorrow may arise by thinking on the death of a beloved person, just as to a mother while thinking on the death of her beloved child. Again, by reflecting on the death of a disliked person, joy may arise, just as to enemies while thinking on the death of their enemies. Through thinking on the death of an indifferent person, however, no emotion will arise, just as to a man whose work consists in cremating the dead at the sight of a dead body. And by reflecting on one's own death fright may arise ... just as at the sight of a murderer with drawn sword one becomes filled with horror. Thus, whenever seeing here or there slain or other dead beings, one should reflect on the death of such deceased persons who once lived in happiness, and one should rouse one's attentiveness, emotion and knowledge and consider thus: 'Death will come, etc.'. ... Only in him who considers in this way, will the hindrances (*nīvaraṇa*, q.v.) be repressed; and through the idea of death attention becomes steadfast, and the exercise reaches neighbourhood-concentration (*upacāra-samādhi*)."

According to VISM. VIII, one may also reflect on death in the following various ways: one may think of it as a murderer with a drawn sword standing in front of oneself; or one may bear in mind that all happiness ends in death; or that even the mightiest beings on this earth are subject to death; or that we must share this body with all those innumerable worms and other tiny beings residing therein; or that life is something dependent on in-and-out breathing, and bound up with it; or that life continues only as long as the elements, food, breath, etc. are properly performing their functions; or that nobody knows when, where, and under what circumstances, death will take place, and what kind of fate we have to expect after death; or, that life is very short and limited. As it is said: 'Short, indeed, is this life of men, limited, fleeting, full or woe and torment; it is just like a dewdrop that vanishes as soon as the sun rises; like a water-bubble; like a furrow drawn in the water; like a torrent dragging everything along and never standing still; like cattle for slaughter that every moment look death in the face" (A. VII, 74).

"The monk devoted to this recollection of death is at all time indefatigable, gains the idea of disgust with regard to all forms of existence, gives up delight in life, detests evil, does not hoard up things, is free from stinginess with regard to the necessities of life, the idea of impermanence (*anicca*) becomes familiar to him; and through pursuing it, the idea of misery (*dukkha*) and of impersonality (*anatta*) become present to him. ... Free from fear and bewilderment will he pass away at death; and should he not yet realise the Deathless State in his lifetime, he will at the dissolution of the body attain to a happy course of existence" (VISM. VIII).

See *Buddhist Reflections on Death*, by V.F. Gunaratna (WHEEL 102/103), and *Buddhism and Death*, by M.O.C. Walshe (WHEEL. 260).

marvel: see *pāṭihāriya*.

mastery (regarding the absorptions): see *vasī*. Eight stages of ~: *abhibhāyatana* (q.v.).

material food: *kabaliṅkārāhāra* (q.v.).

matter (corporeality): see *khandha*, *rūpa-kalāpa*.

matured one, the: *gotrabhū* (q.v.).

maturity-knowledge: *gotrabhū-ñāṇa*, see *visuddhi* (VII).

meaning: evident, and to be inferred; see *neyyatthadhamma*.

meat-eating: just as the karmic, i.e., moral, quality of any action is determined by the quality of volition (*cetanā*) underlying it, and independently of this volition nothing whatever can be called karmically wholesome or unwholesome (*kusala, akusala*), just so it is with the merely external act of meat-eating, this being as such purely non-moral, i.e., karmically neutral (*avyākata*).

"In three circumstances meat-eating is to be rejected: if one has seen, or heard, or suspects (that the animal has been slaughtered expressly for one's own sake)" (M. 55). For if in such a case one should partake of the meat, one would as it were approve the murder of animals, and thus encourage the animal-murderer in his murderous deeds. Besides, that the Buddha never objected, in ordinary circumstances, to meat-eating may be clearly understood from many passages of the suttas (e.g. A. V. 44; VIII, 12; M. 55, etc.), as also from the Vinaya, where it is related that the Buddha firmly rejected Devadatta's proposal to forbid meat-eating to the monks; further from the fact that ten kinds of meat were (for merely external reasons) forbidden to the monks, namely from elephants, tigers, serpents, etc.

See Āmagandha Sutta (SN.), *Early Buddhism and the Taking of Life*, by I. B. Horner (WHEEL 104).

meditation: see *bhāvanā, jhāna, samādhi*.

mental action: *mano-kamma*, see *karma*.

mental advertence: *mano-dvārāvajjana*, see *āvajjana*.

mental formation: *saṅkhāra* (q.v.), see TAB. II.

mental function: *citta-saṅkhāra*, see *saṅkhāra* (2).

mental image: see *nimitta, kasiṇa, samādhi*.

mental obduracy: *ceto-khila* (q.v.).

merit, the four streams of: *puñña-dhārā* (q.v.). For transference of merit, see *patti-dāna*.

meritorious action: see *puñña, puñña-kiriya-vatthu*.

message, the ninefold of the Buddhasāsana: see *sāsana*.

messengers, the three divine: see *deva-dūta*.

method, the right: *ñāya*, is a name for the Eightfold Path (see *magga*)

mettā: 'loving kindness', is one of the four sublime abodes (*brahma-vihāra*, q.v.).

micchā-diṭṭhi: *~saṅkappa*, *~vācā etc.*: see *micchā-magga*.

micchā-magga: *Aṭṭhaṅgika*, the 'eightfold wrong path', i.e., (1) wrong view (*micchā-diṭṭhi*), (2) wrong thought (*micchā-saṅkappa*), (3) wrong speech (*micchā-vācā*), (4) wrong bodily action (*micchā-kammanta*), (5) wrong livelihood (*micchā-ājīva*), (6) wrong effort (*micchā-vāyāma*), (7) wrong mindfulness (*micchā-sati*), (8) wrong concentration (*micchā-samādhi*). Just as the eightfold Right Path (*sammā-magga*), so also here the eight links are included in the group of mental formations (*saṅkhārak-khan-dha*; see *khandha*). The links 2, 6, 7, 8, are inseparably bound up with every karmically unwholesome state of consciousness. Often are also present 3, 4, or 5, sometimes link 1.

micchatta: 'wrongnesses' = *micchā-magga* (q.v.).

micchā-vācā: 'wrong speech': false speech (*musāvādā*), tale-bearing (*pisuṇā vācā*), harsh or abusive speech (*pharusā vācā*), idle chatter or gossip (*samphappalāpa*).

middha: 'sloth'. Combined with *thīna*, 'torpor', it forms one of the five hindrances (*nīvaraṇa*, q.v.). Both may be associated with greedy consciousness (see TAB. III and I, 23, 25, 27, 29).

middle path: *majjhimā paṭipadā* (q.v.).

mind: *mano* (q.v.); cf. *nāma*.

mind and corporeality: *nāma-rūpa* (q.v.).

mind-base: *manāyatana*, see *āyatana*.

mind-consciousness-element: *mano-viññāṇadhātu* (q.v.).

mind-element: *mano-dhātu* (q.v.).

mindfulness: *sati* (q.v.), see *satipaṭṭhāna*. Right ~: see *sacca*, *magga*.

mind-object: *dhamma*, see *āyatana*. Contemplation of the, see *satipaṭṭhāna* (4).

mind-training, 'higher': *adhicitta-sikkhā*, see *sikkhā*.

miracle: see *pāṭihāriya*.

mirth (in the arahat): see *hasituppāda-citta*.

misapprehension: see *parāmāsa*.

misery, contemplation of: *dukkhānupassanā*, see *ti-lakkhaṇa*.

moha: 'delusion', is one of the three unwholesome roots (*mūla*, q.v.). The best known synonym is *avijjā* (q.v.).

moha-carita: the 'deluded-natured', see *carita*.

momentaneity (of existence): see *maraṇa*.

monkhood, the fruits of: *sāmañña-phala* (q.v.).

monks' community: Saṅgha (q.v.); further see *pabbajjā*, progress of the disciple.

morality: *sīla* (q.v.). Contemplation on, see *anussati* (4).

morality-training, higher: *adhisīla-sikkhā*, see *sikkhā*.

moral rules, the five, eight or ten: see *sikkhā-pada*.

muccitu-kamyatā-ñāṇa: 'knowledge consisting in the desire for deliverance', see *visuddhi* (VI. 6).

muditā: 'altruistic (or sympathetic) joy', is one of the four sublime abodes (*brahma-vihāra*, q.v.).

mudutā (*rūpa-~*, *kāya-~*, *citta-~*): 'elasticity' (of corporeality, mental factors, consciousness); see *khandha* (I) and TAB. II.

SOURCE NOTE: not found, or not found in this form or meaning, in the oldest parts of the Sutta Piṭaka; see *lahutā*.

mūla: 'roots', also called *hetu* (q.v.; see *paccaya*, 1), are those conditions which through their presence determine the actual moral quality of a volitional state (*cetanā*), and the consciousness and mental factors associated therewith, in other words, the quality of karma (q.v.). There are six such roots, three karmically wholesome and three unwholesome roots, viz.,: greed, hate, delusion (*lobha*, *dosa*, *moha*), and greedlessness, hatelessness, undeludedness (*alobha*, *adosa*, *amoha*).

In A. III, 68 it is said that greed arises through unwise reflection on an attractive object, hate through unwise reflection on a repulsive object. Thus, greed (*lobha* or *rāga*) comprises all degrees of 'attractedness' towards an object from the faintest trace of a longing thought up to grossest egoism, while hatred (*dosa*) comprises all degrees of 'repulsion' from the faintest trace of ill-humour up to the highest pitch of hate and wrath.

The three wholesome (*kusala*) roots, greedlessness, etc., though expressed in negative terms, nevertheless possess a distinctly positive character, just as is also often the case with negative terms in other languages, for example, the negative term 'immorality', which has a decidedly positive character.

Thus, greedlessness (*alobha*) is a name for unselfishness, liberality, etc., hatelessness (*adosa*) for kindness or goodwill (*mettā*), undeludedness (*amoha*) for wisdom (*paññā*).

"The perception of impurity is to be developed in order to overcome greed (lust); loving kindness in order to overcome hate; wisdom in order to overcome delusion" (A. VI, 107). "Killing, stealing, sexual misconduct, lying, tale-bearing, harsh language, frivolous talk, covetousness, ill will and wrong views (see *kamma-patha*), these things are due either to greed, or hate, or delusion" (A. X, 174).

"Enraptured with lust (greed), enraged with hate, blinded by delusion, overwhelmed, with mind ensnared, man aims at his own ruin, at others' ruin, at the ruin of both, and he experiences mental pain and grief. And he follows evil ways in deeds, words and thought. ... And he really knows neither his own welfare, nor the welfare of others, nor the welfare of both. These things make him blind and ignorant, hinder his knowledge, are painful, and do not lead him to peace."

The presence or absence of the three unwholesome roots forms part of the mind contemplation in the Satipaṭṭhāna Sutta (M. 10). They are also used for the classification of unwholesome consciousness (see TAB. I).

See *The Roots of Good and Evil*, by Nyanaponika Thera (WHEEL 251/253).

multiformity-perceptions: *nānatta-saññā*, see *jhāna* (5).

mundane: *lokiya* (q.v.).

musāvādā: false speech, see *miccha-vācā*.

mutability, contemplation of: *viparināmānupassanā*: see *vipassanā*.

N

N

nāma: (lit. 'name'): 'mind', mentality. This term is generally used as a collective name for the four mental groups (*arūpino khandha*), viz. feeling (*vedanā*), perception (*saññā*), mental formations (*saṅkhāra*) and consciousness (*viññāṇa*). Within the fourth link (*nāma-rūpa*) in the formula of the *paṭiccasamuppāda* (q.v.), however, it applies only to karma resultant (*vipāka*) feeling and perception and a few karma resultant mental functions inseparable from any consciousness. As it is said (M. 9; D. 15; S. XII, 2): "Feeling (*vedanā*), perception (*saññā*), volition (*cetanā*), impression (*phassa*), mental advertence (*manasikāra*): this, O brother, is called mind (*nāma*)." With the addition of two more mental factors, namely, mental vitality (*jīvita*) and concentration (*samādhi*), here 'stationary phase of mind' (*cittaṭṭhiti*), these seven factors are said in the Abhidhammattha Saṅgaha to be the inseparable mental factors in any state of consciousness.

For the complete list of all the fifty mental formations of the *saṅkhārakkhandha* (not including feeling and perception), see TAB. II.

nāma-kāya: the 'mind-group' (as distinguished from *rūpa-kāya*, the corporeality-group) comprises the four immaterial groups of existence (*arūpino khandhā*; see *khandha*). This twofold grouping, frequent in com., occurs first in D. 15, also in PTS.M. (I, 183); *nāma-kāya* alone is mentioned in SN. 1074.

nāma-rūpa (lit. 'name and form'): 'mind-and-body', mentality and corporeality. It is the fourth link in the dependent origination (see *paṭiccasamuppāda* 3, 4) where it is conditioned by consciousness, and on its part is the condition of the sixfold sense-base. In two texts (D. 14, 15), which contain variations of the dependent origination, the mutual conditioning of consciousness and mind-and-body is described (see also S. XII, 67), and the latter is said to be a condition of sense-impression (*phassa*); so also in SN. 872.

The third of the seven purifications (see *visuddhi*), the purification of views, is defined in VISM. XVIII as the "correct seeing of mind-and-body," and various methods for the discernment of mind-and-body by way of insight-meditation (*vipassanā*, q.v.) are given there. In this context, 'mind' (*nāma* q.v.) comprises all four mental groups, including consciousness.

In five-group-existence (*pañca-vokāra-bhava*, q.v.), mind-and body are inseparable and interdependent; and this has been illustrated by comparing them with two sheaves of reeds propped against each other: when one falls the other will fall, too; and with a blind man with stout legs, carrying on his shoulders a lame cripple with keen eye-sight: only by mutual assistance can they move about efficiently (see VISM. XVIII, 32ff.). On their mutual dependence, see also *paṭicca-samuppāda* (3).

With regard to the impersonality and dependent nature of mind and corporeality it is said:

"Sound is not a thing that dwells inside the conch shell and comes out from time to time, but due to both, the conch-shell and the man that blows it, sound comes to arise: Just so, due to the presence of vitality, heat and consciousness, this body may execute the acts of going, standing, sitting and lying down, and the five sense organs and the mind may perform their various functions" (D. 23).

"Just as a wooden puppet though unsubstantial, lifeless and inactive may by means of pulling strings be made to move about, stand up, and appear full of life and activity; just so are mind and body, as such, something empty, lifeless and inactive; but by means of their mutual working together, this mental and bodily combination may move about, stand up, and appear full of life and activity."

ñāṇa: 'knowledge, comprehension, intelligence, insight', is a synonym for *paññā* (q.v.); see also *vipassanā*.

SOURCE NOTE: of the nine kinds of insight-knowledge constituting the *paṭipadā-ñāṇadassana-visuddhi* (see VISM. XXI), the following six are, as such, enumerated and explained for the first time in PTS.M., namely: *udayabbayānupassanā-ñāṇa* (I. 54–57), *bhaṅgānupassanā-ñāṇa*, (ib. 57ff.), *bhayatupaṭṭhāna-ñāṇa* (ib. 59ff.), *muccitukamyatā-ñāṇa*, *paṭisaṅkā-ñāṇa*, *saṅkhārupekkhā-ñāṇa* (ib. 60–65). The terms *udayabbaya* and *bhaṅga*, in connection with the five groups of existence, however, are often met with in the old sutta texts. Of the remaining three kinds of knowledge, *ādīnavānupassanā*, *nibbidānupassanā* and *anulomañāṇa*, the first two occur often in the old sutta texts, while *anuloma-ñāṇa*, though only briefly mentioned in the ABH. canon (PATTH.), plays a prominent part in the exegetical literature.

ñāṇadassana-visuddhi: 'purification of knowledge and vision', is the last of the seven purifications and a name for path-knowledge (*magga-ñāṇa*), i.e., the penetrating realisation of the path of stream-winning, once-returning, non-returning or arahatship. VISM. XXII furnishes a detailed explanation of it (see *visuddhi*, VII).

N

In A. IV, 41 *ñāṇadassana* apparently means the divine eye (*dibba-cakkhu*, see *abhiññā*), being produced through concentrating the mind on light.

nānatta-saññā: the 'variety- (or multiformity-) perceptions' are explained under *jhāna* (q.v.).

ñāṇa-vipphārā iddhi: the 'power of penetrating knowledge', is one of the magical powers (*iddhi*, q.v.).

ñāta-pariññā: 'full understanding (or comprehension) of the known', is one of the three kinds of full understanding (*pariññā* q.v.).

natthika-diṭṭhi: 'nihilistic view' (a doctrine that all values are baseless, that nothing is knowable or can be communicated, and that life itself is meaningless), see *diṭṭhi*.

natthi-paccaya: 'absence-condition', is one of the twenty-four conditions (*paccaya*, q.v.).

SOURCE NOTE: not found, or not found in this form or meaning, in the oldest parts of the Sutta Piṭaka.

natural morality: *pakati-sīla* (q.v.).

navaṅga-buddha (or **satthu-**) **sāsana**: see *sāsana*.

nava-sattāvāsa: see *sattāvāsa*.

naya-vipassanā: see *kalāpa* (2).

ñāya: 'right method', is often used as a name for the Noble Eightfold Path (see *magga*), e.g. in the Satipaṭṭhāna Sutta (M. 10, D. 22).

neighbourhood-concentration: *upacāra-samādhi* (q.v.).

nekkhamma: 'freedom from sensual lust', renunciation. Though apparently from *nir* + √ *kram*, 'to go forth (into the homeless state of a monk)', this term is in the Pali texts nevertheless used as if it were derived from *kāma*, lust, and always as an antonym to *kāma*. It is one of the perfections (see *pāramī*). ~ *saṅkappa*, thought free from lust, or thought of renunciation, is one of the three kinds of right thought (*sammā-saṅkappa*), the second link of the Noble Eightfold Path (see *magga*, 2), its antonym being *kāmasaṅkappa*, lustful thought.

nesajjikaṅga: one of the thirteen *dhutaṅga* (q.v.).

neutral, karmically: *avyākata* (q.v.); ~ feelings, see *vedanā*.

n'eva-saññā-n'āsaññāyatana: the 'sphere of neither-perception-nor-non-perception', is the name for the fourth absorption of the immaterial sphere (*arūpāvacara*), a semi-conscious state, which is surpassed only by the state of complete suspense of consciousness, called 'attainment of extinction' (*nirodha-samāpatti*, q.v.). See *jhāna* (8).

n'eva-sekha-n'āsekha: 'neither in training nor beyond training', i.e., neither learner nor master. Thus is called the worldling (*puthujjana*, q.v.), for he is neither pursuing the threefold training (*sikkhā* q.v.) in morality, mental culture and wisdom, on the level of the first three paths of sanctity, nor has he completed his training as an arahat. see *sekha*.

SOURCE NOTE: while the terms *sekha* and *asekha* occur frequently in the old sutta texts (e.g. A. II, 4: *sekho ca asekho ca imasmiṃ loke … āhuneyyā*, etc.), the term *n'eva-sekha-n'āsekha* is perhaps mentioned for the first time in PUG. of the ABH. canon.

neyya: 'requiring guidance', is said of a person "who through advice and questioning, through wise consideration, and through frequenting noble-minded friends, having intercourse with them, associating with them, gradually comes to penetrate the truth" (PUG. 162). Cf. *ugghaṭitaññū*.

neyyattha-dhamma: a 'teaching the meaning of which is implicit, or has to be inferred' as contrasted with a 'teaching with an explicit or evident meaning' (*nītatthadhamma*).

In A. I, 60 (PTS) it is said, "Whoso declares a sutta with an implicit meaning as a sutta with explicit meaning (and conversely), such a one makes a false statement with regard to the Blessed One." See *paramattha*.

Nibbāna, (SKR. *Nirvāna*): lit. 'extinction' (*nir* + √ *vā*, to cease blowing, to become extinguished); according to the commentaries, 'freedom from desire' (*nir* + *vana*). Nibbāna constitutes the highest and ultimate goal of all Buddhist aspirations, i.e., absolute extinction of that life-affirming will manifested as greed, hate and delusion, and convulsively clinging to existence; and therewith also the ultimate and absolute deliverance from all future rebirth, old age, disease and death, from all suffering and misery. Cf. *parinibbāna*.

"Extinction of greed, extinction of hate, extinction of delusion: this is called Nibbāna" (S. XXXVIII. 1). The two aspects of Nibbāna are:

(1) The full extinction of defilements (*kilesa-parinibbāna*), also called *sa-upādi-sesa-nibbāna* (see IT. 41), i.e., 'Nibbāna with the groups of existence still

remaining' (see *upādi*). This takes place at the attainment of arahatship, or perfect holiness (see *ariya-puggala*).

(2) The full extinction of the groups of existence (*khandha -parinibbāna*), also called *an-upādi-sesa-nibbāna* (see IT. 41, A. IV, 118), i.e., 'Nibbāna without the groups remaining', in other words, the coming to rest, or rather the 'no-more-continuing' of this physical-mental process of existence. This takes place at the death of the arahat. (see Nibbāna).

Sometimes both aspects take place at one and the same moment, i.e., at the death of the arahat; see *sama-sīsī*.

"This, O monks, truly is the peace, this is the highest, namely the end of all formations, the forsaking of every substratum of rebirth, the fading away of craving, detachment, extinction, Nibbāna" (A. III, 32).

"Enraptured with lust (*rāga*), enraged with anger (*dosa*), blinded by delusion (*moha*), overwhelmed, with mind ensnared, man aims at his own ruin, at the ruin of others, at the ruin of both, and he experiences mental pain and grief. But if lust, anger and delusion are given up, man aims neither at his own ruin, nor at the ruin of others, nor at the ruin of both, and he experiences no mental pain and grief. Thus is Nibbāna visible in this life, immediate, inviting, attractive, and comprehensible to the wise" (A. III, 55).

"Just as a rock of one solid mass remains unshaken by the wind, even so neither visible forms, nor sounds, nor odours, nor tastes, nor bodily impressions, neither the desired nor the undesired, can cause such a one to waver. Steadfast is his mind, gained is deliverance" (A. VI, 55).

"Verily, there is an unborn, unoriginated, uncreated, unformed. If there were not this unborn, unoriginated, uncreated, unformed, escape from the world of the born, the originated, the created, the formed, would not be possible" (UD. VIII, 3).

One cannot too often and too emphatically stress the fact that not only for the actual realisation of the goal of Nibbāna, but also for a theoretical understanding of it, it is an indispensable preliminary condition to grasp fully the truth of *anatta* (q.v.), the egolessness and insubstantiality of all forms of existence. Without such an understanding, one will necessarily misconceive Nibbāna—according to one's either materialistic or metaphysical leanings—either as annihilation of an ego, or as an eternal state of existence into which an ego or self enters or with which it merges. Hence it is said:

"Mere suffering exists, no sufferer is found;
The deed is, but no doer of the deed is there;
Nibbāna is, but not the man that enters it;
The path is, but no traveller on it is seen." (VISM. XVI)

LITERATURE: for texts on Nibbāna, see P. TO D., 36ff. See VISM. XVI. 64ff. *Anatta and Nibbāna*, by Nyanaponika Thera (WHEEL 11); *The Buddhist Doctrine of Nibbāna*, by Ven. P. Vajiranana & F. Story (WHEEL 165/166).

SOURCE NOTE: the two terms *kilesa-* and *khandha-parinibbāna* (or *-nibbāna*) are found only in the com.; their corresponding two aspects *sa-upādisesa* and *anupādisesa-nibbāna*, however, are mentioned and explained in IT. 44.

nibbatti: 'arising', 'rebirth', is a synonym for *paṭisandhi* (q.v.).

nibbedha-bhāgiya-sīla (*-samādhi, -paññā*): 'morality (concentration, wisdom) connected with penetration'; see *hāna-bhāgiya-sīla*.

nibbidānupassanā-ñāṇa: 'contemplation of aversion', is one of the eighteen chief kinds of insight; see *vipassanā* (4), *samatha-vipassanā* (2), *visuddhi* (VI, 5).

nicca-saññā (*-citta, -diṭṭhi*): perception (or consciousness, or view) of permanency, is one of the four perversions (*vipallāsa*, q.v.).

nihilistic view: *natthika-diṭṭhi*, see *diṭṭhi*.

nīla-kasiṇa: 'blue-kasina exercise' see *kasiṇa*.

nimitta: mark, sign; image; target, object; cause, condition. These meanings are used in, and adapted to, many contexts of which only the doctrinal ones are mentioned here.

1. 'Mental (reflex-) image', obtained in meditation. In full clarity, it will appear in the mind by successful practice of certain concentration-exercises and will then appear as vividly as if seen by the eye. The object perceived at the very beginning of concentration is called the preparatory image (*parikamma-nimitta*). The still unsteady and unclear image, which arises when the mind has reached a weak degree of concentration, is called the acquired image (*uggaha-nimitta*). An entirely clear and immovable image arising at a higher degree of concentration is the counter-image (*paṭibhāga-nimitta*). As soon as this image arises, the stage of neighbourhood (or access) concentration (*upacāra-samādhi*) is reached. For further details, see *kasiṇa, samādhi*.

2 'Sign of (previous) kamma' (*kamma-nimitta*) and 'sign of (the future) destiny' (*gati-nimitta*); these arise as mental objects of the last karmic consciousness before death (*maraṇāsanna-kamma*; see *karma*, III, 3). Usages (1) and (2) are commentarial. In sutta usage, the term occurs, e.g. as:

3. 'Outward appearance': of one who has sense-control it is said- that "he does not seize upon the general appearance' of an object (*na nimittaggāhī*; M. 38, D. 2; expl. VISM. I, 54ff.; see *sīla*).

4. 'Object': the six objects, i.e., visual, etc. (*rūpa-nimitta*; S. XXII, 3). Also, when in explanation of *animitta-cetovimutti*, signless deliverance of mind (see *cetovimutti*, *vimokkha*), it is said, *sabba-nimittānaṃ amanasikārā*, it refers to the six sense-objects (com. to M. 43), and has therefore to be rendered "by paying no attention to any object (or object-ideas)." A pleasant or beautiful object (*subha-nimitta*, q.v.) is a condition to the arising of the hindrance of sense-desire; a 'repellent object' (*paṭigha-nimitta*) for the hindrance of ill will; contemplation on the impurity of an object (*asubha-nimitta*; see *asubha*) is an antidote to sense desire.

5. In PTS.M. II, in a repetitive series of terms, *nimitta* appears together with *uppādo* (origin of existence), *pavattaṃ* (continuity of existence), and may then be rendered by 'condition of existence' (see P. TO D., 194ff.).

SOURCE NOTE: as signifying the mental reflex-image occurring in meditation, this term, singly or in compounds (*parikamma-~*, *uggaha-~*, *paṭibhāga-~*), is found only in the com., VISM., etc. The same holds good for *kamma-~*, *gati-~*

Nimmāna-rati: the name of a class of heavenly beings of the sensuous sphere, see *deva*.

nine abodes of beings: see *sattāvāsa*.

ninefold dispensation: see *sāsana*.

nippapañca: see *papañca*.

nipphanna-rūpa: 'produced corporeality', is identical with *rūpa-rūpa*, 'corporeality proper', i.e., material or actual corporeality, as contrasted with 'unproduced corporeality' (*anipphanna-rūpa*), consisting of mere qualities or modes of corporeality, e.g. impermanence, etc., which are also enumerated among the twenty-eight phenomena of the corporeality group. See *khandha*, Summary I; VISM. XIV, 73.

niraya: lit. 'the downward-path', the nether or infernal world, usually translated by 'hell', is one of the four lower courses of existence (*apāya*, q.v.). The Buddhists are well aware that on account of the universal sway of impermanence a life in hell, just as in heaven, cannot last eternally, but will after exhaustion of the karma which has caused the respective form of rebirth, necessarily be followed again by a new death and a new rebirth, according to the stored-up karma.

nirodha: 'extinction', see *nirodha-samāpatti*, *anupubba-nirodha*.

nirodhānupassanā: 'contemplation of extinction', is one of the eighteen chief kinds of insight (*vipassanā* q.v.). See *ānāpāna-sati* (15).

nirodha-samāpatti: 'attainment of extinction' (s. XIV, 11), also called *saññā-vedayita-nirodha*, 'extinction of feeling and perception', is the temporary suspension of all consciousness and mental activity, following immediately upon the semi-conscious state called 'sphere of neither-perception-nor-non-perception' (see *jhāna*, 8). The absolutely necessary preconditions to its attainment are said to be perfect mastery of all the eight absorptions (*jhāna*), as well as the previous attainment of non-returner-ship or arahatship (see *ariya-puggala*).

According to VISM. XXIII, the entering into this state takes place in the following way: by means of mental tranquillity (*samatha*) and insight (*vipassanā*) one has to pass through all the eight absorptions one after the other up to the sphere of neither-perception-nor-non-perception and then one has to bring this state to an end. If, namely, according to the VISM., the disciple (non-returner or arahat) passes through the absorption merely by means of tranquillity, i.e., concentration, he will only attain the sphere of neither-perception-nor-non-perception, and then come to a standstill; if, on the other hand, he proceeds only with insight, he will reach the fruition (*phala*) of non-returner-ship or arahatship. He, however, who by means of both faculties has risen from absorption to absorption and, having made the necessary preparations, brings the sphere of neither-perception-nor-non-perception to an end, such a one reaches the state of extinction. While the disciple is passing through the eight absorptions, he each time emerges from the absorption attained, and regards with his insight all the mental phenomena constituting that special absorption, as impermanent, miserable and impersonal. Then he again enters the next higher absorption, and thus, after each absorption practising insight, he at last reaches the state of neither-perception-nor-non-perception, and thereafter the full extinction.

This state, according to the com., may last for seven days or even longer. Immediately at the rising from this state, however, there arises in the non-returner the fruition of non-returner-ship (*anāgāmī-phala*), in the arahat the fruition of arahatship (*arahatta-phala*).

With regard to the difference existing between the monk abiding in this state of extinction on the one hand, and a dead person on the other hand, M. 43 says: "In him who is dead, and whose life has come to an end, the bodily (in-and-outbreathing), verbal (thought conception and discursive thinking), and mental functions (see *saṅkhāra*, 2) have become suspended and come to a standstill, life is exhausted, the vital heat extinguished, the faculties are destroyed. Also in the monk who has reached 'extinction of perception and feeling' (*saññā-vedayita-nirodha*), the bodily, verbal and mental functions have been suspended and come to a standstill, but life is not exhausted, the vital heat not extinguished, and the faculties are not destroyed."

For details, see VISM. XXIII; for texts see P. TO D. 206.

nirutti-paṭisambhidā: the 'analytical knowledge of language', is one of the four *paṭisambhidā* (q.v.).

nirvāṇa: (SKR.) Nibbāna (q.v.).

nissaraṇa-pahāna: 'overcoming by escape', is one of the five kinds of overcoming (*pahāna* q.v.).

SOURCE NOTE: not found, or not found in this form or meaning, in the oldest parts of the Sutta Piṭaka.

nissaya: 'foundation'. The two wrong foundations of morality are craving (*taṇhā-nissaya*) and views (*diṭṭhi-nissaya*). Hence there are two wrong bases of morality: morality based on craving (*taṇhā-nissita-sīla*) and morality based on views (*diṭṭhi-nissita-sīla*).

"'Based on craving' is that kind of morality which has come about by the desire for a happy existence, e.g.: 'O that by this morality I might become a godlike or heavenly being!' (A. IX, 172). 'Based on views' is that morality which has been induced by the view that through the observation of certain moral rules purification may be attained" (VISM. I).

SOURCE NOTE: these two terms, in combination with *taṇhā* and *diṭṭhi*, probably belong to the commentarial literature, e.g. VISM. I.

nissaya-paccaya: 'support', base, foundation, is one of the twenty-four conditions (see *paccaya*, 8).

nītattha-dhamma: a 'doctrine with evident meaning', contrasted with a 'doctrine with a meaning to be inferred' (*neyyattha-dhamma*, q.v.). See also *paramattha*.

nīvaraṇa: 'hindrances', are five qualities which are obstacles to the mind and blind our mental vision. In the presence of them we cannot reach neighbourhood-concentration (*upacāra-samādhi*) and full concentration (*appanā-samādhi*), and are unable to discern clearly the truth. They are:

1. sensuous desire (*kāmacchanda*),
2. ill will (*vyāpāda*),
3. sloth and torpor (*thīna-middha*),
4. restlessness and scruples (*uddhacca-kukkucca*), and
5. sceptical doubt (*vicikicchā*; q.v.).

In the beautiful similes in A. V, 193, sensuous desire is compared with water mixed with manifold colours, ill will with boiling water, sloth and torpor with water covered by moss, restlessness and scruples with agitated water whipped by the wind, sceptical doubt with turbid and muddy water. Just as in such water one cannot perceive one's own reflection, so in the presence of these five mental hindrances, one cannot clearly discern one's own benefit, nor that of others, nor that of both.

Regarding the temporary suspension of the five hindrances on entering the first absorption, the stereotype sutta text (e g., A. IX, 40) runs as follows:

"He has cast away sensuous desire; he dwells with a heart free from sensuous desire; from desire he cleanses his heart.

"He has cast away ill will; he dwells with a heart free from ill will, cherishing love and compassion toward all living beings, he cleanses his heart from ill will.

"He has cast away sloth and torpor; he dwells free from sloth and torpor; loving the light, with watchful mind, with clear consciousness, he cleanses his mind from sloth and torpor.

"He has cast away restlessness and scruples; dwelling with mind undisturbed, with heart full of peace, he cleanses his mind from restlessness and scruples.

"He has cast away sceptical doubt; dwelling free from doubt, full of confidence in the good, he cleanses his heart from doubt. "He has put aside these five hindrances, and come to know these paralysing defilements of the mind. And far from sensual impressions, far from unwholesome things, he enters into the first absorption, etc."

The overcoming of these five hindrances by the absorptions is, as already

N

pointed out, a merely temporary suspension, called 'overcoming through repression' (*vikkhambhana-pahāna*). They disappear forever on entering the four supermundane paths (see *ariya-puggala*), i.e., sceptical doubt on attaining stream-Entry; sensuous desire, ill will and mental worry on attaining once-returner; sloth, torpor and restlessness on reaching arahatship.

For their origination and their overcoming, see A. I, 2; VI, 21; S. XLVI, 51. See *The Five Mental Hindrances*, by Nyanaponika Thera (WHEEL 26).

niyāma: the 'fixedness of law' regarding all things; cf. *tathatā*. *Pañca-niyāma* is a commentarial term, signifying the 'fivefold lawfulness' or 'natural order' that governs: (1) temperature, seasons and other physical events (*utu-niyāma*); (2) the plant life (*bīja-~*); (3) karma (*kamma-~*); (4) the mind (*citta-~*), e.g. the lawful sequence of the functions of consciousness (see *viññāṇa-kicca*) in the process of cognition; (5) certain events connected with the Dhamma (*dhamma-~*), e.g. the typical events occurring in the lives of the Buddhas.

SOURCE NOTE: the compound words *utu-*, *bīja-*, *kamma-*, *citta-*, and *dhamma-niyāma*, probably occur for the first time in the com. *Niyāmatā*, however, occurs often in the old sutta texts, e.g. *thitā va sā dhātu dhammaṭṭhitatā dhamma-niyāmatā* ... (A. III. 134. etc.).

niyata-micchā-diṭṭhi: 'wrong views with fixed destiny', are the views of uncausedness of existence (*ahetukadiṭṭhi*), of the inefficacy of action (*akiriya-diṭṭhi*), and nihilism (*natthika-diṭṭhi*). For details, see *diṭṭhi*; and M. 60, com. (WHEEL 98/99).

SOURCE NOTE: this term is apparently mentioned for the first time in DHS. (e.g. § 1028) of the ABH. As a name for the tenth and last of the *akusala-kamma-pathas*, it plays a prominent role in the com.

niyata-puggala: a 'person with a fixed destiny', may be either one who has committed one of the five 'heinous deeds with immediate result' (*ānantarika-kamma*, q.v.), or one who follows 'wrong views with fixed destiny' (*niyata-micchā-diṭṭhi*, q.v.), or one who has reached one of the four stages of holiness (see *ariya-puggala*). About the latter cf. the frequent passage: "Those disciples in whom the three fetters (of personality-belief, sceptical doubt and attachment to mere rules and ritual; see *saṃyojana*) have vanished, they all have entered the stream, have forever escaped the states of woe; fixed is their destiny (*niyata*), assured their final enlightenment."

noble abodes: see *vihāra*.

noble family, passing from ~ to ~: *kolaṅkola*, see *sotāpañña*.

noble persons: *ariya-puggala* (q.v.).

noble power: *ariya-iddhi*, see *iddhi*.

noble truths, the four: *ariya-sacca*, see *sacca*. The twofold knowledge of the ~, see *sacca-ñāṇa*.

noble usages, the four: *ariya-vaṃsa* (q.v.).

non-disappearance: *avigata-paccaya*, is one of the twenty-four conditions (*paccaya*, q.v.).

non-violence: see *avihiṃsā*.

non-self: see *anatta*.

no-upādā-rūpa: 'underived corporeality', designates the four primary elements (*mahābhūta* or *dhātu*), as distinguished from the 'derived corporeality' (*upādā-rūpa*), such as the sensitive organs, etc. Cf. *khandha*, I.

nutriment: see *ojā*, *āhāra*. ~ is one of the twenty-four conditions (*paccaya*, q.v.) ~-produced corporeality, see *samuṭṭhāna*.

O

O

obduracies, the five mental: *ceto-khila* (q.v.).

obhāsa: 'effulgence of light', aura, appearing at times during deep insight (*vipassanā*), may become a 'defilement of insight' (*vipassanūpakkilesa*); cf. *visuddhi*, v.

object: *ārammaṇa* (q.v.); as condition see *paccaya* (2).

obstacles, the ten ~ of meditation: *palibodha* (q.v.). For the five mental obstacles, or hindrances, see *nīvaraṇa*.

odāta-kasiṇa: 'white-kasina-exercise', see *kasiṇa*.

ogha: 'floods', is a name for the four cankers (*āsava*, q.v.).

ojā: 'nutriment' (synonym of *āhāra*, q.v.), is one of those eight minimal constituent parts, or qualities, of all corporeality, to wit: the solid, liquid, heat, motion; colour, odour, taste and nutriment. This is the 'octad with nutriment as the eighth (factor)' (*ojaṭṭhamaka-kalāpa*), also called the 'pure eightfold unit' (*suddhaṭṭhaka-kalāpa*), being the most primitive material combination. For further details, see *rūpa-kalāpa*.

okkanti: 'conception', lit. 'descent', designates the appearance of the embryo in the mother's womb, i.e., the beginning of the birth process (*jāti*, q.v.). "Through the concurrence of three circumstances arises the embryo. When father and mother have united, … and the mother has her time, and the 'genius' (metaphorically for the karma energy) is ready; under these three circumstances does the embryo appear" (M. 38).

old age: *jarā* (q.v.), is one of the three divine messengers (see *devadūta*).

olfactory organ: see *āyatana*.

omāna: 'inferiority-conceit', see *māna*.

once-eater, the practice of the: see *dhutaṅga*.

one-group existence: *eka-vokāra-bhava* (q.v.).

one-pointedness of mind (*citt'ekaggatā*): a name for mental concentration (*samādhi*, q.v.).

opapātika: lit. 'accidental' (from *upapāta*, accident; not from *upapatti*, as P.E.D. has); 'spontaneously born', i.e., born without the instrumentality of parents. This applies to all heavenly and infernal beings. "After the disappearing of the five lower fetters (*saṃyojana*, q.v.), he (the non-returner) appears in a spiritual world (*opapātika*). ... "

open air, practice of living in the: see *dhutaṅga*.

opposite: 'overcoming by the opposite,' see *pahāna*.

orambhāgiya-saṃyojana: the 'lower fetters', i.e., the first five fetters that bind to lower existence; see *saṃyojana*.

origination, dependent: *paṭiccasamuppāda* (q.v.).

origination of corporeality: see *samuṭṭhāna*.

ottappa: 'moral dread', see *hiri-ottappa*.

overcoming, the five kinds of: see *pahāna*. Full understanding consisting in I, see *pariññā*. The effort to ~, see *padhāna*. ~ doubt, the purification by; see *visuddhi*, IV.

P

pabbajjā: lit. 'the going forth', or more fully stated, 'the going forth from home to homelessness' of a monk (*agārasmā anagāriyaṃ pabbajjā*), consists in severing all family and social ties to live the pure life of a monk, in order to realise the goal of final deliverance pointed out by the Enlightened One. Thus, ~ has become the name for admission as a *sāmaṇera*, or novice, i.e., as a candidate for the order of bhikkhus, or monks.

See *Going Forth*, by Sumana Samanera (WHEEL 27/28), and *Ordination in Theravāda Buddhism* (WHEEL 56).

paccavekkhana-ñāṇa: 'retrospective knowledge', refers to the recollected mental image obtained in concentration, or to any inner experience just passed, as for instance, any absorption (*jhāna* q.v.), or any supermundane path, or fruition of the path, etc. (see *ariya-puggala*). As it is said: "At the end of fruitional consciousness, consciousness sinks into the subconscious stream of existence (*bhavaṅga-sota*, q.v.). Then, breaking off the stream of existence, mental advertence (*manodvārāvajjana*) arises at the mind-door, for the purpose of retrospecting the (just passed) path-moment. Now, as soon as this stage has passed, seven moments of impulsive consciousness (*javana-citta*), one after the other, flash up while retrospecting the path. After they again have sunk into the subconscious stream, there arise, for the purpose of retrospecting the fruition of the path the moments of advertence and impulsion, during whose arising the monk is retrospecting the path, retrospecting the fruition, retrospecting the abandoned defilements, retrospecting the still remaining defilements, retrospecting Nibbāna as object. … 'This blessing have I attained'. … 'This and that defilement still remains in me'. … 'This object have I beheld in my mind', etc." (VISM. XXII).

paccavekkhana-suddhi: 'purity of reflection', is a name for wise consideration in using the four requisites allowed to the monk, i.e., robes, food, dwelling, and medicine; see *sīla* (4).

paccaya: 'condition', is something on which something else, the so-called 'conditioned thing', is dependent, and without which the latter cannot be. Manifold are the ways in which one thing, or one occurrence, may be the condition for some other thing, or occurrence. In the Paṭṭhāna, the last book of the Abhidhamma Piṭaka (comprising six large vols. in the Siamese edition), these twenty-four modes of conditionality are enumerated and explained, and then applied to all conceivable mental and physical phenomena and occurrences, and thus their conditioned nature is demonstrated.

The first two volumes of the Paṭṭhāna have been translated into English by the Venerable U Nārada (Mūlapatthāna Sayadaw) of Burma, under the title *Conditional Relations* (Published by the Pali Text Society, London 1969, 1981). For a synopsis of this work, see GUIDE VII.

The twenty-four modes of conditionality are:

1.	Root	condition	: *hetu*	*paccaya*
2.	Object	"	: *ārammaṇa*	"
3.	Predominance	"	: *adhipati*	"
4.	Priority	"	: *anantara*	"
5.	Contiguity"	"	: *samanantara*	"
6.	Co-nascence	"	: *sahajāta*	"
7.	Mutuality	"	: *aññamañña*	"
8.	Support	"	: *nissaya*	"
9.	Decisive Support	"	: *upanissaya*	"
10.	Pre-nascence	"	: *purejāta*	"
11.	Post-nascence	"	: *pacchājāta*	"
12.	Repetition	"	: *āsevana*	"
13.	Karma	"	: *kamma*	"
14.	Karma result	"	: *vipāka*	"
15.	Nutriment	"	: *āhāra*	"
16.	Faculty	"	: *indriya*	"
17.	Jhāna	"	: *jhāna*	"
18.	Path	"	: *magga*	"
19.	Association	"	: *sampayutta*	"
20.	Dissociation	"	: *vippayutta*	"
21.	Presence	"	: *atthi*	"
22.	Absence	"	: *natthi*	"
23.	Disappearance	"	: *vigata*	"
24.	Nondisappearance	"	: *avigata*	"

(1) Root-condition (*hetu-paccaya*) is that condition that resembles the root of a tree. Just as a tree rests on its root, and remains alive only as long as its root is not destroyed, similarly all karmically wholesome and unwholesome mental states are entirely dependent on the simultaneity and presence of their respective roots, i.e., of greed (*lobha*), hate (*dosa*), delusion (*moha*), or

greedlessness (*alobha*), hatelessness (*adosa*), undeludedness (*amoha*). For the definition of these six roots, see *mūla*.

"The roots are a condition by way of root for the (mental) phenomena associated with a root, and for the corporeal phenomena produced thereby (e.g. for bodily expression)" (PATTH.).

(2) Object-condition (*ārammaṇa-paccaya*) is called something which, as object, forms the condition for consciousness and mental phenomena. Thus, the physical object of sight consisting in colour and light ('light-wave'), is the necessary condition and the sine qua non for the arising of eye-consciousness (*cakkhu-viññāṇa*), etc.; sound ('sound wave') for ear-consciousness (*sotā-viññāṇa*), etc.; further, any object arising in the mind is the condition for mind-consciousness (*mano-viññāṇa*). The mind-object may be anything whatever, corporeal or mental, past, present or future, real or imaginary.

(3) Predominance-condition (*adhipati-paccaya*) is the term for four things, on the preponderance and predominance of which are dependent the mental phenomena associated with them, namely: concentrated intention (*chanda*, q.v.), energy (*viriya*, q.v.), consciousness (*citta*) and investigation (*vīmaṃsā*). In one and the same state of consciousness, however, only one of these four phenomena can be predominant at a time. "Whenever such phenomena as consciousness and mental concomitants are arising by giving preponderance to one of these four things, then this phenomenon is for the other phenomena a condition by way of predominance" (PATTH.). Cf. *iddhi-pāda*.

(4–5) Proximity and contiguity (or immediacy) -condition (*anantara* and *samanantara-paccaya*)—both being identical—refer to any state of consciousness and mental phenomena associated with them, which are the conditions for the immediately following stage in the process of consciousness. For example, in the visual process, eye-consciousness is for the immediately following mind-element—performing the function of receiving the visible object—a condition by way of contiguity; and so is this mind-element for the next following mind-consciousness element, performing the function of investigating the object, etc. Cf. *viññāṇa-kicca*.

(6) Co-nascence condition (*sahajāta-paccaya*), i.e., condition by way of simultaneous arising, is a phenomenon that for another one forms, a condition in such a way that, simultaneously with its arising, also the other thing must arise. Thus, for instance, in one and the same moment each of the four mental groups (feeling, perception, mental formations and consciousness) is for

the three other groups a condition by way of co-nascence or co-arising; or again each of the four physical elements (solid, liquid, heat, motion) is such a condition for the other three elements. Only at the moment of conception in the mother's womb does corporeality (physical base of mind) serve for the four mental groups as a condition by way of co-nascence.

(7) Condition by way of mutuality (*aññāmañña-paccaya*). All the just mentioned associated and co-nascent mental phenomena, as well as the four physical elements, are, of course, at the same time also conditioned by way of mutuality, "just like three sticks propped up one by another." The four mental groups are one for another a condition by way of mutuality. So also are the four elements, and also mentality and corporeality at the moment of conception.

(8) Support-condition (*nissaya-paccaya*). This condition refers either to a pre-nascent (see 10) or co-nascent (see 6) phenomenon which is aiding other phenomena in the manner of a foundation or base, just as the trees have the earth as their foundation, or as the oil-painting rests on the canvas. In this way, the five sense organs and the physical base of the mind are for the corresponding six kinds of consciousness a pre-nascent, i.e., previously arisen, conditioned by way of support. Further all co-nascent (see 6) phenomena are mutually (see 7) conditioned by each other by way of support.

(9) Decisive-support (or inducement) condition (*upanissaya-paccaya*) is threefold, namely (a) by way of object (*ārammanūpanissaya-paccaya*), (b) by way of proximity (*anantarūpanissaya*), (c) natural decisive support (*pakati-upanissaya*). These conditions act as strong inducement or cogent reason.

(a) Anything past, present or future, corporeal or mental, real or imaginary, may, as object of our thinking, become a decisive support, or strong inducement, to moral, immoral or karmically neutral states of mind.

Evil things, by wrong thinking about them, become an inducement to immoral life; by right thinking, an inducement to moral life. But good things may be an inducement not only to similarly good things, but also to bad things, such as self-conceit, vanity, envy, etc.

(b) is identical with proximity condition (No. 4).

(c) Faith, virtue, etc., produced in one's own mind, or the influence of climate, food, etc., on one's body and mind, may act as natural and decisive support-conditions. Faith may be a direct and natural inducement to charity, virtue to mental training, etc.; greed to theft, hate to murder; unsuitable food and climate to ill-health; friends to spiritual progress or deterioration.

(10) Pre-nascence-condition (*purejāta-paccaya*) refers to something previously arisen, which forms a base for something arising later on. For example, the five physical sense organs and the physical base of mind, having already arisen at the time of birth, form the condition for the consciousness arising later, and for the mental phenomena associated therewith.

P

(11) Post-nascence-condition (*pacchā-jāta-paccaya*) refers to consciousness and the phenomena therewith associated, because they are—just as is the feeling of hunger—a necessary condition for the preservation of this already arisen body.

(12) Repetition-condition (*āsevana-paccaya*) refers to the karmic consciousness, in which each time the preceding impulsive moments (*javana-citta*, q.v.) are for all the succeeding ones a condition by way of repetition and frequency, just as in learning by heart, through constant repetition, the later recitation becomes gradually easier and easier.

(13) Karma-condition (*kamma-paccaya*). The prenatal karma (i.e., karma-volitions, *kamma-cetanā*, in a previous birth) is the generating condition (cause) of the five sense organs, the fivefold sense-consciousness, and the other karma-produced mental and corporeal phenomena in a later birth. Karmic volition is also a condition by way of karma for the co-nascent mental phenomena associated therewith, but these phenomena are in no way karma results.

(14) Karma result-condition (*vipāka-paccaya*). The karma resultant five kinds of sense-consciousness are a condition by way of karma result for the co-nascent mental and corporeal phenomena.

(15) Nutriment-condition (*āhāra-paccaya*). For the four nutriments, see *āhāra*.

(16) Faculty-condition (*indriya-paccaya*). This condition applies to twenty faculties (*indriya*, q.v.), leaving out No. 7 and 8 from the twenty-two faculties. Of these twenty faculties, the five physical sense organs (1 to 5), in their capacity as faculties, form a condition only for incorporeal phenomena (eye-consciousness etc.); physical vitality (6) and all the remaining faculties, for the co-nascent mental and corporeal phenomena.

(17) Jhāna-condition (*jhāna-paccaya*) is a name for the seven so-called jhāna-factors, as these form a condition to the co-nascent mental and corporeal phenomena, to wit: (1) thought-conception (*vitakka*), (2) discursive thinking (*vicāra*), (3) interest (*pīti*), (4) joy (*sukha*), (5) sadness (*domanassa*), (6) indifference (*upekkhā*), (7) concentration (*samādhi*). (For definition see Pali terms.)

1, 2, 3, 4, 7 are found in four classes of greedy consciousness (see TAB. I. 22–25); 1, 2, 5, 7 in hateful consciousness (IB. 30, 31); 1, 2, 6, 7 in the classes of deluded consciousness (ib. 32, 33). This condition does not only apply to *jhāna*, but also to the general intensifying ('absorbing') impact of these seven factors.

(18) Path-condition (*magga-paccaya*) refers to the twelve path-factors, as these are for the karmically wholesome and unwholesome mental phenomena associated with them, a way of escape from this or that mental constitution, namely: (1) knowledge (*paññā* = *sammā-diṭṭhi*, right understanding), (2) (right or wrong) thought-conception (*vitakka*), (3) right speech (*sammā-vācā*), (4) right bodily action (*sammā-kammanta*), (5) right livelihood (*sammā-ājīva*), (6) (right or wrong) energy (*viriya*), (7) (right or wrong) mindfulness (*sati*), (8) (right or wrong) concentration (*samādhi*), (9) wrong views (*micchā-diṭṭhi*), (10) wrong speech (*micchā-vācā*), (11) wrong bodily action (*micchā-kammanta*), (12) wrong livelihood (*micchā-ājīva*). Cf. *magga*.

(19) Association-condition (*sampayutta-paccaya*) refers to the co-nascent (see 6) and mutually (see 7) conditioned four mental groups (*khandha*), "as they aid each other by their being associated, by having a common physical base, a common object, and by their arising and disappearing simultaneously" (PATTH. com.).

(20) Dissociation-condition (*vippayutta-paccaya*) refers to such phenomena as aid other phenomena by not having the same physical base (eye, etc.) and objects. Thus corporeal phenomena are for mental phenomena, and conversely, a condition by way of dissociation, whether co-nascent or not.

(21) Presence-condition (*atthi-paccaya*) refers to a phenomenon being pre-nascent or co-nascent, which through its presence is a condition for other phenomena. This condition applies to the conditions Nos. 6, 7, 8, 10, 11.

(22) Absence-condition (*natthi-paccaya*) refers to consciousness, etc., which has just passed, and which thus forms the necessary condition for the immediately following stage of consciousness by giving it an opportunity to arise. Cf. No. 4.

(23) Disappearance-condition (*vigata-paccaya*) is identical with No. 22.

(24) Non-disappearance-condition (*avigata-paccaya*) is identical with No. 21.

These twenty-four conditions should be known thoroughly for a detailed understanding of that famous formula of the dependent origination (*paṭicca-samuppāda*, q.v.). Cf. FUND. III, GUIDE 117ff.

See *The Significance of Dependent Origination*, by Nyanatiloka (WHEEL 140).

SOURCE NOTE: this term occurs often in the old sutta texts in such expressions as '*ko hetu, ko paccayo*', '*yaṃ yad eva paccayaṃ paṭicca uppajjati viññāṇaṃ*', *etc.*, or as abl. adverb in '*avijjā paccayā saṅkhārā*'. All the twenty-four *paccayas* are for the first time enumerated, explained and applied to the phenomena of existence in the ABH. canon (PATTH.). Of these twenty-four *paccaya*, five are already mentioned in PTS.M. (II, 49–54, 59ff., 72–77), namely, *sahajāta-~*, *aññamañña-~*, *nissaya-~*, *sampayutta-~*, *vippayutta-~*.

P

1. *Hetu* is already used in the sutta texts as 'condition' in a general and indefinite way, as a synonym of *paccaya*. In the sense of *kusala* and *akusala* roots (*mūla*; see M. 9), however, it is only found in the ABH. canon and com.

2. *Ārammaṇa* has in the 'sutta texts only the meaning of 'foundation', or 'basis', or 'dependent on', e.g. M. 21: '*tadārammaṇañca sabbalokaṃ mettāsahagatena cetasā pharitvā. ...* ' or D. 33; S. XXII. 53: '*viññāṇaṃ ... rūpārammaṇaṃ ... vedanārammaṇaṃ. ...* ' As term for the six objects, *rūpārammaṇa*, *saddārammaṇa*, etc., it is first used in the ABH. canon, though the teaching of dependency of the six kinds of *viññāṇa* on the six sense-objects is an integral part of the suttas. Cf. e.g. M. 38: '*cakkhuñca paṭicca rūpe ca uppajjati viññāṇaṃ sotañca paṭicca sadde ca ...* ' etc.

3. *Adhipati*, as a philosophical term, occurs for the first time in the ABH. canon (esp. PATTH.). The four *adhipati* are in the suttas called *iddhipāda* (e.g. S. LI. 11). In the old sutta texts, three *adhipateyya* are however mentioned: *atta-*, *loka-*, *dhamma-* (A. III, 38).

4. & 5. *Anantara-* and *samanantara-paccaya* occur, as *paccaya*, for the first time in the ABH. canon (esp. PATTH.). In a veiled form, however, we find the first term in the old sutta texts (e.g. Ratana Sutta in KHP. And SN.): '*samādhim ānantarikaññamāhu*': the concentration (associated with the *arahatta-magga*), which is called the 'immediate' condition (for *arahatta-phala*).

6. & 7. *Sahajāta* and *aññamañña-paccaya*. Though these terms, as such, are not found in the older sutta texts, still the teaching of the co-nascent and mutual conditionedness of the four mental groups (*vedanā*, *saññā*, *saṅkhāra*, *viññāṇa*) is taught in the old texts, e.g. M. 28, 43; S. XXII, etc.

8. *Nissaya-paccaya* is mentioned in PTS; see first paragraph of these notes, above.

9. *Upanissaya-paccaya*. Though this name is not found in the suttas, the teaching expressed thereby is, however, frequently met with there, sometimes even

in the form of *upanisā* (apparently a contraction of *upanissaya*), e.g. S. XII, 23: '*Yam pi'ssa taṃ bhikkhave khayasmiṃ khaye ñāṇaṃ, taṃ sa-upanisaṃ vadāmi, no anupanisaṃ*'. The terms *pakati-*, *ārammaṇa-* and *anantara-upanissaya* are later developments of the ABH. com.

All the remaining terms are met with only in the ABH. literature though the substance is, perhaps in all cases, already dealt with in the old sutta texts.

P

paccaya-sannissita-sīla: 'morality consisting in the wise use of the monk's requisites', see *sīla* (4).

pacceka-bodhi: 'independent enlightenment', see the *pacceka-buddha* and *bodhi*.

pacceka-buddha: an 'Independently Enlightened One'; or Separately or Individually (=*pacceka*) Enlightened One (renderings by 'Silent' or 'Private Buddha' are not very apt). This is a term for an arahat (see *ariya-puggala*) who has realised Nibbāna without having heard a Buddha's doctrine from others. He comprehends the Four Noble Truths individually (*pacceka*), independent of any teacher, by his own effort. He has, however, not the capacity to proclaim the Teaching effectively to others, and therefore does not become a 'Teacher of gods and men', a Perfect or Universal Buddha (*sammā-sambuddha*). *Paccekabuddhas* are described as frugal of speech, cherishing solitude. According to tradition, they do not arise while the teaching of a Perfect Buddha is known; but for achieving their rank after many'ons of effort, they have to utter an aspiration before a Perfect Buddha.

Canonical references are few; PUG. 29 (defin.); A. II, 56; in M. 116, names of many *Paccekabuddhas* are given; in D. 16 they are said to be worthy of a *thūpa* (*dagoba*); the Treasure-Store Sutta (Nidhikhaṇḍha Sutta, KHP.) mentions *pacceka-bodhi*; the C.NID. ascribes to individual *Paccekabuddhas* the verses of the Rhinoceros Sutta (Khaggavisāṇa Sutta, SN.). see *bodhi*.

See *The Paccekabuddha*, by Ria Kloppenborg (WHEEL 305/307).

pacchājāta-paccaya: 'post-nascence-condition', is one of the twenty-four conditions (*paccaya*, q.v.).

pādakajjhāna: 'foundation-forming absorption', is an absorption used as a foundation, or starting point, for the higher spiritual powers (*abhiññā*, q.v.), or for insight (*vipassanā*, q.v.), leading to the supermundane paths (see *ariya-puggala*). The foundation for the former is the fourth absorption; for insight, however, any absorption is suitable. For details, see *samatha-vipassanā*.

SOURCE NOTE: this term is not found in the sutta canon, nor apparently in the

ABH. canon, but very often used in the exegetical literature. The idea, however, expressed thereby, is implied in many places of the old sutta texts, e.g., A. IX, 36, where it is shown how the *jhānas*, one after the other, may serve as basis, or foundation (as mental object), for *vipassanā*. In many of the old sutta texts it is also shown how the fourth *jhāna* forms the foundation for the attainment of the five higher spiritual powers (*abhiññā*).

pada-parama: 'one for whom the words are the utmost attainment'. "Whoever, though having learned much, speaking much, knowing many things by heart, and discoursing much, has not penetrated the truth, such a man is called by that name" (PUG. 163).

padhāna: 'effort.' The four right efforts (*sammā-padhāna*), forming the sixth stage of the Eightfold Path (i.e., *sammā-vāyāma*, see *magga*) are: (1) the effort to avoid (*saṃvara-padhāna*), (2) to overcome (*pahāna-padhāna*), (3) to develop (*bhāvanā-padhāna*), (4) to maintain (*anurakkhaṇa-padhāna*), i.e., (1) the effort to avoid unwholesome (*akusala*) states, such as evil thoughts, etc. (2) to overcome unwholesome states, (3) to develop wholesome (*kusala*) states, such as the seven elements of enlightenment (*bojjhaṅga*, q.v.), (4) to maintain the wholesome states.

"The monk rouses his will to *avoid* the arising of evil, unwholesome things not yet arisen ... to *overcome* them ... to *develop* wholesome things not yet arisen ... to *maintain* them, and not to let them disappear, but to bring them to growth, to maturity and to the full perfection of development. And he makes effort, stirs up his energy, exerts his mind and strives" (A. IV, 13).

(1) "What now, O monks, is the effort to avoid? Perceiving a form, or a sound, or an odour, or a taste, or a bodily or mental impression, the monk neither adheres to the whole nor to its parts. And he strives to ward off that through which evil and unwholesome things might arise, such as greed and sorrow, if he remained with unguarded senses; and he watches over his senses, restrains his senses. This is called the effort to avoid.

(2) "What now is the effort to overcome? The monk does not retain any thought of sensual lust, or any other evil, unwholesome states that may have arisen; he abandons them, dispels them, destroys them, causes them to disappear. This is called the effort to overcome.

(3) "What now is the effort to develop? The monk develops the factors of enlightenment, bent on solitude, on detachment, on extinction, and ending in deliverance, namely: mindfulness (*sati*), investigation of the law (*dhamma-*

vicaya), energy (*viriya*), rapture (*pīti*), tranquillity (*passaddhi*), concentration (*samādhi*), equanimity (*upekkhā*). This is called the effort to develop.

(4) "What now is the effort to maintain? The monk keeps firmly in his mind a favourable object of concentration, such as the mental image of a skeleton, a corpse infested by worms, a corpse blue-black in colour, a festering corpse, a corpse riddled with holes, a corpse swollen up. This is called the effort to maintain" IV, 14).

P

padhāniyaṅga: 'elements of effort', are the following five qualities: faith, health, sincerity, energy, and wisdom (M. 85, 90; A. V. 53). See *pārisuddhi-padhāniyaṅga*.

pāguññatā: 'proficiency', namely, of mental concomitants (*kāya-pāguññatā*), and of consciousness (*cittapāguññatā*), are two mental phenomena associated with all wholesome consciousness. Cf. TAB. II.

SOURCE NOTE: not found, or not found in this form or meaning, in the oldest parts of the Sutta Piṭaka, see *lahutā*.

pahāna: 'overcoming', abandoning. There are five kinds of overcoming: (1) overcoming by repression (*vikkhambhana-pahāna*), i.e., the temporary suspension of the five hindrances (*nīvaraṇa*, q.v.) during the absorptions, (2) overcoming by the opposite (*tadaṅga-pahāna*), (3) overcoming by destruction (*samuccheda-pahāna*), (4) overcoming by tranquillisation (*paṭipassaddhi-pahāna*), (5) overcoming by escape (*nissaraṇa-pahāna*).

(1) "Among these, 'overcoming by repression' is the pushing back of adverse things, such as the five mental hindrances (*nīvaraṇa*, q.v.), etc., through this or that mental concentration (*samādhi*, q.v.), just as a pot thrown into moss-clad water pushes the moss aside. …

(2) "'Overcoming by the opposite' is the overcoming by opposing this or that thing that is to be overcome, by this or that factor of knowledge belonging to insight (*vipassanā* q.v.), just as a lighted lamp dispels the darkness of the night. In this way, the personality-belief (*sakkāya-diṭṭhi*, see *diṭṭhi*) is overcome by determining the mental and corporeal phenomena … the view of uncausedness of existence by investigation into the conditions … the idea of eternity by contemplation of impermanence … the idea of happiness by contemplation of misery. …

(3) "If through the knowledge of the noble path (see *ariya-puggala*) the fetters and other evil things cannot continue any longer, just like a tree destroyed

by lightning, then such an overcoming is called 'overcoming by destruction' "(VISM. XXII, 110ff.).

(4) When, after the disappearing of the fetters at the entrance into the paths, the fetters, from the moment of fruition (*phala*) onwards, are forever extinct and stilled, such overcoming is called the 'overcoming by tranquillisation'.

(5) "The 'overcoming by escape' is identical with the extinction and Nibbāna" (PTS.M. I. 27).

SOURCE NOTE: the five terms, as *vikkhambhana*, etc., are, as such, not found in the old sutta texts, but they are enumerated and explained already in PTS.M. (II. 179ff.).

pahāna-pariññā: see *pariññā*.

pain, feeling of: see *vedanā*.

pakati-sīla: 'natural or genuine morality', is distinct from those outward rules of conduct laid down for either laymen or monks. Those later are the so-called 'prescribed morality' (*paññātti-sīla*). Cf. *sīla*.

pakati-upanissaya: 'direct inducement', see *paccaya*.

palibodha: 'obstacles', is the term for the following things if they obstruct the monk in the strict practice of a subject of meditation: a crowded monastery, travelling, relatives, association with lay folk, gifts, pupils, repairs in the monastery, sickness, study, magical power. The latter, however, may become an obstacle only in developing insight (*vipassanā*, q.v.). See VISM. III, 29ff.

SOURCE NOTE: this tenfold group is perhaps for the first time mentioned in KHP. com. and explained in VISM. III.

paṃsukūlik'aṅga: the 'vow to wear only robes made from picked-up rags', is one of the ascetic rules of purification; see *dhutaṅga*.

pānātipātā veramaṇī: 'abstaining from the killing of living beings', is the first of the five moral rules binding upon all Buddhists; see *sikkhā-pada*.

pañcadvārāvajjana: 'advertence to the five sense-doors', see *viññāṇa-kicca*.

SOURCE NOTE: not found, or not found in this form or meaning, in the oldest parts of the Sutta Piṭaka. see *āvajjana*.

pañca-sīla: see *sikkhā-pada*.

pañca-vokāra-bhava: 'five-group existence', is a name for existence in the sensuous sphere (*kāmāvacara*), or in the fine-material sphere (*rūpāvacara*, see *avacara*), since all the five groups of existence (*khandha*, q.v.) are found there. In the immaterial sphere (*arūpāvacara*, see *avacara*), however, only the four mental groups are found, and in the world of unconscious beings (*asañña-satta*, q.v.) only the one corporeality group. Cf. *ekavokāra-bhava* and *catu-pañca-vokāra-bhava*; further see *avacara*. see: *vokāra*.

P

pañha-byākaraṇa: 'answering questions'. "There are, O monks, four ways of answering questions: there are questions requiring a direct answer; questions requiring an explanation; questions to be answered by counter-questions; questions to be rejected (as wrongly put)." See D. 33; A. III, 68; A. IV, 42.

paññā: 'understanding, knowledge, wisdom, insight', comprises a very wide field. The specific Buddhist knowledge or wisdom, however, as part of the Noble Eightfold Path (*magga*, q.v.) to deliverance, is insight (*vipassanā*, q.v.), i.e., that intuitive knowledge which brings about the four stages of holiness and the realisation of Nibbāna (see *ariya-puggala*), and which consists in the penetration of the impermanence (*anicca*, q.v.), misery (*dukkha*, see *sacca*) and impersonality (*anatta*) of all forms of existence. Further details, see under *ti-lakkhaṇa*.

With regard to the condition of its arising one distinguishes three kinds of knowledge: knowledge based on thinking (*cintā-maya-paññā*), knowledge based on learning (*suta-maya-paññā*), knowledge based on mental development (*bhāvanā-maya-paññā*) (D. 33).

"'Based on thinking' is that knowledge which one has acquired through one's own thinking, without having learnt it from others. 'Based on learning' is that knowledge which one has heard from others and thus acquired through learning. 'Based on mental development' is that knowledge which one has acquired through mental development in this or that way, and which has reached the stage of full concentration" (*appanā*, q.v.) (VISM. XIV).

Wisdom is one of the five mental faculties (see *bala*), one of the three kinds of training (*sikkhā*, q.v.), and one of the perfections (see *pāramī*). For further details, see *vipassanā*, and the detailed exposition in VISM. XIV, 1–32.

paññatti-sīla: 'prescribed morality', is a name for the disciplinary rules of the monk or layman prescribed by the Buddha, as distinguished from natural or genuine morality (*pakati-sīla*; see *sīla*).

paññā-vimutti: 'deliverance through wisdom' (or understanding'), signifies, according to com. to A.V, 142, the wisdom associated with the fruition of holiness (*arahatta-phala*). In PUG. 31 and similarly in M. 70, it is said: "A monk may not have reached in his own person the eight liberations (=*jhāna*, q.v.), but through his wisdom the cankers have come to extinction in him. Such a person is called wisdom-liberated" (*paññā-vimutta*). com. to PUG.: "He may be one of five persons: either a practiser of bare insight (*sukkhavipassako*, q.v.), or one who has attained to holiness after rising from one of the absorptions." See S. XII, 70.

The term is often linked with *ceto-vimutti* (q.v.), 'deliverance of mind'.

P

papañca: (SKR. *prapañca*): in doctrinal usage, it signifies the expansion, differentiation, 'diffuseness' or 'manifoldness' of the world; and it may also refer to the 'phenomenal world' in general, and to the mental attitude of 'worldliness'. In A. IV, 173, it is said: "As far as the field of sixfold sense-impression extends, so far reaches the world of diffuseness (or the phenomenal world; *papañcassa gati*); as far as the world of diffuseness extends, so far extends the field of sixfold sense-impression. Through the complete fading away and cessation of the field of sixfold sense-impression, there comes about the cessation and the coming-to-rest of the world of diffuseness (*papañca-nirodho papañcavupasamo*)."

The opposite term *nippapañca* is a name for Nibbāna (S. LIII), in the sense of 'freedom from samsaric diffuseness'. DHP. 254: "Mankind delights in the diffuseness of the world, the Perfect Ones are free from such diffuseness" (*papañcābhiratā pajā, nippapañcā tathāgatā*). The eighth of the 'thoughts of a great man' (*mahā-purisa-vitakka*; A. VIII, 30) has: "This Dhamma is for one who delights in non-diffuseness (the unworldly, Nibbāna); it is not for him who delights in worldliness (*papañca*)." For the psychological sense of 'differentiation', see M. 18 (Madhupiṇḍika Sutta): "Whatever man conceives (*vitakketi*) that he differentiates (*papañceti*); and what he differentiates, by reason thereof ideas and considerations of differentiation (*papañca-saññā-saṅkhā*) arise in him."

On this text and the term *papañca*, see Dr. Kurt Schmidt in *German Buddhist Writers* (WHEEL 74/75) 61ff. See D. 21 (*Sakka's Quest*; WHEEL 10).

The commentaries often mention a threefold classification, *taṇhā-*, *diṭṭhi-*, *māna-papañca*, which probably means the world's diffuseness created by craving, false views, and conceit. See M. 123; IV, 173; A. VI, 14, SN. 530, 874, 916.

Ñānananda Bhikkhu, in *Concept and Reality: An Essay on Papañca and Papañca-saññā-saṅkhā* (BPS, 1971), suggests that the term refers to man's "tendency towards proliferation in the realm of concepts" and proposes a rendering by "conceptual proliferation," which appears convincing in psychological context, e.g. in two of the texts quoted above, A. IV, 173 and M. 18. The threefold classification of *papañca*, by way of craving, false views and conceit, is explained by the author as three aspects, or instances, of the foremost of delusive conceptualisations, the ego-concept.

parāmāsa: 'adherence', attachment, 'misapprehension', is according to VISM. XXII a name for wrong views; in that sense it occurs in DHS. 1174ff. See *sīlabbataparāmāsa*.

paramattha (*-sacca, -vacana, -desanā*): 'truth (or term, exposition) that is true in the highest (or ultimate) sense', as contrasted with the 'conventional truth' (*vohāra-sacca*), which is also called 'commonly accepted truth' (*sammuti-sacca* —SKR. *saṃvrti-satya*). The Buddha, in explaining his doctrine, sometimes used conventional language and sometimes the philosophical mode of expression which is in accordance with undeluded insight into reality. In that ultimate sense, existence is a mere process of physical and mental phenomena within which, or beyond which, no real ego-entity nor any abiding substance can ever be found. Thus, whenever the suttas speak of man, woman or person, or of the rebirth of a being, this must not be taken as being valid in the ultimate sense, but as a mere conventional mode of speech (*vohāra-vacana*).

It is one of the main characteristics of the Abhidhamma Piṭaka, in distinction from most of the Sutta Piṭaka, that it does not employ conventional language, but deals only with ultimates, or realities in the highest sense (*paramattha-dhammā*). But also in the Sutta Piṭaka there are many expositions in terms of ultimate language (*paramattha-desanā*), namely, wherever these texts deal with the groups (*khandha*), elements (*dhātu*) or sense-bases (*āyatana*), and their components; and wherever the three characteristics (*ti-lakkhaṇa*, q.v.) are applied. The majority of sutta texts, however, use the conventional language, as appropriate in a practical or ethical context, because it "would not be right to say that 'the groups' (*khandha*) feel shame, etc."

It should be noted, however, that also statements of the Buddha couched in conventional language, are called 'truth' (*vohāra-sacca*), being correct on their own level, which does not contradict the fact that such statements ultimately refer to impermanent and impersonal processes.

The two truths—ultimate and conventional—appear in that form only in the commentaries, but are implied in a sutta-distinction of 'explicit (or direct) meaning' (*nītattha*, q.v.) and 'implicit meaning (to be inferred)' (*neyyattha*).

Further, the Buddha repeatedly mentioned his reservations when using conventional speech, e.g. in D. 9: "These are merely names, expressions, turns of speech, designations in common use in the world, which the Perfect One (Tathāgata) uses without misapprehending them." See also S. I. 25.

The term *paramattha*, in the sense here used, occurs in the first para. of the Kathāvatthu, a work of the Abhidhamma Piṭaka (see GUIDE, p. 62). (see *vohāra*).

The commentarial discussions on these truths (com. to D. 9 and M. 5) have not yet been translated in full. On these see K.N. Jayatilleke, *Early Buddhist Theory of Knowledge* (London, 1963), 361ff.

In Mahāyana, the Mādhyamika school has given a prominent place to the teaching of the two truths.

SOURCE NOTE: not found, or not found in this form or meaning, in the oldest parts of the Sutta Piṭaka. see *vohāra-desanā*, SOURCE NOTE.

pāramī (also **pāramitā**): 'perfection'. Ten qualities leading to Buddhahood: (1) perfection in giving (or liberality; *dāna-~*), (2) morality (*sīla-~*), (3) renunciation (*nekkhamma-~*), (4) wisdom (*paññā-~*), (5) energy (*viriya-~*), (6) patience (or forbearance; *khanti-~*), (7) truthfulness (*sacca-~*), (8) resolution (*adhiṭṭhāna-~*), (9) loving kindness (*mettā-~*), (10) equanimity (*upekkhā-~*).

These qualities were developed and brought to maturity by the Bodhisatta in his past existences, and his way of practising them is illustrated in many of the Birth Stories (Jātaka), of which, however, only the verses are regarded as canonical. Apart from the latter, the ten *pāramī* are mentioned in only two other canonical works which are probably apocryphal, the Buddhavaṃsa (in the Story of Sumedha) and the Cariyapiṭaka. A long and methodical exposition of the *pāramī* is given in the concluding Miscellaneous Section (*pakiṇṇakakathā*) of the com. to Cariyapiṭaka.

In VISM. IX it is said that through developing the four sublime states (loving kindness, compassion, altruistic joy, equanimity; see *brahma-vihāra*), one may reach these ten perfections, namely:

"As the Great Beings (*mahā-satta*; a synonym often found in the Mahāyana scriptures for Bodhisatta (q.v.), i.e., 'Enlightenment Being or Being destined for Buddhahood) are concerned about the welfare of living beings, not tolerating the suffering of beings, wishing long duration to the higher states of happiness of beings, and being impartial and just to all beings, therefore (1) they give alms (*dāna*, q.v.) to all beings so that they may be happy, without investigating whether they are worthy or not. (2) By avoiding to do them any harm, they observe morality (*sīla* q.v.). (3) In order to bring morality to perfection, they train themselves in renunciation (*nekkhamma*). (4) In order to understand clearly what is beneficial and injurious to beings, they purify their wisdom (*paññā*). (5) For the sake of the welfare and happiness of others they constantly exert their energy (*viriya*). (6) Though having become heroes through utmost energy, they are nevertheless full of forbearance (*khanti*) towards the manifold failings of beings. (7) Once they have promised to give or do something, they do not break their promise ('truthfulness'; *sacca*). (8) With unshakeable resolution (*adhiṭṭhāna*) they work for the weal and welfare of beings. (9) With unshakeable kindness (*mettā*) they are helpful to all. (10) By reason of their equanimity (*upekkhā*) they do not expect anything in return" (VISM. IX. 24).

In the Mahāyana scriptures, where the *pāramī* occupy a much more prominent place, a partly differing list of six is given: liberality, morality, patience, energy, meditation, and wisdom.

LITERATURE: *Ten Jataka Stories* (illustrating the ten *pāramī*), by I.B. Horner (London 1957, Luzac & Co.); *Buddhavaṃsa & Cariyapitaka*. tr. by I.B. Horner (Minor Anthologies III, Sacred Books of the Buddhists. PTS). Narada Thera, *The Buddha & His Teachings*, Ch. 41; Pāramī (BPS). The treatise on the perfections from the com. to Cariyapitaka has been translated in *The Discourse on the All-Embracing Net of Views* (Brahmajala Sutta, with com.), tr. by Bhikkhu Bodhi (BPS).

SOURCE NOTE: only the com. deals with this subject, apart from the three apocryphal works, Buddhavaṃsa, Cariyapiṭaka, and the Jātaka.

Paranimmita-vasavatti-deva: 'heavenly beings with power over the productions of others', constitute a class of heavenly beings in the sensuous sphere (*kāma-loka*). Māra (q.v.) is said to be their ruler. Cf. *loka*, *deva* I.

parassa ceto-pariya-ñāṇa: 'penetration of the mind of others', is one of the higher powers (*abhiññā*, q.v.).

paricchinnākāsa-kasiṇa: 'limited-space kasina' = space kasina, see *kasiṇa*.

SOURCE NOTE: this term is used in the com. for the term *ākāsa-kasiṇa* used in the older sutta texts.

parihāna-dhamma: 'liable to decline'. "Now, someone reaches the attainments (absorptions: *jhāna*, q.v.) of the fine-material or immaterial sphere (see *avacara*). But he does not reach them according to his wish, and not without trouble and exertion; and not according to his wish with regard to place, object and duration, does he enter them, or rise therefrom. Therefore it is well possible that such a monk, through negligence, may lose these attainments. Such a person is said to be liable to decline" (PUG. 5).

parikamma: 'preparatory-moment': see *javana*.

parikamma-nimitta: 'preparatory image', see *nimitta, kasiṇa*.

parikamma-samādhi: 'preparatory concentration', is the initial and still undeveloped concentration of mind; see *samādhi*.

parinibbāna: 'full Nibbāna', is a synonym for Nibbāna; this term, therefore, does not refer exclusively to the extinction of the five groups of existence at the death of the holy one, though often applied to it. Cf. Nibbāna.

pariññā: 'full understanding', full comprehension. There are three kinds of mundane full understanding (*lokiya*-~), namely: full understanding of the known (*ñāta*-~), f.u. as investigating (*tīraṇa*-~), and full understanding as overcoming (*pahāna*-~) In VISM. XX, 3 it is said:

"Full understanding of the known is the knowledge consisting in the discernment of the specific characteristics of such and such phenomena, as: 'Corporeality has the characteristic of being oppressed; feeling has the characteristic of being felt, etc.'

"Full understanding by investigating is that insight-wisdom (*vipassanā-paññā*; see *vipassanā*), which has the three general characteristics (impermanence, suffering, non-self) as its objects, and which arises when attributing a general characteristic to (physical and mental) phenomena, as for instance: 'Corporeality is impermanent, feeling is impermanent, etc.'

"Full understanding by overcoming is that insight-wisdom which has the above mentioned general characteristics as its objects, and arises after overcoming the idea of permanence, etc."

SOURCE NOTE: *pariññā, ñāta-~, tīraṇa-~, pahāna-~*, belong to the exegetical literature, but they are already implied in PTS.M. I. 87: '*Abhiññā-paññā ñātatthe ñāṇam, pariññāpaññā tīraṇatthe ñāṇam, pahāna-paññā pariccāgatthe ñāṇam … ye ye dhammā abhiññātā honti, te te dhammā ñātā honti … tīritā … pahīnā.*'

pārisuddhi-padhāniyaṅga: the four 'elements of the effort for purity' consist of effort for purity of morality (*sīla-parisuddhi-padhāniyaṅga*), for purity of mind (*citta*), of view (*diṭṭhi*), and of deliverance (*vimutti*). Cf. A. IV, 194.

Another nine factors are enumerated in D. 34, namely the seven 'stages of purification (see *visuddhi*) and the effort for purity of (higher) knowledge (*vijjā*-~) and of deliverance (*vimutti*-~).

pārisuddhi-sīla: 'morality consisting in purity', is fourfold: restraint with regard to the monks' Disciplinary Code, sense restraint, purity of livelihood, morality with regard to the monks' four requisites; for details, see *sīla*.

Parittābha and **Paritta-subha**: two classes of heavenly beings of the fine-material sphere, see *deva* (II).

pariyatti: 'learning the doctrine', the 'wording of the doctrine'. In the 'progress of the disciple' (q.v.), three stages may be distinguished: theory, practice, realisation, i.e., (1) learning the wording of the doctrine (*pariyatti*), (2) practising it (*paṭipatti*), (3) penetrating it (*paṭivedha*) and realising its goal.

SOURCE NOTE: on *pariyatti, paṭipatti, paṭivedha*—the first of these three fundamental terms, especially in this threefold grouping, belongs to the commentarial literature, though the idea expressed thereby is often found in the suttas in such expressions as '*dhammaṃ pariyāpuṇāti suttaṃ geyyaṃ veyyākaraṇaṃ. ...*' The two other terms are found separately in the suttas.

pasāda-rūpa: 'sensitive corporeality', is a name for the five physical sense organs responding to sense-stimuli. Cf. *āyatana*.

passaddhi-sambojjhaṅga: 'tranquillity as a factor of enlightenment', consists in tranquillity of mental factors (*kāya-passaddhi*) and tranquillity of consciousness (*citta-passaddhi*). Cf. *bojjhaṅga*; further TAB. II.

patched-up robes, the practice of wearing: is one of the ascetic rules of purification (*dhutaṅga*, q.v.).

path and non-path, the knowledge and vision regarding: see *visuddhi* (V).

paṭhavī-dhātu: 'earth-element' or 'solid element'. It is cognisable through the sensations of pressure, touch, cold, heat. pain, etc. About the four elements, see *dhātu*, *khandha* (I. A.).

paṭhavī-kasiṇa: 'earth-kasina' (see *kasiṇa*).

path-condition: *magga-paccaya*, is one of the twenty-four conditions (*paccaya*, q.v.).

path-knowledge, the four kinds of: see *visuddhi* (VII).

path-result (fruition): *phala* (q.v.).

paṭibhāga-nimitta: see *nimitta*, *kasiṇa*, *samādhi*.

paṭibhāna-paṭisambhidā: the 'analytical knowledge of ready wit', see *paṭisambhidā*.

paṭiccasamuppāda: 'dependent origination', is the doctrine of the conditionality of all physical and psychical phenomena, a doctrine which, together with that of impersonality (*anatta* q.v.), forms the indispensable condition for the real understanding and realisation of the teaching of the Buddha. It shows the conditionality and dependent nature of that uninterrupted flux of manifold physical and psychical phenomena of existence conventionally called the ego, or man, or animal, etc.

Whereas the doctrine of impersonality, or *anatta*, proceeds analytically, by splitting existence up into the ultimate constituent parts, into mere empty, unsubstantial phenomena or elements, the doctrine of dependent origination, on the other hand, proceeds synthetically, by showing that all these phenomena are, in some way or other, conditionally related with each other. In fact, the entire Abhidhamma Piṭaka, as a whole, treats really of nothing but just these two doctrines: phenomenality, implying impersonality and conditionality of all existence. The former or analytical method is applied in Dhammasaṅgani, the first book of the Abhidhamma Piṭaka; the latter or synthetical method, in Paṭṭhāna, the last book of the Abhidhamma Piṭaka. For a synopsis of these two works, see GUIDE I and VII.

Though this subject has been very frequently treated by Western authors, by far most of them have completely misunderstood the true meaning and purpose of the doctrine of dependent origination, and even the twelve terms themselves have often been rendered wrongly.

The formula of dependent origination runs as follows:

- *Avijiā-paccayā saṅkhārā*: "Through ignorance are conditioned the *saṅkhāras*," i.e., the rebirth-producing volitions (*cetanā*), or 'karma-formations'.
- *Saṅkhāra-paccayā viññāṇaṃ*: "Through the karma formations (in the past life) is conditioned consciousness (in the present life)."
- *Viññāṇa-paccayā nāma-rūpaṃ*: "Through consciousness are conditioned the mental and physical phenomena (*nāma-rūpa*)," i.e., that which makes up our so-called individual existence.
- *Nāma-rūpa-paccayā saḷāyatanaṃ*: "Through the mental and physical phenomena are conditioned the six bases," i.e., the five physical sense organs, and consciousness as the sixth.
- *Saḷāyatana-paccayā phasso*: "Through the six bases is conditioned the (sensorial mental) impression."

- *Phassa-paccayā vedanā*: "Through the impression is conditioned feeling."
- *Vedanā-paccayā taṇhā*: "Through feeling is conditioned craving."
- *Taṇhā-paccayā upādānaṃ*: "Through craving is conditioned clinging."
- *Upādāna-paccayā bhavo*: "Through clinging is conditioned the process of becoming," consisting in the active and the passive life process, i.e., the rebirth-producing karma-process (*kamma-bhava*) and, as its result, the rebirth-process (*upapatti-bhava*).
- *Bhava-paccayā jāti*: "Through the (rebirth-producing karma-) process of becoming is conditioned rebirth."
- *Jāti-paccayā jarāmaraṇaṃ*, etc.: "Through rebirth are conditioned old age and death (sorrow, lamentation, pain, grief and despair). Thus arises this whole mass of suffering again in the future."

The following diagram shows the relationship of dependence between three successive lives:

Past	1 Ignorance (*avijjā*) 2 Karma-formations (*saṅkhārā*)	Karma-process (*kamma-bhava*) five causes: 1, 2, 8, 9, 10
Present	3 Consciousness (*viññāṇa*) 4 Mind & matter (*nāma-rūpa*) 5 Six bases (*āyatana*) 6 Impression (*phassa*) 7 Feeling (*vedanā*)	Rebirth-process (*upapatti-bhava*) five results: 3–7
	8 Craving (*taṇhā*) 9 Clinging (*upādāna*) 10 Process of becoming (*bhava*)	Karma-process (*kamma-bhava*) five causes: 1, 2, 8, 9, 10
Future	11 Rebirth (*jāti*) 12 Old age and death (*jarā-maraṇa*)	Rebirth-Process (*upapatti-bhava*) five results: 3–7

Before taking up the study of the following exposition, it is suggested that the reader first goes thoroughly through the article on the twenty-four conditions (see *paccaya*). For a thorough understanding of the *paṭiccasamuppāda* he should know the main modes of conditioning, as decisive support, co-nascence, pre-nascence, etc.

For a closer study of the subject should be consulted: VISM. XVII; FUND.

III; GUIDE (Ch. VII and Appendix); *Dependent Origination*, by Piyadassi Thera (WHEEL 15); *The Significance of Dependent Origination* (WHEEL 140).

(1)

"Through ignorance are conditioned the karma-formations" (*avijjā-paccayā saṅkhārā*), i.e., all wholesome and unwholesome actions (*karma*, q.v.) of body, speech and mind, are conditioned through ignorance. By 'karma-formations' are meant karmically wholesome and unwholesome volitions (*cetanā*), or volitional activities, in short karma (q.v., and FUND. II).

P

In view of the many misconceptions current in the West, it is necessary to repeat here that karma (q.v.), as a technical term, never signifies anything but moral or immoral action, i.e., the above mentioned volitional activities, or karma-formations, as either causing results in the present life or being the causes of future destiny and rebirth. Thus karma, as a philosophical term, never means the result of action, as often wrongly conceived by Western authors.

Now, in what way are the karma-formations conditioned through ignorance? As concerns the unwholesome karma-formations associated with greed, hate or delusion (*lobha, dosa, moha*), these are always and in all circumstances, conditioned through the simultaneous ignorance inseparably associated therewith. Thus, ignorance is for the unwholesome karma-formations a condition by way of co-nascence (*sahajāta-paccaya*), association (*sampayutta-paccaya*), presence (*atthi-paccaya*), etc. Ignorance further may be for them a condition by way of decisive support or inducement (*upanissaya-paccaya*), if, for instance, ignorance coupled with greed induces a man to commit evil deeds, such as killing, stealing, sexual misconduct, etc. In these cases, therefore, ignorance is a 'natural decisive support' or 'direct inducement' (*pakati-upanissaya-paccaya*). It also may become an indirect inducement, by way of object (*ārammaṇūpanissaya-paccaya*) of our thinking. This takes place, if, for example, someone remembers a former state of ignorance combined with sensual enjoyment, and in doing so karmically unwholesome states spring up, such as sensual desire, grief, etc.

For the wholesome (*kusala*) karma-formations, ignorance can only be a condition by way of decisive support (*upanissaya*), never by way of co-nascence (*sahajāta*), etc., since wholesome consciousness at that very moment, of course, cannot be associated with any unwholesome phenomenon, such as ignorance. Ignorance is a 'natural decisive support' or 'direct inducement' (*pakati-upanissaya*), for example, if, induced by ignorance and vanity, one exerts oneself to attain the absorptions, and thus finally, through perseverance, reaches these wholesome states of mind. Ignorance may also be for wholesome karma-formations a 'decisive support' or 'inducement by way of object' (*ārammaṇūpanissaya*), if, for example, one reflects on ignorance as the root of all misery in the world, and thus finally attains insight and entrance into one of the four supermundane paths of holiness. For ignorance, see *avijjā*; for karma-formations, see *saṅkhāra*.

(2)

"Through the karma-formations is conditioned consciousness" (*saṅkhāra-paccayā viññāṇaṃ*). This proposition teaches that the wholesome and unwholesome karma-formations are the causes of future rebirth in an appropriate sphere (*gati*). The karma-formations of the previous life condition the budding in a new mother's womb of a fresh psycho-physical aggregation of the five groups of existence (see *khandha*), which here are represented by consciousness (*viññāṇa*). All such karma resultant (*vipāka*) consciousness, however, such as eye-consciousness (seeing), etc., as well as all the mental phenomena associated therewith (feeling, etc.), are karmically neutral. It should be understood that already from the very first moment of conception in the mother's womb, this karma resultant consciousness of the embryonic being is functioning.

Against Dr. Paul Dahlke's misconception of the *paṭiccasamuppāda* as "one single karmic moment of personal experience," and of the 'simultaneity' of all the twelve links of this formula, I should like to state here distinctly that the interpretation of the ~ given here as comprising three successive lives not only agrees with all the different schools of Buddhism and all the ancient commentaries, but also is fully identical with the explanations given already in the canonical suttas. Thus, for example, it is said verbatim in Nidāna-Saṃyutta (S. XII, 51): "Once *ignorance* (1) and *clinging* (9) are extinguished, neither karmically meritorious, nor demeritorious, nor imperturbable *karma-formations* (2=10) are produced, and thus no *consciousness* (3=11) will spring up again in a new mother's womb." And further: "For, if consciousness were not to appear in the mother's womb, would in that case *mentality* and *corporeality* (4) arise?" Cf. above diagram.

The purpose of the Buddha in teaching the ~ was to show to suffering mankind how, depending on ignorance and delusion, this present existence and suffering has come about, and how through extinction of ignorance, and of the craving and clinging conditioned thereby, no more rebirth will follow, and thus the standstill of the process of existence will have been realised and therewith the extinction of all suffering.

(3)

"Through consciousness are conditioned corporeality and mentality" (*viññāṇa-paccayā nāma-rūpaṃ*). This proposition implies that without consciousness there can be no mental and physical process of existence. By mentality (*nāma*) is here to be understood the karma resultant (*vipāka*) mental phenomena, such as feeling (*vedanā*), perception (*saññā*), volition (*cetanā*: non-karmic volition is here meant), consciousness-impression (*phassa*), advertence (*manasikāra*) (M. 9; S. XII, 2). For the basic seven mental phenomena inseparably associated with every state of consciousness, see *nāma*. By corporeality (*rūpa*) is meant the four physical elements (see *dhātu*) and the corporeality dependent thereon (see *khandha*, I).

Mentality is always conditioned through consciousness; i.e., consciousness (*viññāṇa*) is for mentality (*nāma*) a condition by way of co-nascence (*sahajāta*), mutuality (*aññamañña*), association (*sampayutta*), etc., since the four mental groups at all times form an inseparable unit.

Consciousness (*viññāṇa*) is for corporeality (*rūpa*) a condition by way of co-nascence only at the moment of conception, thereafter a condition by way of post-nascence (*pacchājāta-paccaya*; *paccaya* 11) and nutriment (*āhāra*), i.e., as a support. Just as the repeatedly arising hunger is a condition and support for the pre-arisen body, so is the consciousness arising afterwards a condition and support for the maintenance of this pre-arisen body.

(4)

"Through mentality and corporeality are conditioned the six bases (*nāma-rūpa paccayā saḷāyatanaṃ*). The six bases are a name for the five physical sense organs and, as sixth, the mind-base (*manāyatana* q.v.), i.e., consciousness.

Mentality (*nāma*; see 3) is for the five physical bases (*āyatana*), or sense organs, a condition by way of post-nascence. Cf. end of 3.

Mentality (*nāma*), i.e., feeling, etc., is for the sixth base, or consciousness—as being always inseparably associated therewith a condition by way of co-nascence, etc.

Corporeality (*rūpa*), here the four elements, are for the five physical bases (*āyatana*), or sense organs, a condition by way of support (*nissaya*).

Corporeality (*rūpa*), here the five physical sense organs, are for the sixth base (*āyatana*), i.e., consciousness, a condition by way of support and pre-nascence (*purejāta-paccaya*).

(5)

"Through the six bases is conditioned the (sensorial and mental) impression" (*saḷāyatana-paccayā phasso*), for without the five physical bases, or sense organs, there can be no sense-impressions; and without the sixth base, or consciousness, there can be no mental impression.

Thus, the five physical bases, eye, etc., are for the corresponding five sense-impressions (visual impression, etc.) a condition by way of support (*nissaya*) and pre-nascence (*purejāta*), whereas the sixth, the mind-base (consciousness), is for the mental impression a condition by way of co-nascence, association, mutuality, etc.

(6)

"Through impression is conditioned feeling" (*phassa-paccayā vedanā*), i.e., the sensorial and the mental impressions are for the feeling associated therewith a condition by way of co-nascence, association, mutuality, etc.

(7)

"Through feeling is conditioned craving" (*vedanā-paccayā taṇhā*). Any (karma resultant) feeling, whether agreeable, disagreeable or neutral, bodily or mental, past or expected, may become for craving a condition of decisive support by way of object (*ārammaṇūpanissaya*). Even physically and mentally painful feeling may, through the desire to be released therefrom, become for craving a condition of decisive support by way of object (*ārammaṇupanis-saya*).

(8)

"Through craving is conditioned clinging" (*taṇhā-paccayā upādānaṃ*). 'Clinging' is explained as an intensified form of craving. It is of four kinds: (1) clinging to sensuality, (2) to erroneous views, (3) to rules and ritual, (4) to personality-belief. Sensuous craving is to (1) a condition of natural decisive support (*pakati-upanissaya*). For (2–4), craving is a condition by way of co-nascence, mutuality, root (*hetu*), etc. It also may be a condition of natural decisive support. For example, through craving for heavenly rebirth, etc. people often may be induced to cling to certain rules and rituals, with the hope of reaching thereby the object of their desires.

(9)

"Through clinging is conditioned the process of becoming" (*upādāna-paccayā bhavo*), i.e., the wholesome and unwholesome active karma-process of becoming (*kamma-bhava*), as well as the karma resultant (*vipāka*) passive process, the so-called 'rebirth-process' (*upapatti-bhava*). The karma-process (*kamma-bhava*) comprises the five karmic causes: ignorance, karma formations, craving, clinging, karma-process (see 1, 2, 8, 9, 10, of the diagram); the rebirth-process (*upapatti-bhava*) comprises the five karma results (see 3–7 of the diagram).

The karma-process is here, correctly speaking, a collective name for generative karmic volition (*kamma-cetanā*) and all the mental phenomena associated therewith, while the second link (karma-formations) designates only karmic volition (see *āyūhana*). Both, however, i.e., the second and tenth proposition, practically state one and the same thing, namely, that karma is the cause of rebirth, as we shall see under 10.

Clinging (*upādāna*) may be an inducement of decisive support (*upanissaya*) to many kinds of wholesome and unwholesome karma. Sensuous clinging (*kāmūpādāna*), i.e., clinging to sensuous objects, for example, may be a direct inducement to murder, theft, unlawful intercourse with the other sex, evil words and thoughts, etc. Clinging to rules and ritual (*sīlabbatūpādāna*) may lead to self-complacency, fanaticism, cruelty, etc. Clinging is also for the evil karma associated therewith, a condition by way of co-nascence, association, etc.

(10)

"Through the process of becoming is conditioned rebirth" (*bhava-paccayā jāti*), i.e., through the wholesome and unwholesome karma-process (*kamma-bhava*) is conditioned the rebirth-process (*upapatti-bhava*). The second and tenth propositions, as already pointed out, practically teach one and the same thing, namely, that karma is the cause of rebirth; in other words, that the karmic volition (*cetanā*) is the seed out of which springs the new life, just as from the mango-seed is generated the new mango-tree.

Hence, the five karmic causes (ignorance, etc.) of the past birth are the condition for the karma results of the present birth; and the five karmic causes of the present birth are the condition for the five karma results of the next birth (see diagram). As it is said in VISM. XVII:

> "Five causes were there in the past,
> Five fruits we find in present life;
> Five causes do we now produce,
> Five fruits we reap in future life."

Now, just as in this process of continually changing mental and bodily phenomena, nothing can be found that would pass from one moment to the next moment, so also there is no enduring entity, ego, or personality, within this process of existence that would transmigrate from one life to the next (see *nāma-rūpa, anatta, paṭisandhi, khandha*). "No being and no living soul passed from the former life to this life, and yet this present embryo could not have entered into existence without the preceding causes" (VISM. XVII). "Many things may serve to illustrate this fact, as for example the echo, the light of a lamp, the impression of a seal, or the image produced by a mirror" (ib.).

"Whosoever is in the dark with regard to the conditionally arisen things, and does not understand that karma originates from ignorance, etc., he thinks that it must be his ego that knows or does not know, acts and causes to act, and that arises at rebirth. Or he thinks that the atoms, or a creator, with the help of this embryonic process, must have formed this body, or that it is the ego endowed with faculties that has impressions, - 254 - feels, desires, clings, continues and enters again into existence in a new birth. Or he thinks that all beings have been born through fate, or fortuitously" (VISM. XVII).

Now, on hearing that Buddhism teaches that everything whatever in the world is determined by conditions some might come to the conclusion that Buddhism teaches some sort of fatalism, and that man has no free will, or that will is not free.

The problem 'whether man has a free will' does not exist for the Buddhist, since he knows that, apart from these ever-changing mental and physical phenomena, no such entity as 'man' can be found, and that 'man' is merely a name not relating to any reality. And the question, 'whether will is free', must be rejected for the reason that 'will', or volition, is a mental phenomenon flashing forth only for a moment, and that as such it had not any existence at the preceding moment. For of a thing which is not, or is not yet, one cannot, properly speaking, ask whether it is or is not free. The only admissible question would be whether the arising of 'will' is independent of conditions, or whether it is conditioned. But the same question would equally apply also to all the other mental phenomena, as well as to all physical phenomena, in other words: to everything and every occurrence whatever. And the answer would be: whether will arises, or whether feeling arises, or whether any other mental or any physical phenomenon arises, the arising of anything whatsoever is dependent on conditions, and without conditions nothing ever can arise or enter into existence.

According to Buddhism, everything mental or physical happens in accordance with laws and conditions; and if it were otherwise, chaos and blind chance would reign. But such a thing is impossible and contradicts all laws of thinking. Cf. FUND. III (end).

(11)

"Through rebirth are conditioned old age and death" (*jātipaccayā jarā-maraṇaṃ*). Without birth there can be no old age and death, no suffering and misery. Thus rebirth is to old age and death, etc. a condition by way of decisive support (*upanissaya*). The Buddha has said (D. 15):

"Profound, Ananda. is this dependent origination, and profound does it appear. It is through not understanding, not penetrating, this law that this world resembles a tangled ball of thread, a bird's nest, a thicket of sedge or reed, and that man does not escape from the lower states of existence, from the course of woe and perdition, suffering from the round of rebirth." And further (M. 28): 'Whoso understands the dependent origination understands the Dhamma; and whoso understands the Dhamma understands the dependent origination."

patience, or forbearance (*khanti*): one of the ten perfections (*pāramī*, q.v.).

paṭigha: 1. In an ethical sense, it means: 'repugnance', grudge, resentment, anger, and is a synonym of *vyāpāda*, 'ill will' (see *nīvaraṇa*) and *dosa*, 'hate' (see *mūla*). It is one of the proclivities (*anusaya*, q.v.).

2. '(Sense-) reaction'. Applied to fivefold sense cognition, ~ occurs in the following contexts:

(a) as *paṭigha-saññā*, 'perception of sense-reaction', said to be absent in the immaterial absorptions (see *jhāna* 5). Alternative renderings: resistance-perception, reflex-perception;

(b) as *paṭigha-samphassa*, '(mental) impression caused by fivefold sensorial reaction' (D. 15); see *phassa*;

(c) as *sappaṭigha-rūpa*, 'reacting corporeality', and *appaṭigha*, 'not reacting', which is an Abhidhammic classification of corporeality, occurring in DHS. 659, 1050. *Sappaṭigha* are called the physical sense organs as reacting (or responding) to sense stimuli; and also the physical sense-objects as impinging (or making an impact) on the sense organs. All other corporeality is *appaṭigha*, non-reacting and non-impinging. These two terms have been variously rendered as resistant and not, responding and not, with and without impact.

pāṭihāriya: 'miracle', marvel. Three marvels are ascribed to the Buddha: the marvel of magic (*iddhi*-~), the marvel of mind-reading (*ādesanā*-~) and the marvel of instruction (*anusāsanī-~*). In D. 11, the Buddha says that he sees danger in the first two and therefore abhors them. In A. III, 61, the 'marvel of instruction' is called the one 'more noble and sublime'. For *iddhi-pāṭihāriya*, see D. 25. See also *yamaka-pāṭihāriya*.

paṭikkūla-saññā: see *kāyagatā-sati*.

pātimokkha: 'disciplinary code', is the name of the code of monks' rules, which on all full-moon and new moon days is recited before the assembled community of fully ordained monks (*bhikkhu*).

See *The Pātimokkha*, romanised Pali text and tr. by Ñāṇamoli Thera (Bangkok 1966, Mahāmakut Buddhist Bookshop).

pātimokkha-saṃvara-sīla: 'morality consisting in restraint with regard to the Disciplinary Code' (see *pātimokkha*). For details, see *sīla*.

paṭinissaggānupassanā: 'contemplation on abandonment', is one of the eighteen kinds of insight (*vipassanā* q.v.). Further cf. the sixteenth exercise of *ānāpāna-sati* (q.v.).

paṭipadā: 1. 'Road', 'path'; for instance in *dukkhanirodha-gāminī-paṭipadā*, 'the road leading to the extinction of suffering' (= the fourth Noble Truth); *majjhimā paṭipadā*, 'the Middle Way'.

2. 'Progress' (see also *paṭipadā-ñāṇadassana-visuddhi*). There are four modes of progress to deliverance: (1) painful progress with slow comprehension (*dukkhā paṭipadā dandhābhiññā*), (2) painful progress with quick comprehension, (3) pleasant progress with slow comprehension, (4) pleasant progress with quick comprehension. In A. IV, 162 it is said:

(1) "Some person possesses by nature excessive greed, excessive hate, excessive delusion, and thereby he often feels pain and sorrow; and also the five mental faculties, as faith, energy, mindfulness, concentration and wisdom (see *indriya* 15–19) are dull in him; and by reason thereof he reaches only slowly the immediacy (*ānantariya*, q.v.) to the cessation of all cankers.

(2) "Some person possesses by nature excessive greed, etc., but the five mental faculties are sharp in him and by reason thereof he reaches quickly the immediacy to the cessation of all cankers. ...

(3) "Some person possesses by nature no excessive greed, etc., but the five mental faculties are dull in him, and by reason thereof he reaches slowly the immediacy to the cessation of all cankers. ...

(4) 'Some person possesses by nature no excessive greed, etc., and the

mental faculties are sharp in him, and by reason thereof he reaches quickly the immediacy to the cessation of all cankers. …

See A. IV, 162, 163, 166–169; DHS. 176ff.; ASL.TR. I, 243; 11, 291, 317.

paṭipadā-ñāṇadassana-visuddhi: 'purification by knowledge and vision of the path-progress' forms the sixth stage of purification (*visuddhi*, q.v.).

P

paṭipannaka: 'path-attainer', is he who had reached one of the four supermundane paths of holiness (see *ariya-puggala*).

SOURCE NOTE: occurs in PUG. 17.

paṭipatti: practice, or 'pursuance' of the teaching, as distinguished from the mere theoretical knowledge of its wording (*pariyatti*, q.v.).

SOURCE NOTE: see *pariyatti*.

paṭipassaddhi-pahāna: 'overcoming (of defilements) by tranquillisation' (see *pahāna*).

paṭisambhidā: 'analytical knowledge' or 'discrimination', is of four kinds: analytical knowledge of the true meaning (*attha-paṭisambhidā*), of the law (*dhamma-paṭisambhidā*), of language (*nirutti-paṭisambhidā*), of ready wit (*paṭibhāna-paṭisambhidā*). As an alternative rendering of the fourth term (*paṭibhāna*), Bhikkhu Ñāṇamoli proposes: perspicuity (in expression and knowledge).

1. The analytical knowledge of the meaning (*attha-~*) is the knowledge with regard to the sense.
2. The analytical knowledge of the law (*dhamma-~*) is the knowledge with regard to the law.
3. The analytical knowledge of language (*nirutti-~*) is the knowledge of the language with regard to those former two things.
4. The analytical knowledge of ready-wit (*patibhāna-~*) is the knowledge about the (former three) kinds of knowledge" (VIBH. XV).

"(1) *attha* (SKR. *artha*, √ *ar*, to reach; result, meaning, purpose, true substance) designates, in short, the fruit (*phala*) of a cause (*hetu*); for since the fruit of a cause results from adhering to the cause, and is reached and effected thereby, therefore it is called result (*attha*). In particular, however, five things are considered as *attha*, namely: everything dependent on conditions, Nibbāna, the meaning of words, karma result, and functional consciousness. When anyone reflects on that meaning any knowledge of his, falling within the category concerned with meaning (or result), is the 'analytical knowledge' of meaning.

"(2) *dhamma* (SKR. *dharma*, √ *dhar*, to bear; bearer, condition, law, phenomenon, thing) is, in short, a name for condition (*paccaya*). … In particular, however, five things are considered as *dhamma*, namely: every cause (*hetu*) producing a result, the noble path, the spoken word, the karmically wholesome, and the karmically unwholesome. When anyone reflects on that law, any knowledge of his, falling within the category concerned with law (or cause), is the 'analytical knowledge' of the law.

In VIBH. it is further said: 'The knowledge of suffering is the 'analytical knowledge' of the true meaning (*attha-paṭisambhidā*), the knowledge of its origin is the 'analytical knowledge' of the law (*dhamma-paṭisambhidā*). The knowledge of the cause is the 'analytical knowledge' of the law (*dhamma-paṭisambhidā*), the knowledge of the result of the cause is the 'analytical knowledge' of the true meaning (*attha-paṭisambhidā*). … That the monk knows the law, the suttas etc. this is called the 'analytical knowledge' of the law (*dhamma-paṭisambhidā*); if however, he understands the meaning of this or that speech … it is called the 'analytical knowledge' of the true meaning (*attha-paṭisambhidā*).'

(3) "'The knowledge of the language concerning those things' means: the language corresponding to reality, and the unfailing mode of expression concerning the true meaning and the law.

(4) "'Knowledge about the kinds of knowledges' is that knowledge which has all knowledges as object and considers them. Or, the analytical knowledge of ready wit (*patibhāna-paṭisambhidā*) means the knowledge of the above mentioned three kinds of knowledge, in all their details, with their objects, functions, etc." (VISM. XIV).

On the seven qualities leading to the attainment of the four 'analytical knowledge', see A. VII, 37. See VISM. XIV, 21ff.; VIBH. XV; PTS.M. Paṭisambhidā Kathā.

paṭisandhi: lit. 'reunion, relinking', i.e., rebirth, is one of the fourteen functions of consciousness (*viññāṇa-kicca*, q.v.). It is a karma resultant type of consciousness and arises at the moment of conception i.e., with the forming of new life in the mother's womb. Immediately afterwards it sinks into the subconscious stream of existence (*bhavaṅga-sota*, q.v.), and conditioned thereby ever and ever again corresponding states of subconsciousness arise. Thus it is really rebirth-consciousness that determines the latent character of a person.

"Neither has this (rebirth-) consciousness transmigrated from the previous existence to this present existence, nor did it arise without such conditions, as karma, karma-formations, propensity, object, etc. That this consciousness has not come from the previous existence to this present existence, yet that it has come into existence by means of conditions included in the previous existence, such as karma (q.v.), etc., this fact may be illustrated by various things, such as the echo, the light of a lamp, the impression of a seal, or the image produced by a mirror. For just as the resounding of the echo is conditioned by a sound, etc., and nowhere a transmigration of sound has taken place, just so it is with this consciousness. Further it is said: 'In this continuous process, no sameness and no otherness can be found.' For if there were full identity (between the different stages), then also milk never could turn into curd. And if there were a complete otherness, then curd could never come from milk. ... If in a continuity of existence any karma result takes place, then this karma result neither belongs to any other being, nor does it come from any other (*kamma*), because absolute sameness and otherness are excluded here" (VISM, XVII 164ff.).

In MIL. it is said:

"Now, Venerable Nāgasena, the one who is reborn, is he the same as the one who has died, or is he another?"

"Neither the same, nor another" (*na ca so na ca añño*).

"Give me an example."

"What do you think, O King: are you now, as a grown-up person, the same that you had been as a little, young and tender babe? "

"No, Venerable Sir. Another person was the little, young and tender babe, but quite a different person am I now as a grown-up man." ...

" ... Is perhaps in the first watch of the night one lamp burning, another one in the middle watch, and again another one in the last watch?"

"No, Venerable Sir. The light during the whole night depends on one and the same lamp."

"Just so, O King, is the chain of phenomena linked together. One phenomenon arises, another vanishes, yet all are linked together, one after the other, without interruption. In this way one reaches the final state of consciousness neither as the same person. nor as another person."

According to the nature of their rebirth-consciousness, beings divide into the following three groups:

1. *ahetu-paṭisandhika*: a 'being reborn without root-conditions', is a being whose consciousness at the moment of rebirth was not accompanied by any of the three noble root-conditions, viz. greedlessness, hatelessness, undeludedness (see *mūla*), i.e., selflessness, kindness, intelligence. Such beings are found in the four lower worlds (*apāya*, q.v.), in which case the function of rebirth is

exercised by the class of consciousness listed in TAB. I as No. 56. But if such beings are born in the sensuous sphere as humans, they will be crippled, blind, deaf, mentally deficient, etc. (Rebirth-consciousness = TAB. I, No. 41)

2. *dvihetu* (or *duhetu*)-*paṭisandhika*: a 'being reborn with only two (noble) root-conditions', i.e., greedlessness and hatelessness. (Rebirth-consciousness = TAB. I, Nos. 44, 45, 48 or 49.)

3. *tihetu-paṭisandhika*: a 'being reborn with three (noble) root-conditions'. Such a being can be found only among men. (Rebirth-consciousness = TAB. 1, Nos. 42, 43, 46, or 47) and higher heavenly beings.

On these three types of rebirth, See ASL.TR. 11, 354–379. see *paṭisandhika*.

In the suttas, the terms for rebirth are chiefly *punabbhava* (q.v.), 'renewed existence', and *abhinibbatti* 'arising'; or both combined as *punabbhavābhinibbatti*.

LITERATURE: VISM. XVII, 133ff., 164ff., 189ff., 289ff.; VISM. XIX, 22ff. *Karma and Rebirth*, by Nyanatiloka Thera (WHEEL 9). *The Case for Rebirth*, by Francis Story (WHEEL 12/13). *Survival and Karma in Buddhist Perspective*, by K.N. Jayatilleke (WHEEL 141/143). *Rebirth Explained*, by V.F. Gunaratna (WHEEL 167/169).

SOURCE NOTE: the term is chiefly a commentarial; but it occurs several times in one of the later books of the Sutta Piṭaka, the Paṭisambhidā Magga (PTS.M. I, 11ff., 52, 59ff.; II, 72ff.). The usual sutta term for 'rebirth' is *punabbhava* ('re-becoming').

paṭisandhika: *ahetu-~*, *dvihetu-~*, and *tihetu-~* (SOURCE NOTE) are purely commentarial terms. For *paṭisandhi-citta*, see *citta-vīthi*.

paṭisaṅkhāna-bala and **bhāvanā-bala**: 'power of reflection', and 'power of mental development'. About these two powers it is said in A. II, 10:

"What, O monks, is the power of reflection? If, O monks, someone thinks thus: 'Bad conduct in deeds, words and thoughts verily bears bad fruits both in this life, as well as in the next life', and in consequence of this consideration, he abandons bad conduct in deeds, words and thoughts, follows good conduct, and keeps his heart pure, this, O monks, is the power of reflection.

"What, O monks, is the power of mental development? If, O monks, a monk develops the factors of enlightenment (*bojjhaṅga*, q.v.), bent on solitude, on detachment, on extinction, and ending in deliverance, namely: mindfulness, investigating of the law, energy, rapture, tranquillity, concentration, and equanimity, this, O monks, is the power of mental development."

P

paṭisaṅkhānupassanā-ñāṇa: 'knowledge consisting in reflective contemplation"; is one of the nine knowledges constituting the 'purification by knowledge and vision of the path-progress' (*paṭipadā-ñāṇadassana-visuddhi*, see *visuddhi* VI), and one of the eighteen chief kinds of insight (*mahāvipassanā*; see *vipassanā*).

P

paṭivedha: 'penetration', signifies the realisation of the truth of the Dhamma, as distinguished from the mere acquisition of its wording (*pariyatti*), or the practice (*paṭipatti*) of it, in other words, realisation as distinguished from theory and practice. Cf. *pariyatti*.

SOURCE NOTE: see *pariyatti*.

patta-piṇḍik'aṅga: the 'exercise of the bowl-eater', is one of the thirteen ascetic purification-exercises (*dhutaṅga*, q.v.), consisting in the vow of using only the alms-bowl for eating, and the rejection of any other vessel.

patti-dāna: lit. 'giving of the acquired', i.e., 'transference of merit.' Though in the older texts very seldom mentioned (e.g. A. VII, 50), it is, however, a widespread custom in all Buddhist countries. It is presumed that moral merit, especially that acquired through giving alms, can be transferred to others, apparently for the reason that one's own good deeds may become to others, especially to departed relatives and friends reborn in the ghost realm, an inducement to a happy and morally wholesome state of mind. Transference of merit is advocated (though without mentioning the term *patti-dāna*) in the Tirokuḍḍa Sutta (KHP. and Petavatthu) and its com. (KHP. TR.). It is one of the ten 'bases of meritorious action' (*puññakiriyavatthu*, q.v.), called there *pattānuppadāna*.

See 'The Doctrine of Reversible Merit' by F. L. Woodward. *Buddhist Review* (London), Vol. I (1914), p. 38.

penetration: see *paṭivedha*, *pariyatti*. For the power of penetrating (*vipphāra*) knowledge and concentration, see *iddhi*. For morality combined with penetration (*nibbedha*), see *hāna-bhāgiya-sīla*, etc. For penetration (*pariya*) of the mind of others, see *abhiññā*.

perfections, the ten: *pāramī* (q.v.).

perfect one, the: Tathāgata (q.v.).

performance and avoidance: *cāritta-vāritta* (q.v.).

permanency, idea of: see *vipallāsa*.

personality: see *sakkāya*. For personality-belief, see *sakkāya diṭṭhi, diṭṭhi, attā, satta, puggala, vipallāsa.*

perversions, the four: *vipallāsa* (q.v.).

peta (SKR. *preta*): lit. 'departed spirit', ghost, see *loka*.

petti-visaya: 'ghost realm', see *loka*.

phala: lit. 'fruit'. 1. result, effect (often together with *hetu*, cause); 2. benefit (e.g. in Sāmañña-phala Sutta, 'The Results, or Benefits, of Recluseship'; D. 2).

2. As 'path-result', or 'fruition', it denotes those moments of supermundane consciousness which flash forth immediately after the moment of path-consciousness (see *ariya-puggala*) and which, till the attainment of the next higher path, may during the practice of insight (*vipassanā*, q.v.) still recur innumerable times. If thus repeated, they are called the 'attainment of fruition (*phala-samāpatti*), which is explained in detail in VISM. XXIII.

pharusā vācā: 'harsh or abusive speech', see *micchā-vācā*.

phassa (fr. *phusati*, to touch): 'sense-impression', contact. The term *samphassa* is used in compounds, e.g. in the following: "There are six classes of sense-impression: visual impression (*cakkhu-samphassa*), impressions of hearing, smelling, tasting, bodily (tactile) impression and mental impression" (M. 9). A twofold division occurs in D. 15: *paṭigha* (q.v.) *-samphassa*, 'impression by sensorial reaction', and *adhivacana-samphassa*, 'verbal (or conceptual, i.e., mental) impression'.

Phassa does not signify physical impact, but is one of the seven constant mental concomitants of consciousness (*cetasika*) and belongs to the group of mental formations (*saṅkhārakkhandha*). In lists of both these categories it is generally mentioned first (e.g. DHS. 1: M. 9), due to its fundamental position in the cognitive process In M. 18 it is thus defined: "Dependent on the eye and the forms, eye-consciousness arises; the coming-together of the three is sense-impression" (similarly stated in the case of the other five senses, including mind). In the dependent origination, it is conditioned by the six sense-bases and is a conditioning factor of feeling (see *paṭicca-samuppāda* 5, 6). Its relation to mind-and-body (*nāma-rūpa*) is described in D. 15, and its influence on feeling and wrong views, in D. 1 (at the end). It is one of the four nutriments (*āhāra*, q.v.), and the first factor in the pentad of sense-impression (*phassa-pañcamaka*), together with feeling, perception, volition and consciousness (see ABH. St., p. 47ff.).

P

Being a key function in the mind's contact with the world of objects and being a potential source of defilements, sense-impression is an important subject for reflective insight contemplation as succinctly formulated in many verses of the SN.: 736/7, 778, 851, 870/72, 923.

picked-up rags, wearing robes made from: see *dhutaṅga*.

piṇḍapātik'aṅga: the 'practice of going for alms', is one of the thirteen ascetic purification-exercises (see *dhutaṅga*).

pisuṇā vācā: tale-bearing; see *musāvādā*.

pīta-kasiṇa: 'yellow-kasina', is one of the kasina exercises; see *kasiṇa*.

pīti: 'rapture', enthusiasm, interest (rendered also as joy, happiness, zest); it is one of the mental factors or concomitants (*cetasika*) and belongs to the group of mental formations (*saṅkhārakkhandha*). Since, in sutta texts, it is often linked in a compound word with 'gladness' (*pāmojja*) or 'happiness' (*sukha*), some Western translations have wrongly taken it as a synonym of these two terms. *Pīti*, however, is not a feeling or a sensation, and hence does not belong to the feeling-group (*vedanākkhandha*), but may be described psychologically as 'joyful interest'. As such it may be associated with wholesome as well as with unwholesome and neutral states of consciousness.

A high degree of rapture is characteristic of certain stages in meditative concentration, in insight practice (*vipassanā*) as well as in the first two absorptions (*jhāna*, q.v.). In the latter it appears as one of the factors of absorption (*jhānaṅga*; see *jhāna*) and is strongest in the second absorption. Five degrees of intensity in meditative rapture are described in VISM. IV. 94ff. It is one of the factors of enlightenment (*bojjhaṅga*, q.v.).

planes of existence, the three: see *avacara*.

pleasantness, idea of: see *vipallāsa*, *subha-nimitta*.

pondering: see *vīmaṃsā*.

ponobbhava: alternate spelling of *punabbhava* (q.v.).

post-nascence: *pacchājāta-paccaya*, one of the twenty-four conditions (*paccaya*, q.v.).

postures, the four bodily: *iriyāpatha* (q.v.).

powers, the five spiritual: see *bala*. For the six higher ~, see *abhiññna*. For the ten ~ of a Buddha, see *dasabala*. For the four roads to ~, see *iddhipāda*. For magical ~, see *iddhi*.

practice: for theory, practice, and realisation, see *pariyatti*.

predominance and **pre-nascence**: *adhipati*, *purejāta*, are two of the twenty-four conditions (*paccaya*, q.v.).

preparatory concentration (and preparatory image, etc.): see *samādhi*, *javana*.

prescribed moral rules: *paññatti-sīla* (q.v.).

proclivities: see *anusaya*.

produced corporeality: *nipphanna-rūpa* (q.v.).

productive karma (or regenerative ~): see *karma*.

proficiency (of mental factors and consciousness): *pāguññatā* (q.v.).

progress: see *paṭipadā*, *abhabbāgamana*. ~ in morality, etc., see *hānabhāgiya*, etc. Purification by knowledge and vision of path-progress, see *visuddhi* (VI). see ~ of the disciple, below.

progress of the disciple, gradual development of the Eightfold Path in the: in many suttas occurs an identical passage that outlines the gradual course of development in the progress of the disciple. There it is shown how this development takes place gradually, and in conformity with laws, from the very first hearing of the doctrine, and from germinating faith and dim comprehension, up to the final realisation of deliverance.

"After hearing the law, he is filled with confidence, and he thinks: 'Full of hindrances is household life, a refuse heap; but the homeless life (of a monk) is like the open air. Not easy is it, when one lives at home, to fulfil in all points the rules of the holy life. How if now I were to cut off hair and beard, put on the yellow robe, and go forth from home to the homeless life?' And after a short time, having given up his possessions, great or little, having forsaken a circle of relations, small or large, he cuts off hair and beard, puts on the yellow robe, and goes forth from home to the homeless life.

Having thus left the world, he fulfils the rules of the monks. He avoids the killing of living beings and abstains from it; without stick or sword, conscientious, full of sympathy, he is desirous of the welfare of all living beings. He avoids stealing … avoids unchastity … avoids lying … tale-bearing … harsh language … vain talk.

"He abstains from destroying vegetal germs and plants; eats only at one time of the day; keeps aloof from dance, song, music and the visiting of shows; rejects floral adornment, perfumes, ointment, as well as any other kind of adornment and embellishment. High and gorgeous beds he does not use. Gold and silver he does not accept … keeps aloof from buying and selling things. …

"He contents himself with the robe that protects his body, and with the alms-bowl with which he keeps himself alive. Wherever he goes, he is provided with these two things, just as a winged bird in flying carries its wings along with him.

"By fulfilling this noble domain of morality (*sīla*) he feels in his heart an irreproachable happiness."

In what follows thereafter it is shown how the disciple watches over his five senses and his mind, and by this noble restraint of the senses (*indriya-saṃvara*) feels in his heart an unblemished happiness; how in all his actions he is ever mindful and clearly conscious; and how, being equipped with this lofty morality (*sīla*), and with this noble restraint of the senses (*indriya-saṃvara*), and with mindfulness and clear consciousness (*sati-sampajañña*), he chooses a secluded dwelling, and freeing his mind from the five hindrances (*nīvaraṇa*, q.v.) he reaches full concentration (*samādhi*, q.v.); and how thereafter, by developing insight (*vipassanā* q.v.) with regard to the impermanence (*anicca*), misery (*dukkha*) and impersonality (*anatta*, q.v.) of all phenomena of existence, he finally realises deliverance from all cankers and defilements, and thus the assurance arises in him:

"For ever am I liberated,
This is the last time I am born,
No new existence waits for me."

Cf. D.1, 2; M. 27, 38, 51, 60, 76; A. IV, 198; X, 99: PUG. 239, etc.

proximity: *anantara*, is one of the twenty-four conditions (*paccaya*, q.v.).

pubbenivāsānussati: 'remembrance of former births', is one of the higher powers (*abhiññā*, q.v.), and a factor of threefold knowledge (*te-vijjā*, q.v.).

puggala: 'individual', 'person', as well as the synonyms: personality, individuality, being (*satta*), self (*attā*), etc., in short all terms designating a personal entity, hence also: I, you, he, man, god, etc., all these, according to Buddhism, are mere names for certain combinations of material and mental processes, and apart from them they have no real existence. They are to be considered as mere 'conventional modes of expression' (*vohāra-vacana*), and on that level they may be used, and are so used in the sutta texts, if taken "without misapprehending them" (see quote from D. 9 under *paramattha*). With such tacit reservations, the term *puggala* occurs quite frequently in the suttas.

In the ultimate sense (*paramattha*, q.v.), however, there exist only ever-changing physical and mental phenomena, flashing up and dying every moment. KATH., in its first section, discusses the question whether "in the absolute sense, any personality (*puggala*) can be found" (see GUIDE, 62ff.). See *paramattha*, *anatta*.

pūjā: (1) honour, respect, homage, (2) worship, devotional observances, devotional offerings; also offerings to monks.

(1) The Mahāmaṅgala Sutta (SN. 259) says that "Honour and respect towards those worthy of it, is conducive to great blessing" (*pūjā ca pūjaniyānaṃ etaṃ maṅgalam uttamaṃ*). See DHP. 195ff.

(2) The Buddha did not think much of mere outer worship. "Not thus, Ananda, is the Tathāgata respected, venerated, esteemed, worshipped and honoured in the highest degree. But, Ananda, whatsoever bhikkhu or bhikkhuni, lay man or lay woman, abides by the Teaching, lives uprightly in the Teaching, walks in the way of the Teaching, it is by him that the Tathāgata is respected, venerated, esteemed, worshipped and honoured in the highest degree" (D. 16). "There are two kinds of worship: in a material way (*āmisa-pūjā*) and through (practice of) the Dhamma (*dhamma-pūjā*). The worship through (practice of) the Dhamma is the better of the two" (A. II).

punabbhava: lit.: re-becoming; 'renewed existence', is a sutta term for 'rebirth', which, in later literature mostly is called *paṭisandhi* (q.v.). The attainment of Sainthood (*arahatta*), implying the end of future rebirths, is often expressed in the words: "This is the last birth. Now there is no more a renewed existence!" (*natthi'dāni punabbhavo*) (M. 26; D. 15; THERAG. 87, 339; SN. 502). The term is often linked with *abhinibbatti* ('arising').

"But how, O brother, does it come to renewed existence and arising in the future (*āyatiṃ punabbhavābhinibbatti*)? Because beings, obstructed by ignorance and fettered by craving, find ever fresh delight now here, now there, for this reason there is renewed existence and arising in the future" (M. 43). See also S.XII. 38. *Abhinibbatti* also stands sometimes alone in signifying 'rebirth', e.g. in A. VI, 61; X, 65.

Cf., in the Second Truth, the adj. *ponobhavika*, 'leading to renewed existence'. See A. III, 76; SN. 163, 273, 514, 733; S. VII, 12; X, 3.

puñña: merit, meritorious, is a popular term for karmically wholesome (*kusala*) action. Opposite terms: *apuñña*, 'demerit'; *pāpa*, 'bad', 'evil'. The value of meritorious action is often stressed, e.g., in the Treasure Store Sutta (see KHP. TR.), Dhp 18, 118, 122. The Community of Holy Monks (*ariya-saṅgha*), the third Refuge (see *ti-saraṇa*), is said to be "the incomparable field of merit in the world" (*anuttaraṃ puññakkhettaṃ lokassa*); see *anussati* 3. The arahats, however, having transcended all life-affirming and rebirth-producing actions, are said to be "beyond merit and demerit"; see SN. 520, 547, 636, 790. Cf. *puññābhisaṅkhāra*, *puññā-dhārā*, and *puñña-kiriya-vatthu*.

P

puññābhisaṅkhāra: 'meritorious karma-formations' of the sensuous and fine-material sphere; see *saṅkhāra* I. 1.

puñña-dhārā: 'streams of merit'. It is said that one produces four streams of merit by offering the four requisites (robes, alms-food, dwelling, medicine) to a monk who has reached the conditionless deliverance of mind; further by being filled with unshakeable faith in the Buddha, his doctrine and community of disciples, and by being perfect in morality (A. IV, 51, 52). A. VIII, 39 describes four further streams of merit.

puñña-kiriya-vatthu: 'bases of meritorious action'. In the suttas, three are mentioned consisting of giving (*liberality; dāna-maya-~*), of morality (*sīla-maya-~*) and of mental development (meditation; *bhāvanāmaya-~*). See D. 33; IT. 60; expl. in A. VIII, 36.

Commentaries have a list of ten (*dasa ~*) which is very popular in Buddhist countries: (1)-(3) as above, (4) reverence (*apaciti*), (5) service (*veyyāvacca*), (6) transference of merit (*puññānuppadāna*), (7) rejoicing in others' merit (*abbhānumodana*), (8) expounding the Doctrine (*desanā*), (9) listening to the Doctrine (*savana*), (10) straightening one's right views (rectification of views; *diṭṭhujukamma*). Expl. in ASL.TR. 209ff.

LITERATURE: see *The Advantages of Merit*, by Bhikkhu Khantipalo (Bodhi Leaves B. 38).

pure abodes: *suddhāvāsa* (q.v.).

purejāta-paccaya: 'pre-nascence', is one of the twenty-four conditions (*paccaya*, q.v.).

purification, the seven stages of: see *visuddhi*.

purisindriya: 'virility', see *bhāva, khandha*.

purity, the elements of the effort for: *pārisuddhipadhāniyaṅga* (q.v.).

puthujjana: lit.: 'one of the many folk', 'worldling', ordinary man, is any layman or monk who is still possessed of all the ten fetters (*saṃyojana*, q.v.) binding to the round of rebirths, and therefore has not yet reached any of the four stages of holiness (see *ariya-puggala*).

"Whoso is neither freed from the three fetters (personality-belief, sceptical doubt, attachment to mere rule and ritual), nor is on the way to lose these three things, such a one is called a worldling" (PUG. 9).

According to com. to M. 9, a 'worldling' may be (1) an outsider (a non-Buddhist) who, if he believed in moral causation, may be said to have right view to that extent; but he has not the 'knowledge conforming to the Truths' (*saccānulomika-ñāṇa*), as has (2) the 'worldling inside the Buddha's Dispensation' (*sāsanika*). A worldling who professes Buddhism, may be either a 'blind worldling' (*andha-~*) who has neither knowledge of, nor interest in the fundamental teaching (the Truths, groups, etc.); or he is a 'noble worldling' (*kalyāṇa-~*), who has such knowledge and earnestly strives to understand and practise the Teaching. See ASL.TR. II, 451 (tr. by 'average man'); com. to M. 1, D. 1.

Q

questions and answers: *pañha-byākaraṇa* (q.v.)

R

radiant gods: *Ābhassara*; cf. *deva*.

rāga: 'lust', 'greed', is a synonym of *lobha* (see *mūla*), *taṇhā* (q.v.) and *abhijjhā* (see *kamma-patha*). For *kāma-*, *rūpa-*, *arūpa-rāga*, see *saṃyojana*.

rāga-carita: the 'greedy-natured', see *carita*.

rapture: *pīti* (q.v.); further see *bojjhaṅga*.

reaction, sense: see *paṭigha*.

ready-wit: see *paṭisambhidā*.

reality: see *paramattha*. Vision and knowledge according to ~ - see *vipassanā* 15.

realisation: for theory, practice, and ~, see *pariyatti*.

rebirth: see *paṭisandhi*, *paṭiccasamuppāda* (3, 10), *karma*, *punabbhava*.

receptive consciousness: *sampaṭicchana-citta* (see *viññāṇa-kicca*).

recollections: see *anussati*.

red-kasina exercise: see *kasiṇa*.

reflecting contemplation: *paṭisaṅkhānupassanā* (see *vipassanā*, 17).

reflection, power of: *paṭisaṅkhāna-bala* (q.v.).

reflex-perceptions: see *paṭigha* (2a).

refuge-formula, the threefold: *ti-saraṇa* (q.v.).

regenerating process: *upapatti-bhava* (see *bhava*).

regenerative karma: *janaka-kamma* (see *karma*).

registering consciousness: *tadārammaṇa-citta* (see *viññāṇa-kicca*).

relative truth: cf. *puggala, paramattha-sacca, desanā, anatta, satta.*

remembrance, of former existences: see *abhiññā* 4.

remorse: *kukkucca* (q.v.).

repetition: *āsevana-paccaya*, is one of the twenty-four conditions (*paccaya*, q.v.).

repression, overcoming by: *vikkhambhana-pahāna* (see *pahāna*).

repugnance: *paṭigha* (q.v.).

resistance-perceptions: see *paṭigha* (2a).

restlessness: *uddhacca* (q.v.).

retrospective knowledge: *paccavekkhana-ñāṇa* (q.v.).

reversible merit: *patti-dāna* (q.v.).

right (view, ~ understanding, ~ speech, etc.): see *magga*.

rise and fall (of phenomena): the knowledge consisting in the contemplation of ~, see *visuddhi* VI, 1.

round of rebirth: see *vaṭṭa* (2), *saṃsāra*. The threefold ~, see *vaṭṭa*, 1.

rukkha-mūlik'aṅga: see *dhutaṅga*.

rules and ritual, clinging to mere: see *saṃyojana, upādāna*.

ruminating-natured: *vitakka-carita* (see *carita*).

rūpa: (1) corporeality (see *khandha* 1); (2) visual object (see *āyatana*); (3) fine-material (see *avacara, jhāna*).

SOURCE NOTE: the terms *nipphanna-rūpa* and *rūpa-rūpa* are used only in the com., although *sappaṭigha* and *pasāda* are already found in the ABH. canon (e.g. DHS. §§ 585, 597ff.), while *upādiṇṇa* occurs repeatedly in the old sutta texts, e.g. M. 28, apparently with the meaning given in the main part of this work. Cf. further *upādā-rūpa*.

R

rūpajjhāna: see *jhāna*.

rūpa-kalāpa: 'corporeal group', material unit, designates a combination of several physical phenomena constituting a temporary unity. Thus, for instance, the so-called 'dead matter' forms the most primitive group, consisting only of eight physical phenomena, called the 'pure eightfold unit' or 'octad' (*suddhaṭṭhaka-kalāpa*), to wit: the four elements (the solid, fluid, heat, motion); colour, smell, taste, nutriment (*paṭhavī, āpo, tejo, vāyo; vaṇṇa, gandha, rasa, ojā*). In VISM., and elsewhere, it is also called *ojaṭṭhamaka-kalāpa*, 'the octad with nutriment as the eighth factor'.

The simplest form of living matter is the 'ninefold vitality unit' or 'life-ennead' (*jīvita-navaka-kalāpa*), formed by adding 'vitality' to the octad. Seven decades, or units of ten (*dasaka-kalāpa*), are formed by adding to the ninefold unit one of the following corporeal phenomena: heart (physical seat of mind), sex, eye, ear, nose, tongue or body. See VISM. XVIII, 4; *Compendium of Buddhist Philosophy* (PTS), 164, 250; ASL.TR., II, 413ff.

R

rūpa-kāya: 'body-group', as distinguished from *nāma-kāya*, 'mind-group' (q.v.). See *nāma-rūpa*.

rūpakkhandha: 'corporeality group', see *khandha* (1).

rūpa-loka: 'fine-material world', see *loka*.

rūpārammaṇa: 'visual object', designates the external of visual physical phenomenon ('light wave') that forms the base consciousness. Cf. *āyatana* (2).

rūpa-rūpa: *nipphanna-rūpa* (q.v.).

rūpāvacara: see *avacara*.

rūpāyatana: see *āyatana* (2).

S

sabba-loke anabhirati-saññā: 'contemplation on disinterestedness regarding the whole world', described in A. X., 60 in the following words: "If, Ananda, the monk gives up his tenacious clinging to the world, his firm grasping and his biases and inclinations of the mind, and turns away from these things, does not cling to them, this, Ananda, is called the contemplation on disinterestedness regarding the whole world."

sabbūpadhi-paṭinissagga: see *upadhi.*

sacca: 'truth'. 1. On the 'two truths', conventional and ultimate, see *paramattha.*

2. 'The Four Noble Truths' (*ariya-sacca*) are the briefest synthesis of the entire teachings of Buddhism, since all those manifold doctrines of the threefold canon are, without any exception, included therein. They are: the truth of suffering, of the origin of suffering, of the extinction of suffering, and of the Eightfold Path leading to the extinction of suffering.

I. The first truth, briefly stated, teaches that all forms of existence whatsoever are unsatisfactory and subject to suffering (*dukkha*).

II. The second truth teaches that all suffering, and all rebirth, is produced by craving (*taṇhā*).

III. The third truth teaches that extinction of craving necessarily results in extinction (*nirodha*) of rebirth and suffering, i.e., Nibbāna (q.v.).

IV. The fourth truth of the Eightfold Path (*magga*) indicates the means by which this extinction is attained.

The stereotype text frequently recurring in the Sutta Piṭaka, runs as follows:

I. "But what, O monks, is the noble truth of suffering? Birth is suffering, decay is suffering, death is suffering; sorrow, lamentation, pain, grief and despair are suffering; in short, the five groups of existence connected with clinging are suffering (cf. *dukkha, dukkhatā*).

II. "But what, O monks, is the noble truth of the origin of suffering? It is that craving which gives rise to fresh rebirth and, bound up with lust and greed, now here, now there, finds ever fresh delight. It is the sensual craving (*kāma-taṇhā*), the craving for existence (*bhava-taṇhā*), the craving for non-existence or self-annihilation (*vibhava-taṇhā*).

III. "But what, O monks, is the noble truth of the extinction of suffering? It is the complete fading away and extinction of this craving, its forsaking and giving up, liberation and detachment from it.

IV. "But what, O monks, is the noble truth of the path leading to the extinction of suffering? It is the Noble Eightfold Path (*ariya-aṭṭhaṅgika-magga*) that leads to the extinction of suffering, namely:

1. Right view	(*sammā-diṭṭhi*)	
2. Right thought	(*sammā-saṅkappa*)	III. Wisdom (*paññā*)
3. Right speech	(*sammā-vācā*)	
4. Right action	(*sammā-kammanta*)	
5. Right livelihood	(*sammā-ājiva*)	I. Morality (*sīla*)
6. Right effort	(*sammā-vāyāma*)	
7. Right mindfulness	(*sammā-sati*)	II. Concentration (*samādhi*)
8. Right concentration	(*sammā-samādhi*)	

1. "What now, O monks, is right view (or right understanding)? It is the understanding of suffering, of the origin of suffering, of the extinction of suffering, and of the path leading to the extinction of suffering.

2. "What now, O monks, is right thought? It is a mind free from sensual lust, ill will and cruelty.

3. "What now, O monks, is right speech? Abstaining from lying, talebearing, harsh words, and foolish babble (cf. *tiracchānakathā*).

4. "What now, O monks, is right action? Abstaining from injuring living beings, from stealing and from sexual misconduct (see *kāmesu micchācāra*).

5. "What now, O monks, is right livelihood? If the noble disciple rejects a wrong living, and gains his living by means of right livelihood (see *magga*, 5).

6. "What now, O monks, is right effort? If the disciple rouses his will to avoid the arising of evil, demeritorious things that have not yet arisen; … if he rouses his will to overcome the evil, demeritorious things that have already arisen; … if he rouses his will to produce meritorious things that have not yet arisen; … if he rouses his will to maintain the meritorious things that have already arisen and not to let them disappear, but to bring them to growth, to maturity and to the full perfection of development; he thus makes effort, stirs up his energy, exerts his mind and strives (see *padhāna*).

7. "What now, O monks is right mindfulness? If the disciple dwells in

contemplation of corporeality ... of feeling ... of mind ... of the mind-objects, ardent, clearly conscious, and mindful after putting away worldly greed and grief (see *satipaṭṭhāna*).

8. "What now, O monks, is right concentration? If the disciple is detached from sensual objects, detached from unwholesome things, and enters into the first absorption ... the second absorption ... the third absorption ... the fourth absorption" (see *jhāna*).

In the Buddha's first sermon, the Dhammacakkappavattana Sutta, it is said that the first truth (suffering) is to be fully understood; the second truth (craving) to be abandoned; the third truth (Nibbāna) to be realised; the fourth truth (the path) to be cultivated.

"The truth of suffering is to be compared with a disease, the truth of the origin of suffering with the cause of the disease, the truth of extinction of suffering with the cure of the disease, the truth of the path with the medicine" (VISM. XVI).

"In the ultimate sense, all these four truths are to be considered as empty of a self, since there is no feeling agent, no doer, no liberated one. no one who follows along the path. Therefore it is said:

'Mere suffering exists, no sufferer is found.
The deed is, but no doer of the deed is there.
Nibbāna is, but not the man that enters it.
The path is, but no traveller on it is seen.
'The first truth and the second truth are empty
Of permanency, joy, of self and beauty;
The Deathless Realm is empty of an ego,
And free from permanency, joy and self, the path.' (VISM. XVI)

It must be pointed out that the first truth does not merely refer to actual suffering, i.e., to suffering as feeling, but that it shows that, in consequence of the universal law of impermanence, all the phenomena of existence whatsoever, even the sublimest states of existence, are subject to change and dissolution, and hence are miserable and unsatisfactory; and that thus, without exception, they all contain in themselves the germ of suffering. Cf. GUIDE, 101ff

Regarding the true nature of the path, see *magga*.

LITERATURE: Dhammacakkappavattana Sutta (in WHEEL 17 and *Bodhi Leaves*); M. 141; Sacca-Saṃyutta (S. LVI); Sacca Vibhaṅga; W. OF B.; VISM. XVI: *The Four Noble Truths*, by Francis Story (WHEEL 34/35); *The Significance of the Four Noble Truths*, by V.F. Gunaratna (WHEEL 123).

S

sacca-ñāṇa: 'knowledge of the truth' (see *sacca*), may be of two kinds: (1) knowledge consisting in understanding (*anubodha-ñāṇa*) and (2) knowledge consisting in penetration (*pativedha-ñāṇa*), i.e., realisation. Cf. *pariyatti*.

"Amongst these, (1) 'knowledge consisting in understanding' is mundane (*lokiya*, q.v.), and its arising with regard to the extinction of suffering, and to the path, is due to hearsay etc. (therefore not due to one's realisation of the supermundane path; see *ariya-puggala*)

(2) 'Knowledge consisting in penetration', however, is supermundane (*lokuttara*), with the extinction of suffering (= Nibbāna) *as* object, it penetrates with its functions the four truths (in one and the same moment), as it is said (S. LVI, 30): "Whosoever, O monks, understands suffering, he also understands the origin of suffering, the extinction of suffering, and the path leading to the extinction of suffering" (VISM. XVI, 84). See *visuddhi* (end of article).

"Of the mundane kinds of knowledge, however, the knowledge of suffering by which (various) prejudices are overcome, dispels the personality-belief (*sakkāya-diṭṭhi*, see *diṭṭhi*). The knowledge of the origin of suffering dispels the annihilation-view (*uccheda-diṭṭhi*, see *diṭṭhi*); the knowledge of extinction of suffering, the eternity-view (*sassata-diṭṭhi*, see *diṭṭhi*); the knowledge of the path, the view of inefficacy of action (*akiriya-diṭṭhi*, see *diṭṭhi*)" (VISM. XVI, 85).

S

saccānulomika-ñāṇa: *anuloma-ñāṇa* (q.v.), *puthujjana*.

sacchikaraṇīyā dhammā: 'things to be realised'. Recollection of former states of existence is to be realised through remembrance (see *abhiññā* 4). The vanishing and reappearing of beings is to be realised through the divine eye (see *abhiññā* 5). The eight deliverances (*vimokkha*, q.v.) are to be realised through the mental group (*kāya*, here feeling, perception, mental formations; see *kāya*). The extinction of cankers is to be realised through insight (*vipassanā*).

saddhā: faith, confidence. A Buddhist is said to have faith if "he believes in the Perfect One's (the Buddha's) enlightenment" (M. 53; A.V, 2), or in the Three Jewels (see *ti-ratana*), by taking his refuge in them (see *ti-saraṇa*). His faith, however, should be "reasoned and rooted in understanding" (*ākāravatī saddhā dassanamūlikā*; M. 47), and he is asked to investigate and test the object of his faith (M. 47, 95). A Buddhist's faith is not in conflict with the spirit of inquiry, and "doubt about dubitable things" (A. II, 65; S. XLII, 13) is admitted and inquiry into them is encouraged. The 'faculty of faith' (*saddhindriya*) should be balanced with that of wisdom (*paññindriya*; see *indriya-samatta*). It is said: "A monk who has understanding, establishes his faith in accordance with that understanding" (S. XLVIII, 45). Through wisdom and understanding, faith becomes an inner certainty and firm conviction based on one's own experience.

Faith is called the seed (SN. V. 77) of all wholesome states because, according to commentarial explanations, it inspires the mind with confidence (*okappana, pasāda*) and determination (*adhimokkha*), for 'launching out' (*pakkhandha na*; see M. 122) to cross the flood of *saṃsāra*.

Unshakeable faith is attained on reaching the first stage of holiness, 'stream-entry' (*sotāpatti*, see *ariya-puggala*), when the fetter of sceptical doubt (*vicikicchā*; see *saṃyojana*) is eliminated. Unshakeable confidence (*avecca-ppasāda*) in the Three Jewels is one of the characteristic qualities of the stream-winner (*sotāpannassa aṅgāni*, q.v.).

Faith is a mental concomitant, present in all karmically wholesome, and its corresponding neutral, consciousness (see TAB. II). It is one of the four streams of merit (*puññadhārā*, q.v.), one of the five spiritual faculties (*indriya*, q.v.), spiritual powers (*bala*, q.v.), elements of exertion (*padhāniyaṅga*, q.v.) and one of the seven treasures (*dhana*, q.v.).

See *Faith in the Buddha's Teaching*, by Soma Thera (WHEEL 262). "Does Saddhā mean Faith?" by Ñānamoli Thera (in WHEEL 52/53).

saddhānusārī and **saddhā-vimutta**: the 'faith-devoted and the 'faith-liberated', are two of the seven kinds of noble disciples (see *ariya-puggala*, B.).

sagga: 'heaven', see *deva* (heavenly beings).

sahajāta-paccaya: 'co-nascence', is one of the twenty-four conditions (*paccaya*, q.v.).

sahetuka-citta: see *hetu*.

sakadāgāmī: the 'once-returner': see *ariya-puggala*, A.

Sakka: the 'King of gods' (*devānam-inda*), is the lord over the celestial beings in the heaven of the Thirty-Three' (*tāvatiṃsa*, see *deva*).

sakkāya: 'existing group'. 'this word is usually translated by 'personality', but according to the commentaries it corresponds to *sat-kāya*, 'existing group', hence not to SKR. *sva-kāya*, 'own group' or 'own body'. In the suttas (e.g. M. 44) it is said to be a name for the five groups of existence (*khandha*): "Sakkāya, O Brother Visākha, is said by the Blessed One to be a name for the five 'groups as objects of clinging' (*upādānakkhandha*), to wit:

corporeality, feeling, perception, mental formations, and consciousness"; see *sakkāya-diṭṭhi.*

sakkāya-diṭṭhi: 'personality-belief', is the first of the ten fetters (*saṃyojana*). It is entirely abandoned only on reaching the path of stream-winning (*sotāpatti-magga*; see *ariya-puggala*). There are twenty kinds of personality-belief, which are obtained by applying four types of that belief to each of the five groups of existence (*khandha*, q.v.): (1–5) the belief to be identical with corporeality, feeling, perception, mental formations or consciousness; (6–10) to be contained in them; (11–15) to be independent of them; (16–20) to be the owner of them (M. 44; S. XXII. 1); see *sakkāya, diṭṭhi, upādāna* 4.

salāyatana: the 'six bases' (of mental activity); see *āyatana, paṭiccasamuppāda.*

samādhi: 'concentration'; lit. 'the (mental) state of being firmly fixed' (*sam* + *ā* + √ *dhā*), is the fixing of the mind on a single object. "One-pointedness of mind (*cittass'ekaggatā*), Brother Visakha, this is called concentration" (M. 44). Concentration—though often very weak—is one of the seven mental concomitants inseparably associated with all consciousness. Cf. *nāma, cetanā.*

S

Right concentration (*sammā-samādhi*), as the last link of the Eightfold Path (see *magga*), is defined as the four meditative absorptions (*jhāna*, q.v.). In a wider sense, comprising also much weaker states of concentration, it is associated with all karmically wholesome (*kusala*) consciousness. Wrong concentration (*micchā-samādhi*) is concentration associated with all karmically unwholesome (*akusala*, q.v.) consciousness. Wherever in the texts this term is not differentiated by 'right' or 'wrong', there 'right' concentration is meant.

In concentration one distinguishes three grades of intensity:

(1) 'Preparatory concentration' (*parikamma-samādhi*) existing at the beginning of the mental exercise.

(2) 'Neighbourhood concentration' (*upacāra-samādhi*), i.e., concentration 'approaching' but not yet attaining the first absorption (*jhāna*, q.v.), which in certain mental exercises is marked by the appearance of the so-called 'counter-image' (*paṭibhāga-nimitta*).

(3) 'Attainment concentration' (*appanā-samādhi*), i.e., that concentration which is present during the absorptions.

Further details, see *bhāvana*, VISM. III and FUND. IV.

Concentration connected with the four noble path-moments (*magga*), and fruition-moments (*phala*), is called supermundane (*lokuttara*), having Nibbāna as object. Any other concentration, even that of the sublimest absorptions is merely mundane (*lokiya*, q.v.).

According to D. 33, the development of concentration (*samādhi-bhāvanā*) may procure a fourfold blessing: (1) present happiness through the four absorptions; (2) knowledge and vision (*ñāṇa-dassana*)—here probably identical with the 'divine eye' (see *abhiññā*) through perception of light (*kasiṇa*); (3) mindfulness and clear comprehension through the clear knowledge of the arising, persisting and vanishing of feelings, perceptions and thoughts; (4) extinction of all cankers (*āsavakkhaya*) through understanding the arising and passing away of the five groups forming the objects of clinging (see *khandha*).

Concentration is one of the seven factors of enlightenment (*bojjhaṅga*, q.v.), one of the five spiritual faculties and powers (see *bala*), and the last link of the Eightfold Path. In the threefold division of the Eightfold Path (morality, concentration and wisdom), it is a collective name for the three last links of the path (see *sikkhā*).

SOURCE NOTE: *parikamma-~*, *upacāra-~*, and *appanā-~* are found only in the com.

S

samādhi-parikkhāra: 'means, or requisites of concentration', are the four foundations of mindfulness (*satipaṭṭhāna* q.v.). See M. 44.

samādhi-samāpatti-kusalatā, *-ṭhiti-kusalatā*, *-uṭṭhāna-kusalatā*: skilfulness in entering into concentration, in remaining in it, and in rising from it. Cf. S. XXXIV, LLff.

samādhi-sambojjhaṅga: 'concentration as a factor of enlightenment' (see *bojjhaṅga*).

samādhi-vipphārā iddhi: the 'power of penetrating concentration', is one of the magical faculties (*iddhi*, q.v.).

samanantara-paccaya: 'contiguity', is one of the twenty-four conditions (*paccaya*, q.v.).

sāmañña-phala: the 'fruits of monkhood', is the name of a famous sutta (D. 2) and also, according to D. 33, a name for the four supermundane fruitions: stream-entry, once-return, non-return, and perfect holiness (see *ariya-puggala*).

samāpatti: 'attainments', is a name for the eight absorptions of the fine-material and immaterial spheres to which occasionally is added as ninth attainment, attainment of extinction (*nirodha-samāpatti*). Cf. *jhāna*.

sama-sīsī: one 'who attains two ends simultaneously', namely: the extinction of cankers and the end of life (see PUG. 19). In A. VIII, 6 it is said: "Such is the case with a monk who dwells in the contemplation of impermanence of all forms of existence, keeping before his eyes their impermanence, perceiving their impermanence, perseveringly, steadfastly, undisturbed, of firm mind, wisely absorbed; and in whom at one and the same time the extinction of cankers and the end of like take place."

SOURCE NOTE: this term seems to be met with for the first time in PUG. 19, while the person indicated is described in A., as discussed above.

samatha: 'tranquillity', serenity, is a synonym of *samādhi* (concentration), *cittekaggatā* (one-pointedness of mind) and *avikkhepa* (undistractedness). It is one of the mental factors in 'wholesome consciousness. Cf. *samatha-vipassanā* and *bhāvanā*.

S

samatha-vipassanā: 'tranquillity and insight', are identical with concentration (*samādhi*, q.v.; see *samatha*) and wisdom (*paññā*, q.v.), and form the two branches of mental development (*bhāvanā*, q.v.).

(1) 'Tranquillity' is all unperturbed, peaceful and lucid state of mind attained by strong mental concentration. Though as a distinct way of practice (see *samatha-yānika*), it aims at the attainment of the meditative absorptions (*jhāna*, q.v.), a high degree of tranquil concentration (though not necessarily that of the absorptions) is indispensable for insight too. Tranquillity frees the mind from impurities and inner obstacles, and gives it greater penetrative strength.

"What now is the power of tranquillity (*samatha-bala*)? It is the one-pointedness and non-distraction of the mind due to freedom from desire (renunciation) ... to freedom from ill will ... to the perception of light (see *aloka-saññā*) ... to non-distraction ... to the defining of phenomena ... to knowledge, gladness, the eight attainments, the ten kasinas, the ten recollections, the nine cemetery contemplations, the thirty-two kinds of respiration-mindfulness ... the one-pointedness and non-distraction of the mind of one contemplating abandonment (relinquishment) while inhaling and exhaling (see *ānāpāna-sati*).

"The power of tranquillity consists of the freedom from perturbation; in the first absorption, from the five hindrances (*nīvaraṇa*, (q.v.); in the second absorption, from thought-conception and discursive thinking; ... in the sphere of neither-perception-nor-non-perception it consists of the freedom from perturbation by the perception of the sphere of nothingness (see *anupubba-nirodha*), which is no longer agitated and irritated by defilements associated with restlessness, nor by the groups of existence" (PTS.M. 1. p. 97).

(2) 'Insight' (see *vipassanā*) is the penetrative understanding by direct meditative experience of the impermanence, unsatisfactoriness and impersonality of all material and mental phenomena of existence. It is insight that leads to entrance into the supermundane states of holiness and to final liberation.

"What now is the power of insight? It is the contemplation of impermanence (*aniccānupassanā*), of misery (*dukkhānupassanā*), impersonality' (*anattā-nupassanā*), of aversion (*nibbidānupassanā*), detachment (*virāgānupassanā*), extinction (*nirodha*), abandonment (*paṭinissagga*), with regard to corporeality, feeling, perception, mental formations and consciousness. ... That in contemplating the impermanence one is no more agitated by the idea of grasping ... no more by ignorance and the defilements associated therewith and no more by the groups of existence: this is called the power of insight" (PTS.M. p. 97).

"Two things are conducive to knowledge: tranquillity and insight. If tranquillity is developed, what profit does it bring? The mind is developed. If the mind is developed, what profit does it bring? All lust is abandoned.

"If insight is developed, what profit does it bring? Wisdom is developed. If wisdom is developed, what profit does it bring? All ignorance is abandoned" (A. II, 2.7).

There is a method of meditative practice where, in alternating sequence, tranquillity-meditation and insight-meditation are developed. It is called 'tranquillity and insight joined in pairs' (*samatha-vipassanāyuganaddha*), the coupling or yoking of tranquillity and insight. He who undertakes it, first enters into the first absorption. After rising from it, he contemplates the mental phenomena that were present in it (feeling, perception, etc.) as impermanent, painful and non-self, and thus he develops insight. Thereupon he enters into the second absorption; and after rising from it, he again considers its constituent phenomena as impermanent, etc. In this way, he passes from one absorption to the next, until at last, during a moment of insight, the intuitive knowledge of the path (of stream-entry, etc.) flashes forth. See A. IV, 170; A.IX, 36; PTS: Yuganaddha Kathā.

samatha-yānika: 'one who takes tranquillity as his vehicle'. This is a name for a person who not only has reached insight but also one or the other of the absorptions, to distinguish him from one 'who practises only insight' (*sukkha-vipassaka*, q.v.).

S

SOURCE NOTE: not found, or not found in this form or meaning, in the oldest parts of the Sutta Piṭaka.

sambodhi: *bodhi* (q.v.).

sambojjhaṅga: *bojjhaṅga* (q.v.).

sammā-diṭṭhi, *-saṅkappa*, *-vaca*, etc: see *magga*.

sammā-magga: see *micchā-magga*.

sammā-padhāna: 'right exertion', is identical with the sixth link of the Eightfold Path (see *magga*, *padhāna*).

sammā-sambodhi: 'Perfect Enlightenment', Universal Buddhahood, is the state attained by a Universal Buddha (*sammā-sambuddha*), i.e., one by whom the liberating law (*dhamma*) which had become lost to the world, has again been discovered, realised and clearly proclaimed to the world.

"Now, someone, in things never heard before, understands by himself the truth, and he therein attains omniscience, and gains mastery in the powers. Such a one is called a Universal Buddha, or Enlightened One" (PUG. 29).

The doctrine characteristic of all the Buddhas, and each time rediscovered by them and fully explained to the world, consists in the four Truths (*sacca*, q.v.) of suffering, its origin, its extinction and the way to its extinction (see *magga*). See *bodhi*.

sammasana: 'comprehension', exploring, 'determining' (*vavatthāna*, q.v.) is a name for the determining of all phenomena of existence as impermanent, miserable and impersonal (*anicca*, *dukkha*, *anatta*), etc., which is the beginning of insight (see PTS.M. I, p. 53; VISM. XX); also called *kalāpa-~* (q.v.), 'comprehension by groups (of existence, i.e., *khandha*).'

SOURCE NOTE: this term, as noun, occurs probably for the first time in PTS.M. I. 53, although as a verb it is found already in the old texts. The same holds good with its synonym *vavatthāna*.

sammatta: the 'state of rightness', are the eight links of the Eightfold Path (D. 33). Cf. *micchātta*.

sammuti-sacca: 'conventional truth', is identical with *vohāra-sacca* (see *paramattha-sacca*).

SOURCE NOTE: *sammuti* is not found, or not found in this form or meaning, in the oldest parts of the Sutta Piṭaka. see *sacca*; see *vohāra-desanā*, SOURCE NOTE.

sampadā: 'attainment, blessing'. The five blessings are said to be faith, morality, learning, liberality, wisdom (A. V, 91). Further: morality, concentration, wisdom, deliverance, the eye of knowledge connected with deliverance (A. V, 92).

sampajañña: 'clarity of consciousness', clear comprehension. This term is frequently met with in combination with mindfulness (*sati*). In D. 22, M. 10 it is said:

"Clearly conscious is he in going and coming, clearly conscious in looking forward and backward, clearly conscious in bending and stretching his body; clearly conscious in eating, drinking, chewing and tasting, clearly conscious in discharging excrement and urine; clearly conscious in walking, standing, sitting, falling asleep and awakening; clearly conscious in speaking and keeping silent." For a definition of the term *satisampajañña*, see PUG. 86.

According to the com., 'clarity of consciousness' is of four kinds: regarding the purpose, the suitability, (inclusion in the meditative) domain, and the undeluded conception of the activity concerned. Explained in detail in com. to Satipaṭṭhāna Sutta. (tr. in *The Way of Mindfulness*, by Soma Thera; BPS).

S

sampaṭicchana-citta: 'receptive consciousness', is the mind-element (*mano-dhātu*) that follows immediately upon the arising of sense-consciousness (visual consciousness, etc.), performing on that occasion the function of receiving the sense-object. Regarding the other functions of consciousness, see *viññāṇa-kicca*.

SOURCE NOTE: not found, or not found in this form or meaning, in the oldest parts of the Sutta Piṭaka. see *citta-vīthi*.

sampayutta-paccaya: 'condition of association', is one of the twenty-four conditions (*paccaya*, q.v.).

samphappalāpa: 'idle chatter or gossip', see *micchā-vācā*.

samphassa: *phassa* (q.v.).

saṃsāra: 'round of rebirth', lit. perpetual wandering', is a name by which is designated the sea of life ever restlessly heaving up and down, the symbol of this continuous process of ever again and again being born, growing old, suffering and dying. More precisely put, *saṃsāra* is the unbroken chain of the fivefold *khandha* combinations, which, constantly changing from moment to moment follow continuously one upon the other through inconceivable periods of time. Of this *saṃsāra*, a single lifetime constitutes only a tiny and fleeting fraction; hence to be able to comprehend the first noble truth of universal suffering, one must let one's gaze rest upon the *saṃsāra*, upon this frightful chain of rebirths, and not merely upon one single lifetime, which, of course, may be sometimes less painful. Cf. *ti-lakkhaṇa, anatta, paramattha, paṭisandhi.*

saṃseva: 'companionship'. (1) "Through companionship with bad men (*asappurisa-~*) comes listening to bad advice, thereby unwise reflection, thereby inattention and mental confusion, thereby lack of sense-control, thereby threefold bad conduct in bodily action, speech and mind, thereby the five hindrances (*nīvaraṇa*, q.v.), thereby craving for existence.

(2) Through companionship with good men (*sappurisa-~*) comes listening to good advice, thereby faith, thereby wise reflection, thereby mindfulness and clarity of consciousness, thereby sense-control, thereby threefold good conduct, thereby the four foundations of mindfulness (*satipaṭṭhāna*, q.v.), thereby the seven factors of enlightenment (*bojjhaṅga*, q.v.), thereby liberation through wisdom (*paññā-vimutti*, q.v.)." Cf. A. X. 62.

S

samuccheda-pahāna: 'overcoming by destruction', is the absolute extinction of certain fetters of existence (*saṃyojana*, q.v.), which takes place by entering into one of the four supermundane paths of holiness (see *ariya-puggala*). Regarding the five kinds of overcoming, see *pahāna*.

samudaya-sacca: 'truth of the origin', i.e., the origin of suffering, is the second of the Four Noble Truths (*sacca*, q.v.).

samuṭṭhāna: 'origination'. There are four kinds of origination of corporeal phenomena, namely: through karma, consciousness, temperature, nutriment. For example, 'karma-produced' (*kamma-~ = kammaja*, karma-born) are the sense organs, sexual characteristics, etc., which, according to their nature, are conditioned either through wholesome or unwholesome karma formations (volitional actions; see *paṭiccasamuppāda*, 2) in a previous existence. 'Mind-produced', i.e., consciousness-produced (*citta-samuṭṭhāna = cittaja*) are bodily and verbal expression (*viññatti*, q.v.). For a detailed exposition, see VISM. XX.

SOURCE NOTE: *kamma-~* (= *kamma-ja*), *utu-~*, *āhāra-~*: these terms are found only in the com. *Citta-samuṭṭhāna-rūpa*, however, occurs already in DHS. (§ 586) of the ABH. canon; and is indicated very often in PATTH., e.g. '*taṃ* (*cittaṃ*) *samuṭṭhānānañ ca rūpānaṃ*'. The teaching of the origin of matter is, of course, already implied in the old sutta texts.

saṃvara-padhāna: 'effort to avoid', see *padhāna*.

saṃvara-sīla: '*indriya-~*', see *sīla*.

saṃvara-suddhi: 'purity of control', is another name for morality consisting of restraint of the senses (*indriya-saṃvara-sīla*; see *sīla*).

saṃvaṭṭa-kappa: see *kappa*.

saṃvega-vatthu: 'the sources of emotion', or of a sense of urgency, are eight: "birth, old age, disease, death, being four; the suffering in the lower states of existence being the fifth; further, the misery of the past rooted in the cycle of rebirth, the misery of the future rooted in the cycle of rebirth, the misery of the present rooted in the search after food" (VISM. III.).

saṃvejanīya-ṭhāna: 'places rousing emotion', are four: the place where the Perfect One was born, (i.e., the Lumbini-grove near Kapilavatthu, at the present frontier of Nepal); the place where he reached Full Enlightenment (i.e., Uruvelā, the modern Ureli, and Buddhagayā, on the Nerañjarā River, the modern Lilanja); the place where he, for the first time, unveiled the Dhamma to the world (i.e., the deer-park at Isipatana near Benares); the place where he entered the final Nibbāna (i.e., Kusinārā). (A. IV, 118).

S

saṃyojana: 'fetters'. There are ten fetters tying beings to the wheel of existence, namely: (1) personality-belief (*sakkāya-diṭṭhi*, q.v.), (2) sceptical doubt (*vicikicchā* q.v.), (3) clinging to mere rules and ritual (*sīlabbata-parāmāsa*; see *upādāna*), (4) sensuous craving (*kāma-rāga*, 4.v.), (5) ill will (*vyāpāda*), (6) craving for fine-material existence (*rūpa-rāga*), (7) craving for immaterial existence (*arūpa-rāga*), (8) conceit (*māna*, q.v.), (9) restlessness (*uddhacca*, q.v.), (10) ignorance (*avijjā*, q.v.). The first five of these are called 'lower fetters' (*orambhāgiya-saṃyojana*), as they tie to the sensuous world. The latter five are called 'higher fetters' (*uddhambhāgiya-saṃyojana*), as they tie to the higher worlds, i.e., the fine-material and immaterial world (A. IX, 67, 68; X. 13; D. 33, etc.).

He who is free from 1–3 is a *sotāpanna*, or stream-winner, i.e., one who has entered the stream to Nibbāna, as it were. He who, besides these three fetters, has overcome four and five in their grosser form, is called a *sakadāgāmī*, a 'once-returner' (to this sensuous world). He who is fully freed from 1–5 is an *anāgāmī*, or 'nonreturner' (to the sensuous world). He who is freed from all the ten fetters is called an arahat, i.e., a perfectly holy one.

For more details, see *ariya-puggala*.

The ten fetters as enumerated in the Abhidhamma, e.g. VIBH. XVII, are: sensuous craving, ill will, conceit, wrong views, sceptical doubt, clinging to mere rules and ritual, craving for existence, envy, stinginess, ignorance.

sañcetanā: *cetanā*, q.v.

saṅgaha-vatthu: the four 'ways of showing favour' are liberality, kindly speech, beneficial actions, impartiality (A. IV, 32; VIII, 24).

saṅgha: (lit., 'congregation' or 'assembly'); the name for the Community of Buddhist monks. As the third of the Three Gems or Jewels (*ti-ratana*, q.v.) and the Three Refuges (*ti-saraṇa*, q.v.), i.e., Buddha, Dhamma, and Saṅgha, it applies to the *ariya-saṅgha*, the community of the saints, i.e., the four noble ones (*ariya-pugga*, q.v.), the stream-winner, etc.

saṅkappa: 'thought', is a synonym of *vitakka* (q.v.). For *sammā-~*, or right thought, see *magga* (2).

saṅkhāra: this term has, according to its context, different shades of meaning, which should be carefully distinguished.

(I)

To its most frequent usages (1–4, following) the general term 'formation' may be applied, with the qualifications required by the context. This term may refer either to the act of 'forming or to the passive state of 'having been formed' or to both.

1. As the second link of the formula of dependent origination, (*paṭicca-samuppāda*, q.v.), *saṅkhāra* has the active aspect, 'forming, and signifies karma (q.v.), i.e., wholesome or unwholesome volitional activity (*cetanā*) of body (*kāya-~*), speech (*vacī-~*) or mind (*citta-* or *mano-~*). This definition occurs, e.g. at S. XII, 2, 27. For ~ in this sense, the word 'karma-formation' has been coined by the author. In other passages, in the same context, ~ is defined by reference to (a) meritorious karma-formations (*puññ'ābhisaṅkhāra*), (b) demeritorious ~ (*apuññ'ābhisaṅkhāra*), (c) imperturbable ~ (*āneñj'ābhisaṅkhāra*), e.g. in S. XII, 51; D. 33. This threefold division covers karmic activity in all spheres of existence: the meritorious karma-formations extend to the sensuous and the fine-material sphere, the demeritorious ones only to the sensuous sphere, and the 'imperturbable' only to the immaterial sphere.

2. The aforementioned three terms, *kāya-*, *vacī-* and *citta-~* are sometimes used in quite a different sense, namely as (1) bodily function, i.e., in-and-

out-breathing (e.g., M. 10), (2) verbal function, i.e., thought-conception and discursive thinking, (3) mental-function, i.e., feeling and perception (e.g., M. 44). see *nirodha-samāpatti*.

3. It also denotes the fourth group of existence (*saṅkhārakkhandha*), and includes all 'mental formations' whether they belong to 'karmically forming' consciousness or not. see *khandha*, TAB. II. and S. XXII, 56, 79.

4. It occurs further in the sense of anything formed (*saṅkhata*, q.v.) and conditioned, and includes all things whatever in the world, all phenomena of existence. This meaning applies, e.g. to the well-known passage, "All formations are impermanent ... subject to suffering" (*sabbe saṅkhāra aniccā ... dukkhā*). In that context, however, ~ is subordinate to the still wider and all-embracing term *dhamma* (thing); for *dhamma* includes also the Unformed or Unconditioned Element (*asaṅkhata-dhātu*), i.e., Nibbāna (e.g. in *sabbe dhammā anattā*, "all things are without a self").

(II)

Saṅkhāra also means sometimes 'volitional effort', e.g., in the formula of the roads to power (*iddhipāda*, q.v.); in *sasaṅkhāra-* and *asaṅkhāra-parinibbāyī* (see *anāgāmī*, q.v.); and in the Abhidhamma terms *asaṅkhārika-* (q.v.) and *sasaṅkhārika-citta*, i.e., without effort, i.e., spontaneously, and with effort, i.e., prompted.

In Western literature, in English as well as in German, *saṅkhāra* is sometimes mistranslated by 'subconscious tendencies' or similarly (e.g. Prof. Beckh: "unterbewußte Bildekräfte," i.e., subconscious formative forces). This misinterpretation derives perhaps from a similar usage in non-Buddhist SKR. literature, and is entirely inapplicable to the connotations of the term in Pali Buddhism, as listed above under I, 1–4. For instance, within the dependent origination, see is neither subconscious nor a mere tendency, but is a fully conscious and active karmic volition. In the context of the five groups of existence (see above I, 3), a very few of the factors from the group of mental formations (*saṅkhārakkhandha*) are also present as concomitants of subconsciousness (see TAB. I–III), but are of course not restricted to it, nor are they mere tendencies.

saṅkhārupekkhā-ñāṇa: the 'equanimity-knowledge with regard to the formations of existence', is one of those kinds of knowledge which form the 'purification by knowledge and vision of the path-progress' (see *visuddhi*, VI, 8). "It is known by three names: in the lowest stage it is called 'knowledge

S

consisting in the desire for deliverance' (*muccitu-kamyatā-ñāṇa*); in the middle stage it is called the 'reflecting contemplation' (*paṭisaṅkhānupassanā-ñāṇa*); in the last stage, however, i.e., after attaining the summit, it is called the "equanimity-knowledge with regard to the formations of existence" (VISM. XXI).

saṅkhata: the 'formed', i.e., anything originated or conditioned, comprises all phenomena of existence. Cf. *saṅkhāra* I, 4; *asaṅkhata*.

saṅkhitta citta: in the Satipaṭṭhāna Sutta, signifies the 'contracted' or 'cramped' mind, not the concentrated (*samāhita*) mind, as often translated by Western authors. Cf. *satipaṭṭhāna* (3).

saññā: 1. 'perception', is one of the five groups of existence (*khandha*, q.v.), and one of the seven mental factors (*cetasika*) that are inseparably bound up with all consciousness (see *cetanā*). It is sixfold as perception of the five physical sense-objects and of mental objects. It is the awareness of an object's distinctive marks ("one perceives blue, yellow, etc.," S. XXII, 79). If, in repeated perception of an object, these marks are recognised, *saññā* functions as 'memory' (see ABH. St., 68ff.).

S

2. *saññā* stands sometimes for consciousness in its entirety, e.g. in *n'eva-saññā-n'āsaññāyatana*, 'the realm of neither-perception-nor-non-perception'; further, in *asaññā-satta*, 'unconscious beings'. In both cases reference is not to 'perception' alone, but also to all other constituents of consciousness. Cf. D. 9.

3. *saññā* may also refer to the 'ideas', which are objects of meditation, e.g. in a group of seven ideas, of impermanence (*anicca-~*), etc. (A. VII, 46); of ten: impurity (*asubha-~*), etc. (A. X, 56), and another set of ten in A. X. 60; or to wrong notions, as in *nicca-*, *subha-~* (the notion of permanence, beauty), etc.

saññā-vedayita-nirodha: *nirodha-samāpatti* (q.v.).

saññā-vipallāsa: 'perversion of perception' (see *vipallāsa*).

saññojana: *saṃyojana* (q.v.).

santāna (or **santati**): 'continuity', may refer to the continuity of consciousness (*citta-~*), of the groups of existence (*khandha -~*), of subconsciousness (*bhavaṅga-~*), of corporeality (*rūpa-~*), to the uninterrupted continuity of the *paṭiccasamuppāda* (q.v.), etc.

SOURCE NOTE: the terms *citta-~*, *rūpa-~*, *khandha -~*, *bhavaṅga-~*, etc., are found, here and there, in the ABH. canon (e.g. DHS. § 634, KATH. 110; see GUIDE V), but they are often met with in the ABH. com. In the suttas (THERAG. 716) is found *saṅkhārasantati*.

santīraṇa-citta: 'investigating consciousness', is one of the stages in the cognitive series. For the fourteen functions of consciousness. see *viññāṇa-kicca*.

SOURCE NOTE: not found, or not found in this form or meaning, in the oldest parts of the Sutta Piṭaka. see *citta-vīthi*.

santuṭṭhitā: 'contentedness', see *ariya-vaṃsa*.

sapadānik'aṅga: see *dhutaṅga*.

sappaṭigha-rūpa: 'corporeality reacting to sense stimuli', refers to the five sense organs (*āyatana*, q.v.). Cf. VIBH. II (see GUIDE II, Chap. II) and VISM. XIV; further see *paṭigha* 2.

saraṇa: see *ti-saraṇa*.

S

sāsana (lit. 'message'): the Dispensation of the Buddha, the Buddhist religion; teaching, doctrine.

Navaṅga-Buddha (or *satthu*)-*sāsana*, the ninefold Dispensation of the Buddha (or the Master) consists of suttas (*sutta*), mixed prose (*geyya*), exegesis (*veyyākaraṇa*), verses (*gāthā*), solemn utterances (*udāna*), sayings of the Blessed One (*itivuttaka*), birth stories (*jātaka*), extraordinary things (*abbhuta-dhamma*), and analysis (*vedalla*). This classification is often found in the suttas (e.g. M. 22). According to the commentaries, the Vinaya and the Abhidhamma Piṭaka also are comprised in that ninefold division (see ASL.TR., I, 33). It is a classification according to literary styles, and not according to given texts or books.

sasaṅkhāra-parinibbāyī: 'one who reaches Nibbāna with exertion', is a name of one of the five kinds of non-returners (*anāgāmī*, q.v.).

sasaṅkhārika-citta (in DHS.: *sasaṅkhārena*): a prepared, or prompted. state of consciousness, arisen after prior deliberation (e.g. weighing of motives) or induced by others (command, advice, persuasion). See TAB. I; exemplified in VISM. XIV, 84ff. Opposite: *asaṅkhārika-citta*, q.v.

sassata-diṭṭhi (-*vāda*): 'eternity-belief', is the belief in a soul or personality existing independently of the five groups of existence, and continuing after death eternally, as distinguished from the 'annihilation-belief' (*uccheda-diṭṭhi*), i.e., the belief in a personality falling at death a prey to absolute annihilation. For more details, see *diṭṭhi*.

sati: 'mindfulness', is one of the five spiritual faculties and powers (see *bala*), one of the seven factors of enlightenment (*bojjhaṅga*, q.v.), and the seventh link of the Eightfold Path (*magga*, q.v.), and is, in its widest sense, one of those mental factors inseparably associated with all karmically wholesome (*kusala*, q.v.) and karma-produced lofty (*sobhana*) consciousness (Cf. TAB. II). For the four foundations of mindfulness see *satipaṭṭhāna*.

satipaṭṭhāna: the four 'foundations of mindfulness', lit. 'awarenesses of mindfulness' (*sati-upaṭṭhāna*), are: contemplation of body, feeling, mind, and mind-objects; cf. *sati*.

A detailed treatment of this subject, so important for the practice of Buddhist mental culture, is given in the two Satipaṭṭhāna Suttas (D. 22; M. 10), which at the start as well as the conclusion, proclaim the weighty words: "The only way that leads to the attainment of purity, to the overcoming of sorrow and lamentation, to the end of pain and grief, to the entering of the right path, and to the realisation of Nibbāna is the four foundations of mindfulness."

After these introductory words, and upon the question which these four are, it is said that the monk dwells in contemplation of the body, the feelings, the mind, and the mind-objects, "ardent, clearly conscious and mindful, after putting away worldly greed and grief."

These four contemplations are in reality not to be taken as merely separate exercises, but on the contrary, at least in many cases, especially in the absorptions, as things inseparably associated with each other. Thereby the Satipaṭṭhāna Sutta forms an illustration of the way in which these four contemplations relating to the five groups of existence (*khandha*, q.v.) simultaneously come to be realised, and finally lead to insight into the impersonality of all existence.

(1) The contemplation of the body (*kāyanupassanā*) consists of the following exercises: mindfulness with regard to in-and-out breathing (*ānāpāna-sati*, q.v.), minding the four postures (*iriyāpatha*, q.v.), mindfulness and clarity of consciousness (*satisampajañña*, q.v.), reflection on the thirty-two parts of the body (see *kāyagatāsati* and *asubha*), analysis of the four physical elements (*dhātuvavatthāna*, q.v.), cemetery meditations (*sīvathikā* q.v.).

(2) All feelings (*vedanānupassanā*) that arise in the meditator he clearly perceives, namely: agreeable and disagreeable feeling of body and mind, sensual and super-sensual feeling, indifferent feeling.

(3) He further clearly perceives and understands any state of consciousness or mind (*cittānupassanā*), whether it is greedy or not, hateful or not, deluded or not, cramped or distracted, developed or undeveloped, surpassable or unsurpassable, concentrated or unconcentrated, liberated or unliberated.

(4) Concerning the mind-objects (*dhammānupassanā*), he knows whether one of the five hindrances (*nīvaraṇa*, q.v.) is present in him or not, knows how it arises, how it is overcome, and how in future it does no more arise. He knows the nature of each of the five groups (*khandha*, q.v.), how they arise, and how they are dissolved. He knows the twelve bases of all mental activity (*āyatana* q.v.): the eye and the visual object, the ear and the audible object, ... mind and mind-object, he knows the fetters (*saṃyojana*, q.v.) based on them, knows how they arise, how they are overcome, and how in future they do no more arise. He knows whether one of the seven factors of enlightenment (*bojjhaṅga*, q.v.) is present in him or not, knows how it arises, and how it comes to full development. Each of the Four Noble Truths (*sacca*, q.v.) he understands according to reality.

S

The four contemplations comprise several exercises, but the Satipaṭṭhāna should not therefore be thought of as a mere collection of meditation subjects, any one of which may be taken out and practised alone. Though most of the exercises appear also elsewhere in the Buddhist scriptures, in the context of this sutta they are chiefly intended for the cultivation of mindfulness and insight, as indicated by the repetitive passage concluding each section of the sutta (see below). The four contemplations cover all the five groups of existence (*khandha*, q.v.), because mindfulness is meant to encompass the whole personality. Hence, for the full development of mindfulness, the practice should extend to all four types of contemplation, though not every single exercise mentioned under these four headings need be taken up. A methodical practice of *satipaṭṭhāna* has to start with one of the exercises out of the group 'contemplation of the body', which will serve as the primary and regular subject of meditation. The other exercises of the group and the other contemplations are to be cultivated when occasion for them arises during meditation and in everyday life.

After each contemplation it is shown how it finally leads to insight-knowledge: "Thus with regard to his own body he contemplates the body, with regard to the bodies of others he contemplates the body, with regard to both he contemplates the body. He beholds how the body arises and how it passes away, beholds the arising and passing away of the body. 'A body is there' (but no living being, no individual, no woman, no man, no self, nothing that belongs to a self; neither a person, nor anything belonging to a person; com.): thus he has established his attentiveness as far as it serves his knowledge and mindfulness, and he lives independent, unattached to anything in the world."

In the same way he contemplates feeling, mind and mind-objects.

In M. 118 it is shown how these four foundations of mindfulness may be brought about by the exercise of mindfulness on in-and-out breathing (*ānāpāna-sati*, q.v.).

LITERATURE: *The Way of Mindfulness*, tr. of the Satipaṭṭhāna Sutta and com., by Soma Thera (3rd ed; Kandy 1967, BPS). *The Heart of Buddhist Meditation*, by Nyanaponika Thera (3rd ed.; London. Rider & Co.). *The Foundations of Mindfulness* (tr. of M. 10), by Nyanasatta Thera (WHEEL 19). *The Satipaṭṭhāna Sutta and its Application to Modern Life*, by V. F. Gunaratna (WHEEL 60). *The Power of Mindfulness*, by Nyanaponika Thera (WHEEL 121/122).

S

sati-sambojjhaṅga: 'mindfulness as a factor of enlightenment' see *bojjhaṅga*.

sati-sampajañña: 'mindfulness and clarity of consciousness, see *sampajañña*.

satta: 'living being'. This term, just like *attā*, *puggala*, *jīva*, and all the other terms denoting 'ego-entity', is to be considered as a merely conventional term (*vohāra-vacana*), not possessing any reality-value. For the impersonality of all existence. see *anatta*, *paramattha*, *puggala*, *jīva*, *satta*, *paṭiccasamuppāda*.

sattakkhattu-parama: 'one with only seven further rebirths at the utmost', is one of the three kinds of stream-winners (*sotāpanna*, q.v.).

sattāvāsa (or **nava sattāvāsa**): '(9) abodes of beings'. In the sutta-texts (e.g. D. 33; A.IX, 24) nine such abodes are mentioned: "There are, O monks, nine abodes of beings, namely:

(1) "There are beings who are different in body and different in perception, such as the human beings, some heavenly beings, and some beings living in the world of suffering (*vinipātika*, q.v.).

(2) "There are beings who are different in body but equal in perception, such as the first-born gods of the Brahma-world (i.e., at the beginning of each new world-formation; see *deva* II).

(3) "There are beings who are equal in body but different in perception, such as the Radiant gods (*Ābhassara*, see *deva* II).

(4) "There are beings who are equal in body and equal in perception, such as the All-Illuminating gods (*Subha-kinha*; see *deva* II).

(5) "There are beings without perception and feeling, such as the unconscious beings (*asaññasatta*, q.v.).

(6) "There are beings who, through the complete overcoming of perceptions of matter (*rūpa-sañña*), the disappearance of perceptions of sense-reaction (*paṭigha-sañña*), and the non-attention to perceptions of variety thinking: 'Boundless is space', are reborn in the sphere of boundless space (see *deva*, III; *jhāna*, 5).

(7) "There are beings who, through the complete overcoming of the sphere of boundless space, thinking: 'Boundless is consciousness', are reborn in the sphere of boundless consciousness (see *jhāna* 6).

(8) "There are beings who, through the complete overcoming of the sphere of boundless consciousness, thinking: 'Nothing is there, are reborn in the sphere of nothingness (see *jhāna*, 7).

(9) "There are beings who, through the complete overcoming of the sphere of nothingness, are reborn in the sphere of neither-perception-nor-non-perception (see *jhāna*, 8)" (A. IX, 24).

According to the com. to A., the beings of the Pure Abodes (*Suddhāvāsa*, q.v.) are not mentioned here, for the reason that they exist only in those world-periods in which Buddhas appear. Cf. *viññāṇaṭhiti*.

S

Sa-upādisesa-nibbāna: see Nibbāna, *upādi*.

sāvaka: 'hearer', i.e., 'disciple', refers, in a restricted sense (then mostly *ariya-sāvaka*, 'noble disciple'), only to the eight kinds of noble disciples (*ariya-puggala*, q.v.).

sāvaka-bodhi: 'enlightenment of the disciple', designates the holiness of the disciple, as distinguished from the holiness of the Pacceka-Buddha (q.v.) and the Sammā-sambuddha (q.v.).

sceptical doubt: *vicikicchā* (q.v.). Cf. *kaṅkhā*.

scruples: *kukkucca* (q.v.).

sekha: a 'noble learner', a disciple in higher training, i.e., one who pursues the three kinds of training (*sikkhā*, q.v.), is one of those seven kinds of noble disciples who have reached one of the four supermundane paths or the three lower fruitions (see *ariya-puggala*), while the one possessed of the fourth fruition, or *arahatta-phala*, is called 'one beyond training' (*asekha*, lit. 'no more learner'). The worldling (*puthujjana*, q.v.) is called 'neither a noble learner, nor perfected in learning' (*n'eva-sekha-nāsekha*). Cf. PUG. 23–25.

self: *attā* (q.v.).

self-annihilation, craving for: *vibhava-taṇhā* (see *taṇhā*).

self-confidence: *vesārajja* (q.v.).

self-mortification: *atta-kilamatha* (q.v.).

senāsana: 'dwelling place', is one of the four requisites of the monk's life (see *sīla* 4). To be suitable for spiritual training, it should possess five advantages. As it is said (A.X, 11): "But how, O monks, does the dwelling place possess five advantages? Such a dwelling place is not too far, nor too near (to the village), is suitable for going (on almsround) and returning. In the daytime it is not much crowded, and at night without noise and bustle. One is not much molested there by gadflies, mosquitoes, wind, sun and creeping things. While living there, the monk without difficulty obtains robes, alms-food, dwelling, and the necessary medicines. There are elder monks living there, with great learning, well versed in the message, masters of the Law (*dhamma*), of the Discipline (*vinaya*) and of the tables of contents (i.e., either the twofold Abhidhamma matrix, or the bhikkhu and bhikkhuni Pātimokkha; see *pātimokkha*). And he approaches them from time to time, questions them, asks them for explanations, etc.

sense organs and **objects**: see *āyatana*, *dhātu*.

sense-stimuli, corporeality responding to: see *āyatana*.

sensitive corporeality: *pasāda-rūpa* (q.v.).

sensuality (subj. & obj.): *kāma* (q.v.).

sensuous clinging: *kāmūpādāna*, see *upādāna*.

sensuous craving: *kāma-taṇhā* (*-rāga*), is one of the ten fetters (*saṃyojana*, q.v.), and one of the three kinds of craving (*taṇhā*, q.v.).

sensuous sphere (-world): see *avacara*, *loka*.

serenity: see *samatha*.

seven rebirths at the utmost: see *sotāpanna*.

sex: see *bhāva*.

sexual intercourse, unlawful: see *kāmesu micchācāra*.

shame: *hiri* (q.v.).

shamelessness: *ahirika* (q.v.).

signless (*animitta*): see *ceto-vimutti, vimokkha, vipassanā*.

sikkhā: the 'training', which the Buddha's disciple has to undergo, is threefold: training in higher morality (*adhisīla-sikkhā*), in higher mentality (*adhicitta-sikkhā*), and in higher wisdom (*adhipaññā-sikkhā*). This threefold training refers to the threefold division of the Eightfold Path (*magga*, q.v.) in morality, concentration and wisdom (*sīla, samādhi, paññā*). In D. 16 and A. IV, 1 it is said:

"It is through not understanding, not penetrating noble morality … noble concentration … noble wisdom … noble deliverance that I, as well as you, have had for such a long time to pass through this round of rebirths."

"This then is morality, this concentration, this wisdom, this deliverance. Being endowed with morality, concentration brings high fruit and blessing. Being endowed with concentration, wisdom brings high fruit and blessing. Being endowed with wisdom, the mind becomes freed from all cankers (*āsava* q.v.) namely, from the sensuous canker (*kāmāsava*), from the canker of existence (*bhavasava*) from the canker of opinions (*diṭṭhāsava*) from the canker of ignorance (*avijjāsava*).

S

sikkhā-pada: 'steps of training', moral rules.

The five moral rules, also called *pañca-sīla* which are binding on all Buddhist laymen, are: (1) abstaining from killing any living being, (2) from stealing, (3) from sexual misconduct, (4) from lying, (5) from the use of intoxicants.(see *surāmeraya* etc.)

The ten rules (*dasa-sīla*) are binding on all novices and monks, namely: (1) abstaining from killing, (2) from stealing, (3) from unchastity, (4) from lying, (5) from the use of intoxicants, (6) from eating after midday, (7) from dancing, singing, music and shows, (8) from garlands, scents, cosmetics and adornments, etc., (9) from luxurious beds, (10) from accepting gold and silver.

In the eight rules (*aṭṭha-sīla*) which on full and new moon days, and on the first and last quarter of the moon, are observed by many lay-followers (*upāsaka*, q.v.), the seventh and eighth of the above ten rules are fused into one as the seventh rule, while the ninth becomes the eighth.

sīla: 'morality', 'virtue', is a mode of mind and volition (*cetana*, q.v.) manifested in speech or bodily action (see *karma*). It is the foundation of the whole Buddhist practice, and therewith the first of the three kinds of training (*sikkhā*, q.v.) that form the threefold division of the Eightfold Path (see *magga*), i.e., morality, concentration and wisdom.

Buddhist morality is not, as it may appear from the negative formulations in the suttas, something negative. And it does not consist in the mere not committing of evil actions, but is in each instance the clearly conscious and intentional restraint from the bad actions in question and corresponds to the simultaneously arising volition.

Morality of the Eightfold Path, namely, right speech, right action and right livelihood, is called 'genuine or natural morality' *pakati-sīla*), as distinguished from the external rules for monks or laymen, the so-called 'prescribed morality' (*paññatti-sīla*, q.v.), which, as such, is karmically neutral.

"What now is karmically wholesome morality (*kusala-sīla*)? It is the wholesome bodily action (*kāyakamma*, see *karma*), wholesome verbal action (*vacīkamma*, see *karma*), and also the purity with regard to livelihood which I call morality" (M. 78). Cf. *magga*, 3–5.

For the five, eight, and ten rules, see *sikkhā-pada*. Further cf. *cāritta*- and *vāritta-sīla*.

The four kinds of morality consisting of purification (*catupārisuddhi-sīla*) *are*: (1) restraint with regard to the monks' Disciplinary Code, (2) restraint of the senses, (3) purification of livelihood, (4) morality with regard to the four requisites (of the monk).

(1) Restraint with regard to the Disciplinary Code (*pātimokkha-saṃvara-sīla*). "Here the monk is restrained in accordance with the monks' Disciplinary Code, is perfect in conduct and behaviour, and perceiving danger even in the least offences, he trains himself in the rules he has taken upon him" (A. V, 87, 109, 114, etc.).

(2) Restraint of the senses (*indriya-saṃvara-sīla*). "Whenever the monk perceives a form with the eye, a sound with the ear, an odour with the nose, a taste with the tongue, an impression with the body, an object with the mind, he neither adheres to the appearance as a whole, nor to its parts. And he strives to ward off that through which evil and unwholesome things, greed and sorrow, would arise, if he remained with unguarded senses; and he watches over his senses, restrains his senses" (M. 38).

(3) Purification of livelihood (*ājīva-pārisuddhi-sīla*). It consists therein that the monk does not acquire his livelihood in a way unbefitting to a monk.

(4) Morality with regard to the four requisites (*paccaya-sannissita-sīla*). It consists therein that the monk is guided by the right mental attitude when making use of the four requisites: robes, alms-food, dwelling and medicine. "Wisely reflecting he makes use of his robes … merely to protect himself against cold and heat, etc. Wisely reflecting he makes use of his alms-food … merely as a prop and support to this body. … Wisely reflecting he makes use of his dwelling … merely to keep off the dangers of weather and to enjoy solitude. … Wisely reflecting he makes use of the necessary medicines, merely to suppress feelings of sickness that arise, and to reach perfect freedom from suffering" (cf. M. 2).

About these four kinds of morality, VISM. I gives a detailed exposition.

SOURCE NOTE: *paccayasannissita-*, *paccāvekkhaṇa-sīla*:, etc., are terms used in the com. for the proper contemplation (*paṭisaṅkhā yoniso*) of the four requisites of a monk, often dealt with in the old texts (e.g. M. 2). Also the three other *pārisuddhi-sīla*, as *pātimokkhasaṃvara-*, *indriya-*, and *ājīvapārisuddhi-sīla*, though under these names perhaps only known in the com., are fully dealt with in the old texts, e.g. M. 53, D. 2, M. 2, etc. The terms *paṇṇatti-* and *paññatti-sīla* are used only in the com.

S

sīlabbata-parāmāsa (and **-upādāna**): 'attachment (or clinging) to mere rules and ritual', is the third of the ten fetters (*saṃyojana*, q.v.), and one of the four kinds of clinging (*upādāna*, q.v.). It disappears on attaining to stream-entry (*sotāpatti*). For definition, see *upādāna*.

sīla-samādhi-paññā: see *sikkhā*, *magga*.

silent buddha: *pacceka-buddha* (q.v.).

sitting position, sleeping in: see *dhutaṅga*.

sīvathikā: 'cemetery contemplations', as described in D. 22 and M. 10, have as their objects a corpse one or two or three days old, swollen up, blue-black in colour, full of corruption; a corpse eaten by crows, etc.; a framework of bones; flesh hanging from it, bespattered with blood, held together by the sinews; without flesh and blood, but still held together by the sinews; bones scattered in all direction; bleached and resembling shells; heaped together after the lapse of years; weathered and crumbled to dust. At the end of each of these contemplations there follows the conclusion: "This body of mine also has this nature, has this destiny, cannot escape it." Similar are the ten objects of loathsomeness (*asubha* q.v.).

skilful: *kusala* (q.v.).

sloth: *middha*, see *nīvaraṇa*.

sobhana: 'lofty', beautiful, pure, are called, in ABH. S., all states of consciousness excepting the unwholesome and those without roots (*ahetuka*). *Sobhana-sādhāraṇa* are called the mental factors (*cetasika*) common to all lofty consciousness; see TAB. II.

somanassa: lit. 'glad-minded-ness' (*su* + *manas* + *ya*), gladness, joy; identical with 'mentally agreeable feeling' (*cetasikā sukhā vedanā*), belongs to the feeling-group (*vedanākkhandha*, see *khandha* II), and is enumerated amongst the twenty-two faculties (*indriya*, q.v.). It may or may not be associated with karmically wholesome consciousness (see TAB. I. 1–4, 9–12, 18–21), with karmically unwholesome consciousness (greedy c., ib. 22–25), and with karmically neutral consciousness (ib. 40, 42–45, 57–60, 66–69, 72–76, 81–84). *Somanassa* is not identical with *pīti* (q.v.).

S

somanassūpavicāra: 'indulging in gladness', see *manopavicāra*.

something: *kiñcana* (q.v.).

sotāpanna: the 'stream-winner', is the lowest of the eight noble disciples (see *ariya-puggala*). Three kinds are to be distinguished: the one 'with seven rebirths at the utmost' (*sattakkhattu-parama*), the one 'passing from one noble family to another' (*kolaṅkola*), the one 'germinating only once more' (*ekabījī*). As it is said (e.g. PUG. 37–39; A. III, 87):

(1) "If a man, after the disappearance of the three fetters (personality-belief, sceptical doubt, attachment to rules and ritual; see *saṃyojana*), has entered the stream (to Nibbāna), he is no more subject to rebirth in lower worlds, is firmly established, destined to full enlightenment. After having passed amongst the heavenly and human beings only seven times more through the round of rebirths, he puts an end to suffering. Such a man is called 'one with seven births at the utmost' (*sattakkhattu-parama*).

(2) "If a man, after the disappearance of the three fetters, ... is destined to full enlightenment, he, after having passed among noble families two or three times through the round of rebirths, puts an end to suffering. Such a man is called 'one passing from one noble family to another' (*kolaṅkola*).

(3) "If a man, after the disappearance of the three fetters, ... is destined to full enlightenment, he, after having only once more returned to human

existence, puts an end to suffering. Such a man is called 'one germinating only once more' (*eka-bījī*). See *Sotāpatti-Saṃyutta* (S. LV).

sotāpannassa aṅgāni: the 'characteristic qualities of a stream-winner' are four: unshakeable faith towards the Enlightened One, unshakeable faith towards the Doctrine, unshakeable faith towards the Order, and perfect morality. Explained in S. LV, I, D. 33, in S. XLVII, 8 and in *Netti-ppakaraṇa* these four qualities are called *sotāpattiyaṅga* (q.v.).

sotāpatti: 'stream-entry'; see *sotāpanna*; see *-magga*, *-phala*, 'path and fruition of stream-entry'; see *ariya-puggala*.

sotāpattiyaṅga: the four (preliminary) 'conditions to stream-entry' are: companionship with good persons, hearing the Good Law, wise reflection, living in conformity with the Law (S. LV, 5; D. 33). Cf. *sotāpannassa aṅgāni*.

space: see *ākāsa*.

spheres (of existence): *avacara* (q.v.). The four immaterial ~ (*āyatana*): see *jhāna* (5–8).

spiritual faculties: see *indriya* (15–19), *indriya-samatta*, *bala*.

spontaneously born beings: *opapātika* (q.v.).

stains, the three: *mala* (q.v.).

standstill (of morality etc.): see *hāna-bhāgiya-sīla*. ~ of existence: *vivaṭṭa* (q.v.).

stinginess: *macchariya* (q.v.); cf. TAB. II.

stored-up karma: *kaṭattā*, see *karma*.

stream-entry: see *sotāpanna*, *ariya-puggala*.

streams of merit: *puññadhārā* (q.v.).

stream-winner: see *sotāpanna*, *ariya-puggala*.

stupid-natured: see *carita*.

subconscious stream (of existence): *bhavaṅga-sota* (q.v.).

Subha-kiṇha (or **-kiṇṇa**): see *deva*, II.

subha-nimitta: 'beautiful (or attractive) object of mind'; it may become an inducement to the arising of sense-desire (*kāmacchanda*; see *nīvaraṇa*): "No other thing do I know, O monks, through which in such a degree sense-desire may arise, and once arisen will continue to grow, as an attractive object. Whoso does not wisely consider an attractive object, in him sense desire will arise, and once arisen will continue to grow" (A.I., 2).

subha-saññā, -citta, -diṭṭhi: 'the perception (consciousness or view) of beauty (or purity)' in what is actually devoid of it (*asubhe subha-saññā*), is one of the four perversions (*vipallāsa*, q.v.).

sublime abodes (or states): *brahma-vihāra* (q.v.).

substrata of existence: *upadhi* (q.v.).

sucarita: 'good conduct', is threefold, in body, speech and mind, and comprises the ten wholesome courses of action (see *kamma-patha*). According to A.X, 61, it has sense-control as its condition. See D. 33, A. II, 17; III, 2.

successive births, karma ripening in: see *karma*.

suchness: *tathatā* (q.v.).

Sudassa, Sudassī: see *suddhāvāsa*.

suddhāvāsa: the 'Pure Abodes', are a group of five heavens belonging to the fine-material world (*rūpa-loka*, see *loka*), where only the non-returners (see *anāgāmī*, q.v.) are reborn, and in which they attain arahatship and Nibbāna (*ariya-puggala*). The names of the inhabitants of these Pure Abodes are: *Aviha, Atappa, Sudassa, Sudassī, Akaniṭṭha*. Cf. *anāgāmī*.

suddha-vipassanā-yānika: *sukkha-vipassaka* (q.v.).

suffering: for the four Truths of suffering, see *sacca*; further see *ti-lakkhaṇa*.

sugati: 'happy course of existence', see *gati*.

sukha: pleasant, happy; happiness, pleasure, joy, bliss. It is one of the three feelings (see *vedanā*) and may be either bodily or mental. The texts distinguish between the happiness of the senses and the happiness of renunciation (A. II), worldly (carnal; *sāmisa*) and unworldly (non-carnal; *nirāmisa*) happiness (M. 10). See A. II, ch. VIII. Happiness is an indispensable condition for attaining concentration of mind (*samādhi*, q.v.), and therefore it is one of the five factors (or constituents) of the first absorption (*jhānaṅga*; see *jhāna*) and is present up to the third absorption inclusively. "The mind of the happy one has concentration as its fruit and reward" (A.X, 1). "In him who is filled with happiness, right concentration has found a foundation" (A.X, 3).

sukha-saññā, -citta, -diṭṭhi: 'the perception (consciousness or view) of happiness' in what is actually suffering (*dukkhe sukha-saññā*), i.e., any form of existence, it is one of the perversions (*vipallāsa*, q.v.).

sukkha-vipassaka: 'one supported by bare insight', is the commentarial term for one who, without having attained any of the meditative absorptions (*jhāna*, q.v.), has realised only by the support of insight (*vipassanā*, q.v.) one or several of the supermundane paths (see *ariya-puggala*). In VISM. XVIII, he is called *suddha-vipassanā-yānika*, as distinguished from 'one who has tranquillity as vehicle' (*samathayānika*, q.v.). Though the primary meaning of *sukkha* as intended here is as stated above, subcommentaries (e.g. D. Tīkā) employ also the literal meaning of *sukkha*, i.e., 'dry':

"His insight is dry, rough, unmoistened by the moisture of tranquillity meditation." This justifies a frequent rendering of this term by 'dry-visioned' or 'having dry insight', which, however, should not lead to misconceptions about the nature of insight meditation as being 'dry' or 'merely intellectual', while in fact the development of insight will produce rapture (*pīti*) and a sense of urgency (*saṃvega*) in the meditator.

SOURCE NOTE: also *suddha-vipassanā-yānika*; these terms are used only in the com., as also their counterpart *samathayānika*.

suñña (adj.), **suññatā** (noun): void (ness), empty (emptiness). As a doctrinal term it refers, in Theravāda, exclusively to the *anatta* doctrine,.i.e., the unsubstantiality of all phenomena: "Void is the world ... because it is void of a self and anything belonging to a self" (*suññam attena vā attaniyena vā*; S. XXXV, 85); also stated of the five groups of existence (*khandha*, q.v.) in the same text. See also M. 43, M. 106. In C.NID. (quoted in VISM. XXI, 55), it is said: "Eye ... mind, visual objects ... mind-objects, visual consciousness ... mind-consciousness, corporeality ... consciousness, etc., are void of self and anything belonging to a self; void of permanency and of anything lasting, eternal or immutable. ... They are coreless: without a core of permanency, or core of happiness or core of self." In M. 121, the voiding of the mind of the cankers, in the attainment of arahatship, is regarded as the "fully purified and incomparably highest (concept of) voidness. See SN. V. 1119; M. 121; M. 122 (WHEEL 87); PTS.M. II: Suñña-kathā; VISM. XXI, 53ff.

suññatānupassanā: 'contemplation of emptiness' (see *suñña*), is one of the eighteen chief kinds of insight (*vipassanā*, q.v.). Cf. VISM. XXI.

suññatā-vimokkha: 'emptiness-deliverance', see *vimokkha*.

superiority-conceit: see *māna.*

supermundane: *lokuttara* (q.v.); ~ faculties, see *indriya* (20–22).

supernormal: *mahaggata* (q.v.); ~ knowledges, see *abhiññā.*

support, and **decisive support**: (*nissaya, upanissaya*) are two of the twenty-four conditions (see *paccaya*).

supportive karma: *upatthambhaka-kamma,* see *karma.*

suppressive karma: *upapīḷaka-kamma,* see *karma.*

surāmeraya-majja-pamādaṭṭhānā veramaṇī sikkhā-padaṃ samādiyāmi: "I take upon myself the vow to abstain from taking intoxicants and drugs that lead to moral carelessness." This is the wording of the last of the five moral rules (see *sikkhā-pada*) binding on all Buddhists.

S

susānik'aṅga: see *dhutaṅga.*

suta-mayā paññā: 'knowledge based on learning', see *paññā.*

T

tadaṅga-pahāna: 'overcoming by the opposite', is one of the five kinds of overcoming (*pahāna*, q.v.).

tadārammaṇa-citta: 'registering consciousness' (see TAB. i, 40–49, 56), is the last stage in the complete process of cognition (*citta-vīthi*) immediately before sinking into the subconscious. It does not occur with the consciousness of the absorptions nor with supermundane consciousness, but only with large or distinct objects of the sensuous sphere. Cf. *viññāṇa-kicca*.

SOURCE NOTE: not found, or not found in this form or meaning, in the oldest parts of the Sutta Piṭaka. see *citta-vīthi*.

taints: *āsava* (q.v.).

talk, low: *tiracchāna-kathā* (q.v.).

taṇhā: (lit. 'thirst'): 'craving', is the chief root of suffering, and of the ever-continuing cycle of rebirths. "What, O monks, is the origin of suffering? It is that craving which gives rise to ever-fresh rebirth and, bound up with pleasure and lust, now here, now there, finds ever fresh delight. It is the sensual craving (*kāma-taṇhā*), the craving for existence (*bhava-taṇhā*), the craving for non-existence (*vibhava-taṇhā*)" (D. 22). ~ is the eighth link in the formula of the dependent origination (*paṭiccasamuppāda*, q.v.). Cf. *sacca*.

Corresponding to the six sense-objects, there are six kinds of craving: craving for visible objects, for sounds, odours, tastes, bodily impressions, mental impressions (*rūpa-, sadda-, gandha-, rasa-, phoṭṭhabba-, dhamma-taṇhā*). (M. 9; D. 15)

Corresponding to the threefold existence, there are three kinds: craving for sensual existence (*kāma-taṇhā*), for fine-material existence (*rūpa-taṇhā*), for immaterial existence (*arūpa-taṇhā*). (D. 33) There are eighteen 'thought-channels of craving' (*taṇhā-vicarita*) induced internally, and eighteen induced externally; and as occurring in past, present and future, they total 108; see A. IV, 199; VIBH., Ch. 17 (Khuddakavatthu-Vibhaṅga).

According to the Dependent Origination, craving is conditioned by feeling; on this see D. 22 (section on the Second Truth).

Of craving for existence (*bhava-taṇhā*) it is said (A. X, 62): "No first beginning of the craving for existence can be perceived, O monks, before which it was not and after which it came to be. But it can he perceived that craving for existence has its specific condition. I say, O monks, that also craving for existence has its condition that feeds it (*sāhāraṃ*) and is not without it. And what is it? 'Ignorance', one has to reply." Craving for existence and ignorance are called "the outstanding causes that lead to happy and unhappy destinies (courses of existence)" (see VISM. XVII, 36–42).

The most frequent synonyms of *taṇhā* are *rāga* (q.v.) and *lobha* (see *mūla*).

taṇhakkhaya: 'extinction of craving', is identical with 'extinction of cankers' (*āsavakkhaya*) and the attainment of perfect holiness or arahatship. Cf. *ariya-puggala*.

taṇhā-nissita-sīla: 'morality based on craving' (see *nissaya*).

Tathāgata: the 'Perfect One', lit. the one who has 'thus gone', or 'thus come', is an epithet of the Buddha used by him when speaking of himself.

To the often asked questions, whether the Tathāgata still exists after death, or not, it is said (e.g. S. XXII, 85, 86) that, in the highest sense (*paramattha*, q.v.) the Tathāgata cannot, even at lifetime, be discovered, how much less after death, and that neither the five groups of existence (*khandha*, q.v.) are to be regarded as the Tathāgata, nor can the Tathāgata be found outside these corporeal and mental phenomena. The meaning intended here is that there exist only these ever-changing corporeal and mental phenomena, arising and vanishing from moment to moment, but no separate entity, no personality.

When the commentaries in this connection explain Tathāgata by 'living being' (*satta*), they mean to say that here the questioners are using the merely conventional expression, Tathāgata, in the sense of a really existing entity.

Cf. *anatta, paramattha, puggala, jīva, satta*.

A commentarial treatise on "The Meaning of the Word 'Tathāgata'" is included in *The All-Embracing Net of Views* (Brahmajāla Sutta), tr. Bhikkhu Bodhi (BPS).

Tathāgata-bala: the 'ten powers of the Perfect One', see *dasa-bala*.

tathatā: 'suchness', designates the firmly fixed nature (*bhāva*) of all things whatever. The only passage in the canon where the word occurs in this sense, is found in KATH. 186 (see GUIDE, p. 83). On the Mahāyana term *tathatā*, see Suzuki, *Awakening of Faith*, 53ff.

SOURCE NOTE: this term, with the meaning in question, occurs perhaps only once in the canon, namely in KATH. (see GUIDE 83). Whether it is found also somewhere in the com., I am unable to say.

tatra-majjhattatā: 'equanimity, equipoise, mental balance' (lit., 'remaining here and there in the middle'), is the name for a high ethical quality belonging to the *saṅkhārakkhandha* (see *khandha*) and is mostly known by the name *upekkhā*. In its widest sense it is associated with all pure consciousness (see TAB. II). "*Tatramajjhattatā* is called the 'keeping in the middle of all things'. It has as characteristic that it effects the balance of consciousness and mental factors; as nature (function; *rasa*), that it prevents excessiveness and deficiency, or that it puts an end to partiality; as manifestation, that it keeps the proper middle" (VISM. XIV).

SOURCE NOTE: occurs probably for the first time in the ABH. canon (e.g. PATTH.; cf. GUIDE 110).

Tāvatiṃsa: 'the Thirty-three (gods)', a class of heavenly beings in the sensuous sphere; see *deva* (I).

te-cīvarik'aṅga: 'practice of the three-rober', is one of the ascetic means for purification (*dhutaṅga*, q.v.).

tejo-dhātu: 'fire-element, heat-element', see *dhātu*.

tejo-kasiṇa: 'fire-kasina', is one of the ten kasina exercises, see *kasiṇa*.

temperature: *utu* (q.v.). For corporeality produced by temperature, see *samuṭṭhāna*.

tendencies: *anusaya* (q.v.).

terror, awareness of: one of the insight-knowledges, see *visuddhi* VI. 3.

te-vijjā: 'one endowed with the threefold (higher) knowledge'. In Brahmanism means 'knower of the three Vedas' (*tri-vidyā*), in Buddhism means one who has realised three kinds of knowledge, to wit: remembrance of former rebirths, the divine eye, extinction of all cankers. For details, see *abhiññā*, 4–6. Cf. Tevijjā Sutta, D. 13 (WHEEL 57/58).

Theravada: 'Doctrine of the Elders', is a name of the oldest form of the Buddha's teachings, handed down in the Pali language. According to tradition, its name is derived from the fact of having been fixed by 500 holy elders of the Order, soon after the passing away of the Master.

Theravāda is the only one of the old schools of Buddhism that has survived among those which Mahāyānists have called 'Hīnayāna'. It is sometimes called Southern Buddhism or Pali Buddhism. It is found today in

Sri Lanka, Burma, Thailand, Cambodia, Laos, and Chittagong (East Bengal.). Cf. GUIDE, 60.

SOURCE NOTE: this term was already used by the Buddha himself in speaking of the doctrine of Ālāra-Kālāma (see M. 26). As a name for the Buddha's doctrine it belongs to the commentarial literature.

thīna-middha: 'sloth and torpor', constitute the third of the five hindrances (*nīvaraṇa*, q.v.). They may or may not, be associated with greedy consciousness (see TAB. 23, 25, 27, 29 and II).

thinking, wisdom based on: *cintāmaya-paññā*: see *paññā*.

ṭhiti-bhāgiya-sīla, **-samādhi**, **-paññā**: 'static morality, static concentration, static wisdom', see *hāna-bhāgiya-sīla*.

thought, **thought-conception**: see *vitakka*.

thought, right: *sammā-saṅkappa*;.see *sacca*, *magga*.

ties, the four: *gantha* (q.v.).

T

ti-hetu-paṭisandhika: see *paṭisandhi*.

ti-lakkhaṇa: the 'three characteristics of existence', or signata, are impermanence (*anicca*, q.v.), suffering or misery (*dukkha*, q.v.; see *sacca*, *dukkhatā*), non-self (*anatta*, q.v.).

"Whether Perfect Ones appear in the world, or whether Perfect Ones do not appear in the world, it still remains a firm condition, an immutable fact and fixed law: that all formations are impermanent, that all formations are subject to suffering, that everything is without a self" (A. III, 134).

"What do you think, O monks: Is corporeality (*rūpa*) permanent or impermanent?—Impermanent, O Venerable One.

Are feeling (*vedanā*), perception (*saññā*), mental formations (*saṅkhāra*) and consciousness (*viññāṇa*), permanent or impermanent?—Impermanent, O Venerable One.

"But that which is impermanent, is it something pleasant or painful?—It is painful, O Venerable One.

"But, of what is impermanent, painful and subject to change, could it be rightly said, 'This belongs to me, this am I, this is my ego'?—No, Venerable One.

"Therefore, whatever there is of corporeality, feeling, perception, mental formations and consciousness, whether past, present or future, one's own or external, gross or subtle, lofty or low, far or near, of all these things one should understand, according to reality and true wisdom: 'This does not belong to me, this am I not, this is not my ego'" (S. XXII, 59).

"In one who understands eye, ear, nose, tongue, body and all the remaining formations as impermanent, painful and non-self, in him the fetters (*saṃyojana*, q.v.) are dissolved" (S. XXXV, 53).

It is the full comprehension of the three characteristics by direct meditative experience which constitutes liberating insight. About their relation to the three gateways of liberation', see *vimokkha* I. For further details, see *anicca, dukkha, anatta, vipassanā*.

LITERATURE: *The Three Signata*, by Prof. O.H. de A. Wijesekera (WHEEL 20). *The Three Basic Facts of Existence*: I-III (WHEEL BPS), VISM. XX, 13ff., 18ff.; XXI, 47ff., 67ff.

Tipiṭaka: 'The Three Baskets', is the name for the three main divisions of the Pali canon: the Basket of Discipline (Vinaya Piṭaka), the Basket of Discourses (Sutta Piṭaka) and the Basket of Philosophy (Abhidhamma Piṭaka).

tiracchāna-kathā: 'low talk', lit. 'beastly talk', is the name in the sutta-texts for the following: "Talk about kings and robbers, ministers and armies, danger and war, eating and drinking, clothes and dwellings, garlands and scents, relations, chariots, villages and markets, towns and districts, women and heroes, street talks, talks by the well, talk about those departed in days gone by, tittle-tattle, talks about world and sea, about gain and loss" (A.X, 69 etc.).

In the commentaries four further kinds are enumerated, thus bringing the number to thirty-two, as mostly counted, namely: talk about sensuous enjoyment, self-mortification, eternity and self-annihilation.

tiracchāna-yoni: 'animal womb'; birth as animal. The animal kingdom belongs to the sensuous world (see *loka*), is one of the four lower worlds (see *apāya*) and one of the three woeful forms of existence (see *gati*).

tīrana-pariññā: 'full understanding by investigating', see *pariññā*.

ti-ratana: 'Three Jewels' or Three Gems, which by all Buddhists are revered as the most venerable things, are the Buddha, the Dhamma and the Holy Saṅgha.' i.e.,: the Enlightened One; the law of deliverance discovered, realised and proclaimed by him; and the Community of Holy Disciples and those who live in accordance with the Law. The contemplations of the three Jewels belong to the ten contemplations (*anussati* q.v.).

ti-saraṇa: 'threefold refuge', in which every faithful adherent of the Buddha puts his whole trust, consists in the Buddha, the Dhamma and the Saṅgha (see *ti-ratana*).

The Buddha, or Enlightened One, is the teacher who by himself has discovered, realised and proclaimed to the world the law of deliverance. The Dhamma is the law of deliverance. The Saṅgha is the community of the disciples, who have realised or are striving to realise the law of deliverance.

The threefold Refuge in Pali, by the uttering of which one may also outwardly profess one's faith, is still the same as in the Buddha's time, namely:

Buddhaṃ saraṇaṃ gacchāmi
Dhammaṃ saraṇaṃ gacchāmi
Saṅghaṃ saraṇaṃ gacchāmi

I take my refuge in the Buddha.
I take my refuge in the Dhamma.
I take my refuge in the Saṅgha.

LITERATURE: *The Threefold Refuge* by Nyanaponika Thera (WHEEL 76). *Devotion in Buddhism* (WHEEL 18). *Going for Refuge*, by Bhikkhu Bodhi (WHEEL 282/284). KHP. TR. 4ff.

T

titthāyatana: the three 'articles of (heretical) belief'. which in A. III, 61 are declared as leading to inactivity, are: (1) the belief that all happiness and woe are produced through former karma (prenatal actions; see *karma*); (2) that everything is uncaused; (3) that everything is created by God.

(1) is the teaching of Nigaṇṭha-Nāthaputta, the leader of the Nigaṇṭhas, the modern Jains. The fault with this doctrine is that it does not account for that happiness and woe which either are the result of the present life's good or bad action, or are associated with the corresponding action. (2) is the doctrine of Makkhali Gosāla; see *diṭṭhi*.

According to the above three doctrines, man is not responsible for his actions, so that all moral exertions become useless.

torpor: *thīna*, see *thīna-middha* (q.v.).

training, the threefold: *sikkhā* (q.v.). The steps of ~: *sikkhā-pada*, (q.v.).

trance: *jhāna* (q.v.).

tranquillity (of mind): see *samatha, samatha-vipa ssanā, bhāvanā, bojjhaṅga*. 'One who has taken ~ as his vehicle': *samathayānika* (q.v.).

tranquilisation, overcoming (of defilements) by way of: see *pahāna*.

transference of merit: *patti-dāna* (q.v.).

transformation, power of: see *iddhi*.

transitoriness: *anicca* (q.v.).

treasures, the seven: see *dhana* (q.v.).

tree, living under: one of the ascetic practices (*dhutaṅga*, q.v.).

truths, the Four Noble: *sacca* (q.v.). Twofold knowledge of the ~, see *saccañāṇa*.

turning away, contemplation of the: *vivaṭṭanupassanā*, see *vipassanā*.

Tusita: a class of heavenly beings in the sensuous plane, see *deva* (1).

twin miracle: *yamaka-pāṭihāriya* (q.v.).

U

ubhato-bhāga-vimutta: the 'both-ways-liberated one', is the name of one class of noble disciples (*ariya-puggala*, q.v.). He is liberated in two ways, namely, by way of all eight absorptions (*jhāna*, q.v.) as well as by the supermundane path (*sotāpatti, etc.*) based on insight (*vipassanā*, q.v.). In M. 70 it is said:

"Who, O monks, is a both-ways-liberated one? If someone in his own person has reached the eight liberations (absorptions), and through wise penetration the cankers (*āsava*, q.v.) have become extinguished, such a one is called a both-ways-liberated one." Cf. D. 15.

In the widest sense, one is both-ways-liberated if one has reached one or the other of the absorptions, and one or the other of the supermundane paths (cf. A. IX, 44).

The first liberation is also called 'liberation of mind' (*cetovimutti*), the latter liberation through wisdom' (*paññā-vimutti*).

The first liberation, however, is merely temporary, being a liberation through repression (*vikkhambhanavimutti* = *vikkhambhana-pahāna*: see *pahāna*).

uccheda-diṭṭhi: 'annihilation-view', see *diṭṭhi*.

U

udayabbayānupassanā-ñāṇa: 'knowledge consisting in the contemplation of rise and fall', is the first of the nine insight-knowledges constituting the purification by knowledge and vision of the path-progress'. For details, see *visuddhi*, VI. 1.

uddhacca: 'restlessness', belongs to the ten fetters (*saṃyojana*, q.v.), and to the five hindrances (*nīvaraṇa*, q.v.). It is one of those four mental factors inseparably associated with all unwholesome consciousness (*akusala-sādhāraṇa*, q.v.). Cf. TAB. II.

uddhambhāgiya-saṃyojana: the five 'higher fetters', see *saṃyojana*.

uddhaṃsota-akaniṭṭhagāmī: 'passing upstream to the highest gods', is one of the five kinds of non-returners (*anāgāmī*, q.v.).

uggaha-nimitta: see *nimitta*.

ugghaṭitaññu: 'one who already during a given explanation comes to penetrate the truth' (PUG.). This is one of four types of persons classified according to their ability of acquiring insight, mentioned in A. IV, 133. Cf. also *vipacitaññu*, *neyya*, *pada-parama*.

See *The Requisites of Enlightenment*, by Ledi Sayadaw (WHEEL 171/174) 1ff.

ujukatā: (*kāya-*, *citta-*): 'uprightness' (of mental factors and of consciousness), is associated with all pure consciousness. Cf. TAB. II.

SOURCE NOTE: not found, or not found in this form or meaning, in the oldest parts of the Sutta Piṭaka; see *lahutā*.

unconditioned, the: *asaṅkhata* (q.v.). Contemplation of the ~ (= *animitta*), see *vipassanā*.

unconscious beings: *asaññā-satta* (q.v.).

understanding: see *diṭṭhi*, *ñāṇa*, *paññā*, *pariññā*. Right ~, see *magga* (1), *sacca* (IV. 1).

unit: see *kalāpa*, *rūpa-kalāpa*.

unprepared, unprompted: see *asaṅkhārika-citta*.

unshakeable deliverance: see *ceto-vimutti*.

unshakeable one, the: *akuppa-dhamma* (q.v.).

unthinkable things, the four: *acinteyya* (q.v.).

unwholesome, karmically: *akusala* (q.v.).

upacāra: 'moment of access', see *javana*.

upacāra-samādhi: 'neighbourhood- or access-concentration', is the degree of concentration just before entering any of the absorptions, or *jhānas*. It still belongs to the sensuous sphere (*kāmāvacara*; see *avacara*).

upacaya, *rūpassa*: 'growth of corporeality', see *khandha* I.

SOURCE NOTE: is an ABH. term but already alluded to in the old sutta texts, e.g. M. 149: '*āyatiṃ pañcūpādānakkhandhā upacayaṃ gacchanti*', or in D.2: '*ayaṃ kāyo ... odana-kummās'upacayo*'.

upacchedaka-kamma: 'destructive karma', see *karma*.

upādāna: 'clinging', according to VISM. XVII, is an intensified degree of craving (*taṇhā*, q.v.). The four kinds of clinging are: (1) sensuous clinging (*kāmupādāna*), (2) clinging to views (*diṭṭhupādāna*), (3) clinging to mere rules and ritual (*sīlabbatupādāna*), and (4) clinging to the personality-belief (*atta-vādupādāna*).

(1) "What now is the sensuous clinging? Whatever with regard to sensuous objects there exists of sensuous lust, sensuous desire, sensuous attachment, sensuous passion, sensuous deludedness, sensuous fetters: this is called sensuous clinging.

(2) "What is the clinging to views? 'Alms and offerings are useless; there is no fruit and result for good and bad deeds: all such view and wrong conceptions are called the clinging to views.

(3) "What is the clinging to mere rules and ritual? The holding firmly to the view that through mere rules and ritual one may reach purification: this is called the clinging to mere rules and ritual.

(4) "What is the clinging to the personality-belief? The twenty kinds of ego-views with regard to the groups of existence (see *sakkāya-diṭṭhi*): these are called the clinging to the personality-belief" (DHS. 1214–17).

This traditional fourfold division of clinging is not quite satisfactory. Besides *kamupādāna* we should expect either *rūpupādāna* and *arūpupādāna*, or simply *bhavupādāna*. Though the *anāgāmī* is entirely free from the traditional four kinds of *upādāna*, he is not freed from rebirth, as he still possesses *bhavupādāna*. The com. to VISM. XVII, in trying to get out of this dilemma, explains *kāmupādāna* as including here all the remaining kinds of clinging.

'Clinging' is the common rendering for ~, though 'grasping' would come closer to the literal meaning of it, which is 'uptake'; see *Three Cardinal Discourses* (WHEEL 17), p.19.

upādānakkhandha: the five 'groups of clinging', or more clearly stated in accordance with VISM., 'the five groups of existence which form the objects of clinging'. Cf. M. 44, and see *khandha*.

upādā-rūpa: 'derived corporeality', signifies the twenty-four secondary corporeal phenomena dependent on the four primary physical elements, i.e., the sense organs and sense-objects, etc. See *khandha* I.

SOURCE NOTE: ~ is, as such, an ABH. term, but it is used with the same meaning in the sutta texts, e.g. in M. 9: '*catunnañ ca mahābhūtānaṃ upādāya rūpaṃ*'. *Upādā* is an abbreviation of *upādāya* (gerund).

upadhi: 'substratum of existence'. In the com. there are enumerated four kinds: the five groups (*khandha*, q.v.), sensuous desire (*kāma*), mental defilements (*kilesa*, q.v.), karma (q.v.). In the suttas it occurs frequently in SN. (VV. 33, 364, 546, 728), and, with reference to Nibbāna, in the phrase "the abandoning of all substrata" (*sabbūpadhi-paṭinissagga*; D. 14). See *viveka* (3).

upādi: lit. 'something which one grasps, to which one clings, i.e., the five groups of existence (*khandha*, q.v.). In the suttas, the word is mostly used in such expressions as "One of the two fruits may be expected: either perfect wisdom or, if the groups are still remaining (*sati upādisese*, 'if there is a remainder of groups'), the fruit of *anāgāmī*" (D. 22). Further (A. IV. 118): "Here the Perfect One has passed into the Nibbāna-element in which no more groups are remaining (*anupādi-sesa*)." Cf. Nibbāna.

upādiṇṇa-rūpa: 'karmically acquired corporeality', or 'matter clung-to (by karma)', is identical with karma-produced corporeality (*kammaja-rūpa*; see *samuṭṭhāna*). In VISM. XIV it is said: "That corporeality which, later on, we shall refer to as 'karma-produced' (*kammaja*), is, for its being dependent on previous (pre-natal) karma, called 'karmically acquired'." The term (*upādinna*) occurs so in the suttas, e.g. M. 28 (WHEEL 101), 62, 140. See DHS. §990; Khandha VIBH.

upaghātaka-kamma: 'destructive karma', see *karma*.

upahacca-parinibbāyī: 'one who reaches Nibbāna within the first half of life', is one of the five kinds of *anāgāmī* (q.v.).

upakkilesa: 'impurities', corruptions, imperfections (a frequent rendering by 'defilements' is better reserved for *kilesa*, q.v.).

A list of sixteen moral 'impurities of the mind' (*cittassa upakkilesa*) is mentioned and explained in M. 7 & 8 (WHEEL. 61/62): 1. covetousness and unrighteous greed (*abhijjhā-visamalobha*), 2. ill will (*vyāpāda*), 3. anger (*kodha*), 4. hostility (*upanāha*), 5. denigration (*makkha*), 6. domineering (*palāsa*), 7. envy (*issā*), 8. stinginess (*macchariya*), 9. hypocrisy (*māyā*), 10. fraud (*sāṭheyya*), 11. obstinacy (*thambha*), 12. presumption (*sārambha*), 13. conceit (*māna*), 14. arrogance (*atimāna*), 15. vanity (*madu*), 16. negligence (*pamāda*).

There are three groups of *upakkilesa* pertaining to meditation:

(a) Nine mental imperfections occurring in 'one devoted to higher mental training' (*adhicitta*); three coarse ones—evil conduct in deeds, words and thoughts; three medium—thoughts of sensual desire, ill will and cruelty; three subtle—thoughts about one's relatives, one's country and one's reputation (A. III, 100).

U

(b) Eighteen imperfections in the practice of mindfulness of breathing (*ānāpāna-sati*, q.v.), mentioned in PTS.M., Ānāpāna-kathā (tr. in *Mindfulness of Breathing*, by Ñāṇamoli Thera (p. 60; BPS).

(c) Ten 'imperfections of insight' (-meditation, *vipassanūpakkilesa*); see *visuddhi* v.

upanissaya-paccaya: 'decisive support' or 'inducement', is one of the twenty-four conditions (*paccaya*, q.v.).

upapajja-vedanīya-kamma: 'karma ripening in the next birth', see *karma*.

upapatti-bhava: 'rebirth-process', see *bhava*.

upapīḷaka-kamma: 'suppressive *kamma*', see *karma*.

upāsaka: lit. 'sitting close by', i.e., a 'lay adherent', is any lay follower who is filled with faith and has taken refuge in the Buddha, his doctrine and his community of noble disciples (A. VIII, 25). His virtue is regarded as pure if he observes the five Precepts (*pañca-sīla*; see *sikkhā-pada*). He should avoid the following wrong ways of livelihood: trading in arms, in living beings, meat, alcohol, and poison (A.V, 177). See also A. VIII, 75.

upasamānussati: 'recollection of the peace of Nibbāna', is the last of the ten recollections (*anussati*, q.v.). "Whatsoever, O monks, there are of things, as highest of them is considered detachment (*virāga*), i.e., the crushing of conceit, the stilling of thirst, the uprooting of clinging, the breaking through the round of rebirths, cessation of craving, detachment, extinction, Nibbāna" (A. IV, 34).

upāsikā: 'female adherent', see *upāsaka*.

upatthambhaka-kamma: 'supportive karma', see *karma*.

upavicāra: see *manopavicāra*.

upekkhā: 'equanimity', also called *tatramajjhattatā* (q.v.), is an ethical quality belonging to the *saṅkhāra*-group (see *khandha*) and should therefore not be confounded with indifferent feeling (*adukkha-masukhā vedanā*) which sometimes also is called *upekkhā* (see *vedanā*).

Upekkhā is one of the four sublime abodes (*brahma-vihāra*, q.v.), and of the factors of enlightenment (*bojjhaṅga*, q.v.). See VISM. IV, 156ff.

upekkhā-ñāṇa: *saṅkhārupekkhā-ñāṇa* (q.v.).

upekkhā-sambojjhaṅga: 'equanimity as a factor of enlightenment', see *bojjhaṅga*.

upekkhā-sukha: 'equanimous happiness,' is the feeling of happiness accompanied by a high degree of equanimity (*upekkhā*) as, e.g. in the third absorption (*jhāna* q.v.).

upekkhā-vedanā: see *vedanā*.

upekkhindriya: the 'faculty of indifference', is one of the five elements of feeling (M. 115) and therefore not to be confounded with the ethical quality 'equanimity', also called *upekkhā* (q.v.).

upekkhopavicāra: 'indulging in indifference', see *manopavicāra*.

uposatha: lit. 'fasting', i.e., 'fasting day', is the full-moon day, the new-moon day, and the two days of the first and last moon-quarters. On full-moon and new-moon days, the Disciplinary Code, the *Pātimokkha*, is read before the assembled community of monks (*bhikkhu*), while on the mentioned four moon-days many of the faithful lay devotees go to visit the monasteries, and there take upon themselves the observance of the eight rules (*aṭṭha-sīla*; *sikkhā-pada*). See A. VIII, 41ff.

uprightness: *ujukatā* (q.v.).

upstream to the highest gods, passing: see *anāgāmī*.

usages, the four noble: *ariya-vaṃsa* (q.v.).

utu: temperature, heat, is identical with the heat element (*tejodhātu*, q.v.).

utu-samuṭṭhāna (= *utuja*)-**rūpa**: 'corporeality produced by temperature', see *samuṭṭhāna*.

V

vācā: 'speech'. On right sp., see *magga* (3), *sacca* (IV.3). Low talk, see *tiracchāna-kathā*.

vacī-kamma: 'verbal action', see *karma, kamma-patha*.

vacī-saṅkhāra: 'verbal karma-formation', or 'verbal function'.

(1) For verbal karma-formation, see *saṅkhāra* (I. 1).

(2) For verbal function (of mind), i.e., thought-conception and discursive thinking, see *saṅkhāra* (I. 2).

vacī-viññatti: see *viññatti*.

vanishing, contemplation of: *vayānupassanā*, is one of the eighteen chief kinds of insight (*vipassāna*, q.v.).

vanishing and reappearing: knowledge of the ~ of beings according to karma, is identical with the divine eye (see *abhiññā* 5).

vāritta-sīla: 'morality consisting in avoiding' (evil things), as distinguished from 'morality consisting in performing' (good things). See *cāritta-vāritta*.

SOURCE NOTE: not found, or not found in this form or meaning, in the oldest parts of the Sutta Piṭaka; see *cāritta*.

V

vasī: 'mastery'. VISM. IV speaks of five kinds, which anyone who wishes to develop the absorptions (*jhāna*, q.v.) should acquire first of all, with regard to the first absorption, namely: mastery in adverting to it (*āvajjana-vasī*), in entering it (*samāpajjana-vasī*), in determining it (*adhiṭṭhāna-vasī*), in rising therefrom (*vuṭṭhāna-vasī*), in retrospection (*paccavekkhana-vasī*).

"If wherever, whenever, and for whatever duration desired, one enters the first absorption, and at one's entering it, no slowness is experienced, this is called mastery in entering the absorption, etc. In an analogous way, the four remaining kinds are to be explained" (VISM. IV, 131ff.; XXIII, 27ff.).

SOURCE NOTE: the five kinds of *vasī* are probably found first in the VISM.

vaṭṭa: 1. 'round', 2. 'round of rebirths'.

(1) With reference to the dependent origination (*paṭiccasamuppāda*, q.v.), VISM. XVII speaks of three rounds: the karma round (*kamma-vaṭṭa*) comprising

the karma-formations and the karma-process (second and tenth links); the round of defilements (*kilesa-vaṭṭa*) comprising ignorance, craving and clinging (first, eighth, and ninth links); the round of results (*vipāka-vaṭṭa*) comprising consciousness, mind and corporeality, six bases, impression, feeling (third through seventh links). Cf. *paṭiccasamuppāda* (diagram).

(2) round of rebirth = *saṃsāra* (q.v.).

vatthu: 'physical base', i.e., the six physical organs on which the mental process is based, are the five physical sense organs and, according to the com., the heart (*hadaya-vatthu*, q.v.) as the sixth. This sixth *vatthu* must not be confounded with the sixth *āyatana*, which is a collective name for all consciousness whatever.

SOURCE NOTE: ~ as a general term for the five sense organs (*cakkhu-vatthu*, etc.) is frequent in the com., and often used together with *ārammaṇa* (object). This usage, however, is already indicated in the ABH. canon: '*Cakkhum p'etaṃ ... vatthum p'etaṃ*' (DHS. § 597; VIBH., p.71, PTS): '*cakkhuviññāṇassa vatthu*' (DHS. §§ 679ff.).

vatthu-kāma: 'objective sensuality', the five sense-objects, see *kāma*.

vavatthāna: 'determining', defining. In its application to insight meditation, this term occurred first in PTS.M. (I, p. 53); but in a verbal form, as a past participle, already in M. 111: *tyassa dhammā anupadavavatthitā honti*, "these things (the mental factors) were determined by him (i.e., Sāriputta) successively" (see ABH. St., p. 54). In VISM. XX, 130, it is said: 'The determining of the truth of suffering is effected with the determining of mind-and-body in the purification of view (see *visuddhi* III). The determining of the truth of origination is effected with the discerning of conditions in the purification by transcending doubt (see *visuddhi* IV). The determining of the truth of the path is effected by emphasis on the right path in the purification by knowledge and vision of what is path and non-path (see *visuddhi* V). Thus the determining of the three truths (suffering, origin, path) has been first effected by means of mundane (*lokiya*, q.v.) knowledge only." See *sammasana*, *visuddhi*.

For the determining of the four physical elements, see *dhātuvavatthāna*.

vayānupassanā: 'contemplation of vanishing', is one of the eighteen chief kinds of insight (*vipassanā*, q.v.).

vāyo-dhātu: 'wind-element', see *dhātu*.

vāyo-kasiṇa: 'wind-kasina', is one of the kasina exercises (*kasiṇa*, q.v.).

vedanā: 'feeling', sensation, is the second of the five groups of existence (see *khandha* II). According to its nature, it may be divided into five classes: (1) bodily agreeable feeling (*kāyikā sukhā-vedanā* = *sukha*); (2) bodily disagreeable feeling (*kāyikā dukkhā-vedanā* = *dukkhā*); (3) mentally agreeable feeling (*cetasikā sukhā-vedanā* = *somanassa*); (4) mentally disagreeable feeling (*cetasikā dukkhā-vedanā* = *domanassa*); (5) indifferent or neutral (*adukkha-m-asukhā vedanā* = *upekkhā*, q.v.). With regard to the six senses, one distinguishes six kinds of feeling: feeling associated with seeing, hearing, smelling, tasting, bodily impression and mental impression. The textual wording of it is 'feeling arisen through visual contact' (*cakkhu-samphassajā vedanā*; S. XXII, 55; D. 22), etc.

Feeling is one of the seven mental factors inseparably associated with all consciousness whatever, see *nāma*. In the formula of the dependent origination (*paṭiccasamuppāda*, q.v.), feeling is the condition for the arising of craving (*taṇhā*). The above-mentioned five kinds of feeling are enumerated amongst the twenty-two faculties (*indriya*, q.v.). See

M. 59; *Contemplation of Feeling* (Vedanā Saṃyutta), by Nyanaponika Thera (WHEEL 303/304).

vedanānupassanā: 'contemplation of feeling', is one of the four foundations of mindfulness (*satipaṭṭhāna* q.v.).

Vehapphala: a class of heavenly beings in the fine-material world, see *deva*.

verbal action: *vacī-kamma*, see *karma*.

verbal functions of mind: *vacī-saṅkhāra*, see *saṅkhāra*.

vesārajja: 'self-confidence' of a Buddha is fourfold. He is confident: 1. to have attained to a perfect Enlightenment of which it cannot be said that it omits anything essential to it; 2. to have destroyed all cankers (*āsava*), leaving none that can be said to be undestroyed by him; 3. that what were declared by him as obstacles to liberation are undeniably such; 4. that his teaching fulfils its purpose of actually leading to final liberation from suffering. See A. IV, 8; VII, 58; M. 12.

vibhajja-vāda: 'analytical or discriminating doctrine' is an early name for the original Buddha-doctrine, called Theravāda. The term *vibhajja-vādī* occurs in M. 99 and A. X, 94, though not in the sense of a separate school, but as a characteristic of the Buddha himself: "Now, by blaming what is blamable and praising what is praiseworthy, the Blessed One is a 'discriminating teacher' (*vibhajja-vadī*) and is not one-sided in his teaching" (A. X, 94).

Buddhaghosa, in the introduction to his com. on the Kathāvatthu, says that in Asoka's time, when the Saṅgha prospered, many heretics took ordination as Buddhist monks but continued to spread their wrong doctrines. For purifying the Saṅgha, Asoka, together with the venerable Moggaliputtatissa, summoned assembly of the bhikkhus. When each of the assembled was individually questioned by the king about what the Buddha taught, those who said that he was an eternalist (*sassata-vadī*), etc. were expelled. The genuine bhikkhus replied that the Buddha was a *vibhajja-vadī*, an 'analyst' or 'discriminating teacher'; and when, on the king's question, Moggaliputtatissa confirmed that this was the correct view, those monks were admitted to the *uposatha* (q.v.) assembly of the Saṅgha, and from their midst the participants of the third Council at Pātaliputta were selected. See *Mahāvaṃsa*, tr. by Wilh. Geiger, Ch. V, v. 268ff.

vibhava-diṭṭhi: *uccheda-diṭṭhi*, see *diṭṭhi*.

vibhava-taṇhā: 'craving for non-existence', or for self-annihilation; see *taṇhā*.

vicāra: 'discursive thinking', see *vitakka-vicāra*.

vicikicchā: 'sceptical doubt', is one of the five mental hindrances (*nīvaraṇa*, q.v.) and one of the three fetters (*saṃyojana*, q.v.), which disappear forever at stream-entry, the first stage of holiness (see *ariya-puggala*). As a fetter, it refers to sceptical doubt about the Master (the Buddha), the Teaching, the Saṅgha, and the training; about things past and future, and conditionality (DHS. 1004; cf. A.X., 71). It also applies to uncertainty whether things are wholesome or not, to be practised or not, of high or low value, etc. According to VISM. XIV, 177, *vicikicchā* is the lack of desire to think (things out i.e., to come to a conclusion; *vigata-cikicchā*, desiderative to √ *cit*, to think); it has the nature of wavering, and its manifestation is indecision and a divided attitude; its proximate cause is unwise attention to matters of doubt. It is associated with one of the two classes of unwholesome consciousness rooted in delusion (TAB. I, No. 32). See also *kaṅkhā*.

view, right: *sammā-diṭṭhi*; see *diṭṭhi*, *magga* 1, *sacca* IV, 1. For wrong view, see *diṭṭhi*.

vigata-paccaya: 'disappearance', is one of the twenty-four conditions (*paccaya*, q.v.).

vihāra: 'abode' There are three abodes: the heavenly abode (*dibba-vihāra*), the divine abode (*brahma-vihāra*, q.v.), the noble abode (*ariya-vihāra*). See A. III, 63; D. 33.

vijjā: '(higher) knowledge', gnosis. For the threefold ~, see *abhiññā* and *te-vijjā*. Cf. *vijjā-caraṇa*.

vijjā-caraṇa: 'knowledge and conduct'. This expression occurs in those passages in the suttas where the qualities of a Buddha are described, namely: "Truly, the Blessed One is holy, is fully enlightened, perfect in knowledge and conduct ... ". According to VISM. VII, 1 and D. 3, knowledge (*vijjā*) refers here either to the threefold knowledge (see *te-vijjā*), or to the eight kinds of knowledge, namely: the six higher spiritual powers (*abhiññā*, q.v.), insight (*vipassanā*, q.v.), and magical power (*iddhi*, q.v.); while conduct (*caraṇa*) refers to fifteen things: moral restraint, watching over the sense-doors, moderation in eating, wakefulness, faith, moral shame, moral dread, great learning, energy, mindfulness, wisdom, and the four absorptions.

vikkhambhana-pahāna: 'overcoming by repression' (or 'suspension'), is one of the five kinds of overcoming (*pahāna*, q.v.). Cf. M. 20 (tr. in WHEEL 21).

vikubbanā-iddhi: the 'power of transformation', is one of the magical faculties (*iddhi*, q.v.).

vimaṃsā: 'investigation, inquiry, pondering', is one of the four roads to power (*iddhi-pāda*, q.v.) and one of the four factors of predominance (see *paccaya*, 3).

V

vimokkha: 'liberation' (deliverance). I. the three; II. the eight.

I.

The three liberations are: (1) the conditionless (or signless) liberation (*animitta-~*), (2) the desireless liberation (*apaṇihita-~*), (3) the emptiness (or void) liberation (*suññatā-~*). They are also called 'the triple gateway to liberation' (*~-mukha*; VISM. XXI, 66ff.), as they are three different approaches to the paths of holiness. See *visuddhi* VI, 8. Cf. VISM. XXI, 6ff., 121ff.; PTS.M. II. Vimokkha-Kathā.

(1) "Whosoever being filled with determination (*adhimokkha*, q.v.), considers all formations as impermanent (*anicca*), such a one attains the conditionless liberation. (2) Whosoever being filled with tranquillity, considers all formations as painful (*dukkha*), such a one attains the desireless liberation. (3) Whosoever being filled with wisdom, considers all formations as without a self (*anatta*), such a one attains the emptiness liberation" (VISM. XXI, 70 = PTS.M. II, p. 58).

(1) and (2) are mentioned and explained in M. 43, under the name of deliverances of mind (*ceto-vimutti*, q.v.). (2) and (3) appear in DHS. (344ff., 353ff.) in the section on supermundane consciousness (see ASL.TR., 299ff.).

II.

The eight liberations (*aṭṭha-vimokkha*) occur frequently in the texts (A. VIII, 66; D. 16, etc.) and are described as follows:

"There are eight liberations, O monks. Which are these?

(1) "While remaining in the fine-material sphere (*rūpī*), one perceives corporeal forms: this is the first liberation.

(2) "Not perceiving corporeal forms on one's own person, one perceives corporeal forms externally: this is the second liberation.

(3) "By thinking of the beautiful, one is filled with confidence: this is the third liberation.

(4) "Through the total overcoming of the corporeality-perceptions, the vanishing of the reflex-perceptions, and the non-attention to the multiformity-perceptions, with the idea 'Unbounded is space', one reaches the sphere of unbounded space (*ākāsānañcāyatana*) and abides therein: this is the fourth liberation.

(5) "Through the total overcoming of the sphere of unbounded space, and with the idea 'Unbounded is consciousness', one reaches the sphere of unbounded consciousness (*viññāṇañcāyatana*) and abides therein: this is the fifth liberation.

(6) "Through the total overcoming of the sphere of unbounded consciousness, and with the idea 'Nothing is there', one reaches the sphere of nothingness (*ākiñcaññāyatana*) and abides therein: this is the sixth liberation.

(7) "Through the total overcoming of the sphere of nothingness, one reaches the sphere of neither-perception-nor-non-perception (*n'evasaññānāsaññāyat ana*) and abides therein: this is the seventh liberation.

(8) "Through the total overcoming of the sphere of neither-perception-nor-non-perception, one reaches the extinction of perception and feeling (see *nirodha-samāpatti*): this is the eighth liberation.

These, O monks, are the eight kinds of liberation."

For (1–3), see *abhibhāyatana*; for (4–7), see *jhāna*; for (8), see *nirodha-samāpatti*.

V

By (3) is meant the attainment of the fine-material absorptions (*jhāna*, q.v.) by means of concentrating the mind on perfectly pure and bright colours as objects of the kasina (q.v.). According to PTS.M. this mental state is produced also by concentrating the mind on the four sublime states, i.e., all-embracing kindness, compassion, sympathetic joy and equanimity, in consequence of which all beings appear perfectly pure and glorified, and thus the mind turns to the beautiful.

See PTS.M. II, Vimokkha-kathā; ASL.TR., p. 255.

SOURCE NOTE: the three, i.e., *suññatā-~*, *animitta-~*, *appaṇihita-~*: are for the first time described and enumerated in PTS.M. II, 351. As *suññatā-samādhi*, etc., however, they are already given at D. 33.

vimutti: 'deliverance', is of two kinds: deliverance of mind (*ceto-vimutti*, q.v.) and deliverance through wisdom (*paññā-vimutti*, q.v.).

'Deliverance of mind', in the highest sense, is that kind of concentration (*samādhi*) which is bound up with the path of arahatship (*arahatta-magga*); 'deliverance through wisdom' is the knowledge (*ñāṇa*) bound up with the fruition of arahatship (*arahatta-phala*). Cf. A. V, 142.

There are also five kinds of deliverance, identical with the five kinds of overcoming (*pahāna*, q.v.).

vinipāta: 'world of suffering', is another name for the four woeful courses (*duggati*; see *gati*) of existence, and for the four lower worlds (*apāya*, q.v.).

The stream-winner (*sotāpanna*, q.v.) is no longer subject to rebirth in them (*avinipāta-dhamma*).

V

viññāṇa: 'consciousness', is one of the five groups of existence (aggregates; *khandha*, q.v.); one of the four nutriments (*āhāra*, q.v.); the third link of the dependent origination (*paṭiccasamuppāda*, q.v.); the fifth in the sixfold division of elements (*dhātu*, q.v.).

Viewed as one of the five groups (*khandha*), it is inseparably linked with the three other mental groups (feeling, perception and formations) and furnishes the bare cognition of the object, while the other three contribute more specific functions. Its ethical and karmic character, and its greater or lesser degree of intensity and clarity, are chiefly determined by the mental formations associated with it.

Just like the other groups of existence, consciousness is a flux (*viññāṇa-sota*, 'stream of c.') and does not constitute an abiding mind-substance; nor is it a transmigrating entity or soul. The three characteristics (see *ti-lakkhaṇa*), impermanence, suffering and no-self, are frequently applied to it in the texts (e.g., in the Anattalakkhaṇa Sutta, S.XXII, 59). The Buddha often stressed that "apart from conditions, there is no arising of consciousness' (M. 38); and all these statements about its nature hold good for the entire range of consciousness, be it "past, future or presently arisen, gross or subtle, in oneself or external, inferior or lofty, far or near" (S. XXII, 59).

According to the six senses it divides into six kinds, viz. eye- (or visual) consciousness (*cakkhu-~*), etc. About the dependent arising of these six kinds of consciousness, VISM. XV, 39 says: 'Conditioned through the eye, the visible object, light and attention, eye-consciousness arises. Conditioned through the ear, the audible object, the ear-passage and attention, ear-consciousness arises. Conditioned, through the nose, the olfactive object, air and attention, nose-consciousness arises. Conditioned through the tongue, the gustative object, humidity and attention, tongue-consciousness arises. Conditioned through the body, bodily impression, the earth-element and attention, body-consciousness arises. Conditioned through the subconscious mind (*bhavaṅga-mano*), the mind-object and attention, mind-consciousness arises."

The Abhidhamma literature distinguishes eighty-nine classes of consciousness, being either karmically wholesome, unwholesome or neutral, and belonging either to the sense-sphere, the fine-material or the immaterial sphere, or to supermundane consciousness. See Table I.

viññāṇa-kicca: 'functions of consciousness', as exercised within a process of consciousness or cognitive series (*citta-vīthi*). In the Abhidhamma com. and VISM. XIV the following functions are mentioned: rebirth (*paṭisandhi*), subconsciousness (*bhavaṅga*), advertence (*āvajjana*), seeing, hearing, smelling, tasting, body-consciousness; receiving (*sampaṭicchana*), investigating (*santīraṇa*), determining (*votthapana*), impulsion (*javana*), registering (*tadārammaṇa*), dying (*cuti*).

A single unit of sense-perception (e.g. visual consciousness), being conditioned through a sense organ and its corresponding object, forms in reality an extremely complex process, in which all the single phases of consciousness follow one upon another in rapid succession, while performing their respective functions, e.g.:

"As soon as a visible object has entered the range of vision, it acts on the sensitive eye-organ (*cakkhu-pasāda*), and conditioned thereby an excitation of the subconscious stream (*bhavaṅga-sota*) takes place.

"As soon, however, as subconsciousness is broken off, the functional mind-element (see TAB. I, 70), grasping the object and breaking through the subconscious stream, performs the function of 'adverting' the mind towards the object (*āvajjana*).

"Immediately thereupon there arises at the eye-door, and based on the sensitive eye-organ, the eye-consciousness, while performing the function of 'seeing' (*dassana*). …

Immediately thereafter there arises the mind-element (TAB. I, 39, 55) performing the function of 'receiving' (*sampaṭicchana*) the object of that consciousness. …

"Immediately thereafter there arises … the mind-consciousness-element (TAB. I, 40, 41, 56), while 'investigating' (*santīraṇa*) the object received by the mind-element. …

"Immediately thereafter there arises the functional, rootless mind-consciousness-element (TAB. I, 71), accompanied by indifference, while performing the function of 'determining' (*votthapana*) the object. …

"Now, if the object is large, then immediately afterwards there flash forth six or seven 'impulsive moments' (*javana-citta*), constituted by one of the eight wholesome, or tywelve unwholesome, or nine functional classes of consciousness (TAB. I, 1–8; 22–23; 72–80). "Now, if at the end of the impulsive moments, the object at the five-sense doors is very large, and at the mind-door clear, then there arises, once or twice, one of the eight root-accompanied, karma resultant classes of consciousness (TAB. I, 42–49) of the sense-sphere, or one of the three rootless karma resultant mind-consciousness-elements (TAB. I, 40, 41, 56). … Because this consciousness after the vanishing of the impulsive moments, possesses the faculty continuing with the object of the subconsciousness, taking the object of the subconsciousness as its own object, therefore it is called 'registering' (*tadārammaṇa*, lit. 'that object', or 'having that as object')" (VISM. XIV, 115ff.).

If, however, the sense-object is weak, then it reaches merely the stage of 'impulsion' (*javana*), or of 'determining' (*votthapana*); if very weak, only an excitation of the subconsciousness takes place. The process of the inner or mind-consciousness, i.e., without participation of the five physical senses, is as follows: in the case that the mind-object entering the mind-door is distinct, then it passes through the stages of 'advertence at the mind-door' (*manodvārāvajjana*), the 'impulsive stage' and the 'registering stage', before finally sinking into the subconscious stream. see *citta-vīthi*.

LITERATURE: *Aids to the Abhidhamma Philosophy*, by Dr. C.B. Dharmasena (with colour chart of the Cognitive Series; WHEEL 63/64). *The Psychology and Philosophy of Buddhism*, by Dr. W.F. Javasuriya (Buddhist Missionary Society, Kuala Lumpur, Malaysia).

viññāṇañcāyatana: 'sphere of boundless consciousness', is a name for the second meditative absorption in the immaterial sphere (see *jhāna*, 6).

viññāṇaṭhiti: 'abodes or supports of consciousness'. The texts describe seven such abodes (e.g. A. VII, 41):

(1) "There are beings who are different in body and different in perception, such as men, some heavenly beings, and some beings living in states of suffering (see *Apāya*). This is the first abode of consciousness.

(2) "There are beings who are different in body but equal in perception, such as the first-born gods of the Brahma-world (see *deva* II). This is the second abode of consciousness.

(3) "There are beings who are equal in body but different in perception, such as the Radiant Gods (Ābhassara-deva). This is the third abode of consciousness.

(4) "There are beings who are equal in body and equal in perception, such as the All-illuminating Gods (Subhakiṇha-deva). This is the fourth abode of consciousness.

(5) "There are beings ... reborn in the sphere of boundless space. This is the fifth abode of consciousness.

(6) "There are beings ... reborn in the sphere of boundless consciousness. This is the sixth abode of consciousness.

(7) There are beings ... reborn in the sphere of nothingness. This is the seventh abode of consciousness"

About the three last-named spheres, see *jhāna* (5–7). Cf. *sattāvāsa*.

In D. 33 there are mentioned four *viññāṇaṭhiti*, apparently in the sense of 'bases' of consciousness, namely: corporeality, feeling, perception, mental formations, which in S. XXII, 53 are further explained.

viññatti: (lit. 'making known') 'intimation', is an Abhidhamma term for bodily expression (*kāya-viññatti*) and verbal expression (*vacī-viññatti*), both belonging to the corporeality-group. They are produced by the co-nascent volition, and are therefore, as such, purely physical and not to be confounded with karma (q.v.), which as such is something mental. Cf. KATH. 80, 100, 101, 103, 194 (see GUIDE V).

"One speaks of 'bodily expression', because it makes known an intention by means of bodily movement, and can itself be understood by the bodily movement which is said to be corporeal.

"'Verbal expression' is so called because it makes known an intention by means of a speech-produced noise" (VISM. XIV).

SOURCE NOTE: *kāya-~* and *vacī-~*, seem to occur for the first time in DHS. (§§ 665,718) of the ABH. canon.

vipacitaññu (or *vipañcitaññu*): 'one who realises the truth after explanation.' Thus is called one who realises the truth only after detailed explanation of that which already had been said to him in a concise form. Cf. *ugghaṭitaññu*.

vipāka: 'karma result', is any karmically (morally) neutral mental phenomenon (e.g. bodily agreeable or painful feeling, sense-consciousness, etc.), which is the result of wholesome or unwholesome volitional action (karma, q.v.) through body, speech or mind, done either in this or some previous life. Totally wrong is the belief that, according to Buddhism, everything is the result of previous action. Never, for example, is any karmically wholesome or unwholesome volitional action the result of former action, being in reality itself karma. On this subject see *titthāyatana*, *karma*, TAB. I; Fund II. Cf. A. III, 101; KATH. 162 (GUIDE, p. 80).

Karma-produced (*kammaja* or *kamma-samuṭṭhāna*) corporeal things are never called *kamma-vipāka*, as this term may be applied only to mental phenomena.

V

vipāka-paccaya: 'karma result condition' is one of the twenty-four conditions (*paccaya*, q.v.).

vipallāsa: 'perversions' or 'distortions'. "There are four perversions which may be either of perception (*saññā-vipallāsa*), of consciousness (*citta* v.) or of views (*diṭṭhi-~*). And which are these four? To regard what is impermanent (*anicca*) as permanent; what is painful (*dukkha*) as pleasant (or happiness-yielding); what is without a self (*anatta*) as a self; what is impure (ugly: *asubha*) as pure or beautiful" (A. IV, 49). See *Manual of Insight*, by Ledi Sayadaw (WHEEL 31/32), p.5.

"Of the perversions, the following are eliminated by the first path-knowledge (*sotāpatti*): the perversions of perception, consciousness and views, that the impermanent is permanent and what is not a self is a self; further, the perversion of views that the painful is pleasant, and the impure is pure. By the third path-knowledge (*anāgāmītā*) are eliminated: the perversions of perception and consciousness that the impure is pure. By the fourth path-knowledge (*arahatta*) are eliminated the perversions of perception and consciousness that the painful is pleasant" (VISM. XXII, 68).

vipariṇāmānupassanā: 'contemplation of change' (of all things), is one of the eighteen chief kinds of insight (*vipassanā*, q.v.).

vipassanā: 'insight', is the intuitive light flashing forth and exposing the truth of the impermanence, the suffering and the impersonal and unsubstantial nature of all corporeal and mental phenomena of existence. It is insight-wisdom (*vipassanā-paññā*) that is the decisive liberating factor in Buddhism, though it has to be developed along with the two other trainings in morality and concentration. The culmination of insight practice (see *visuddhi* VI) leads directly to the stages of holiness (see *visuddhi* VII).

Insight is not the result of a mere intellectual understanding, but is won through direct meditative observation of one's own bodily and mental processes. In the commentaries and the VISM., the sequence in developing insight-meditation is given as follows: 1. discernment of the corporeal (*rūpa*), 2. of the mental (*nāma*), 3. contemplation of both (*nāma-rūpa*; i.e., of their pairwise occurrence in actual events, and their interdependence), 4. both viewed as conditioned (application of the dependent origination, *paṭiccasamuppāda*), 5. application of the three characteristics (impermanence, etc.) to mind-and-body-cum-conditions.

The stages of gradually growing insight are described in the nine insight-knowledges (*vipassanā-ñāṇa*), constituting the sixth stage of purification, beginning with the 'knowledge of rise and fall' and ending with the 'adaptation to Truth'. For details, see *visuddhi* VI and VISM. XXI.

Eighteen chief kinds of insight-knowledge (or principal insights, *mahā-vipassanā) are* listed and described in VISM. XXII, 113:(1) contemplation of impermanence (*aniccānupassanā*), (2) of suffering (*dukkhānupassanā*), (3) of no self (*anattānupassanā*), (4) of aversion (*nibbidānupassanā*). (5) of detachment (*virāgānupassanā*), (6) of extinction (*nirodhānupassanā*), (7) of abandoning (*paṭinissaggānupassanā*), (8) of waning (*khayānupassanā*), (9) of vanishing (*vayānupassanā*), (10) of change (*vipariṇāmānupassanā*), (11) of the unconditioned (or signless, *animittānupassanā*), (12) of desirelessness (*appaṇihitānupassanā*), (13) of emptiness (*suññatāupassanā*), (14) insight into phenomena which is higher wisdom (*adhipaññā-dhamma-vipassanā*), (15) knowledge and vision according to reality (*yathābhūta-ñāṇadassana*), (16) contemplation of misery (or danger, *ādīnavānupassanā*), (17) reflecting contemplation (*paṭisaṅkhānupassanā*), (18) contemplation of turning away (*vivaṭṭānupassanā*).

Through these 18, the adverse ideas and views are overcome, for which reason this way of overcoming is called 'overcoming by the opposite' (*tadaṅga-pahāna*, overcoming this factor by that). Thus (1) dispels the idea of permanence. (2) the idea of happiness, (3) the idea of self, (4) lust, (5) greed, (6) origination, (7) grasping, (8) the idea of compactness, (9) karma-accumulation, (10) the idea of lastingness, (11) the conditions, (12) delight, (13) adherence, (14) grasping and adherence to the idea of substance, (15) attachment and adherence, (17) thoughtlessness, (18) dispels entanglement and clinging.

Insight may be either mundane (*lokiya*, q.v.) or supermundane (*lokuttara*, q.v.). Supermundane insight is of three kinds: (1) joined with one of the four supermundane paths, (2) joined with one of the fruitions of these paths, (3) regarding the extinction, or rather suspension, of consciousness (see *nirodha-samāpatti*). See *samatha-vipassanā*, *visuddhi*, III-VII.

LITERATURE: *Manual of Insight*, by Ledi Sayadaw (WHEEL 31/32). *Practical Insight Meditation* and *Progress of Insight*, both by Mahāsi Sayadaw (BPS). *The Experience of Insight*, by Joseph Goldstein (BPS).

SOURCE NOTE: ~ is frequently found in the older sutta texts (e.g. A. II, 32; S. XLV, 159), also together with *samatha*. The nine and eighteen insight-knowledges (*vipassanā-ñāṇa* and *mahā-vipassanā*), however, occur in the Sutta Piṭaka only in the PTS.M., Ñānakathā, where they are enumerated and explained, though without any group name being attached to them.

V

vipassanā-yānika: *sukkha-vipassaka* (q.v.).

vipassanūpakkilesa: 'imperfections of insight', see *visuddhi*.

SOURCE NOTE: the group of ten is mentioned for the first time in PTS.M. II, 102, and it is said that the mind may become defiled thereby (*kilissati*), but the above term is not used for the ten. This is probably done for the first time in VISM. XX.

vipatti: 'aberration' or 'deviation', may be: deviation from morality (*sīla-vipatti*), or deviation from understanding (*diṭṭhivi-patti*).

"To deviate in deeds, or in words, or in both deeds and words: this is called deviation from morality.

"'Alms and offerings are useless, there is no fruit and result of good and bad actions, there are no such things as this and the next life'. ... Such wrong views are called deviation from understanding." (PUG. 67, 68)

vippayutta-paccaya: 'dissociation', is one of the twenty-four conditions (*paccaya*, q.v.).

virāga: 'fading away', detachment; absence of lust, dispassionateness. Appears frequently together with *nirodha*, 'cessation' (1) as a name for Nibbāna, (2) in the contemplations (a) forming the fourth tetrad in the exercises in mindfulness of breathing (see *ānāpāna-sati* 14), (b) of the eighteen principal insights (No. 5); see *vipassanā*.

According to com., it may mean (1) the momentary destruction of phenomena, or (2) the ultimate 'fading away', i.e., Nibbāna. In the aforementioned two contemplations, it means the understanding of both, and the path attained by such understanding.

virāgānupassanā: see *virāga*.

virati: the three 'abstentions' or abstinences, are: abstention from wrong speech, wrong (bodily) action and wrong livelihood; corresponding to right speech, action and livelihood of the Eightfold Path (see *magga*, 3–5). By abstention is not simply meant the non-occurrence of the evil things in question, but the deliberate abstaining therefrom, whenever occasion arises. They belong to the 'secondary' (not constant) mental concomitants obtaining in lofty consciousness (see TAB. II). Cf. *sīla*.

virility: see *bhāva*.

viriya: 'energy', lit. 'virility', 'manliness' or 'heroism' (from *vīra*, man, hero; Lat. *vir*; cf. *virtus*), is one of the five spiritual faculties and powers (see *bala*), one of the seven factors of enlightenment (see *bojjhaṅga*) and identical with right effort of the Eightold Path (see *magga*). For further explanations, see *padhāna*.

viriya-sambojjhaṅga: 'energy as a factor of enlightenment', is one of the seven factors of enlightenment (*bojjhaṅga*, q.v.).

virtue: see *sīla*.

visesa-bhāgiya-sīla: (*-samādhi*, *-paññā*): morality (concentration, wisdom) connected with progress'. For details, see *hānabhāgiya-sīla*.

visible object: see *āyatana*.

visuddhi: 'purification', purity. The 'seven stages of purification' (*satta-visuddhi*) form the substructure of Upatissa's *Vimutti-Magga* (The Path To Freedom), preserved only in Chinese, as well as of Buddhaghosa's

V

monumental work, *Visuddhi-Magga* (The Path of Purification), based on the former work.

The only place in the canon where these seven kinds of purification are mentioned is M. 24, "The Simile of the Stage-coach" (see P. TO D. 64), wherein their purpose and goal are illustrated. There it is said that the real and ultimate goal does not consist in purification of morality, or of mind, or of view, etc., but in total deliverance and extinction. Now, just as one mounts the first coach and travels to the second coach, then mounts the second coach and travels with it to the third coach, etc., in exactly the same way the goal of (I) the purification of morality (*sīla-visuddhi*) is (II) the purification of mind (*citta-visuddhi*); its goal: (III) the purification of view (*diṭṭhi-visuddhi*); its goal: (IV) the purification by overcoming doubt (*kaṅkhāvitaraṇa-visuddhi*); its goal: (V) the purification by knowledge and vision of what is path and non-path (*maggāmagga-ñāṇadassana-visuddhi*); its goal: (VI) the purification by knowledge and vision of the path-progress (*paṭipadā-ñāṇadassana-visuddhi*); its goal: (VII) the purification of knowledge and vision (*ñāṇadassana-visuddhi*); but the goal of this purification is deliverance freed from all clinging.

(I)

"Purification of morality (*sīla-visuddhi*) consists of the fourfold purity of morality (*catu-pārisuddhi-sīla*), namely: restraint with regard to the Disciplinary Code (*pātimokkhasaṃvara-sīla*), sense-restraint (*indriysaṃvara-sīla*), purity of livelihood (*ājīvapārisuddhi-sīla*), morality with regard to the four requisites (*paccaya-sannissita-sīla*)" (VISM. XVIII). On these four terms, see *sīla*. In the case of a layman, it entails the observance of whatever moral rules (5 or more) he has taken upon himself.

(II)

"Purification of mind (*citta-visuddhi*) is a name for the eight attainments (= absorptions: *jhāna*, q.v.), as well as for neighbourhood-concentration (*upacāra-samādhi*; see *samādhi*)." (IB.).

(III)

"By purification of view (*diṭṭhi-visuddhi*) is meant the understanding, according to reality, of mind and corporeality (*nāma-rūpa*, q.v.) ... which is founded on undeludedness (wisdom) as base, and which in manifold ways determines mind and corporeality after overcoming all belief in a personality (*attā*: self, ego.)." (IB.).

(IV)

"By purification by overcoming doubt (*kaṅkhā-vitaraṇa-visuddhi*) is meant the understanding which, by grasping the conditions of this mind and corporeality, has escaped from all doubt with regard to the three times (past, present, future)." (IB. XIX)

(V)

"By purification by knowledge and vision of what is path and non-path (*maggāmagga-ñāṇadassana-visuddhi*) is meant that understanding which knows the right path from the wrong path: 'This is the right path, that the wrong path.'" (ib. XX) In order to attain this fifth stage of purification, one at first should develop methodical insight (*nayavipassanā*), i.e., through contemplation of the five groups of existence (*khandha*, q.v.). For whosoever does not yet possess a perfectly developed insight, to him such phenomena as effulgence of light, etc. (see below), arising during insight, may become impediments in the three kinds of full understanding here considered (see *pariññā*).

'As soon as the manifold ways and characteristics of the four Truths (*sacca*) and the dependent origination (*paṭiccasamuppāda*) have become clear to the meditating disciple, he says to himself: Thus do these things never before arisen arise, and having arisen they disappear again. Thus do the formations of existence ever and again arise as something quite new. But not only are they something new, they are moreover also of limited duration, like a dew-drop at sunrise, like a bubble, like a line drawn with a stick in the water, like a mustard seed placed on the point of an arrow, or like a flash of lightning. Also as something unsubstantial and empty do they appear, as jugglery, as a mirage. ... Merely something subject to vanishing arises, and having arisen disappears again.'"

During such insight practice, however, may arise the ten imperfections (or defilements) of insight (*vipassanāpakkilesa*): effulgence of light (*obhāsa*), knowledge (*ñāṇa*), rapture (*pīti*), tranquillity (*passaddhi*), happiness (*sukha*), determination (*adhimokkha*), energy (*paggaha*), awareness (*upaṭṭhāna*), delight (*nikanti*). See VISM. XX, 105ff.

Excepting the last one, 'delight', they are not imperfections or defilements in themselves, but may become a basis for them through the arising of pride or delight or by a wrong conclusion that one of the holy paths has been attained. He, however, who is watchful and experienced in insight practice, will know that these states of mind do not indicate attainment of the true path, but are only symptoms or concomitants of insight meditation.

"Thus far the meditating disciple has determined three of the truths, namely while determining the corporeal and mental phenomena he has, through purification of view (*diṭṭhi-visuddhi*), determined the 'truth of suffering'. While grasping the conditions he has, through purification by overcoming doubt (*kaṅkhāvitaraṇa-visuddhi*), determined the 'truth of the origin of suffering'. While determining the right path, he has, through purification by knowledge and vision of what is path and non-path (*maggāmagga-ñāṇadassana-visuddhi*), determined the 'truth of the path' (leading to the extinction of suffering)."

(VI)

Purification by knowledge and vision of the path-progress (*paṭipadā-ñāṇadassana-visuddhi*) is the insight perfected in eight kinds of knowledge, together with the ninth knowledge, the 'knowledge adapting itself to truth'.

By the eight kinds of knowledge are here meant the following, which are freed from defilements, follow the right process, and are considered as insight, namely:

1. knowledge consisting in contemplation of rise and fall (*udayabbayānu-passanā-ñāṇa*),
2. in contemplation of dissolution (*bhaṅgānupassanā-ñāṇa*),
3. in awareness of terror (or the fearful) (*bhayatūpaṭṭhānā-ñāṇa*),
4. in contemplation of misery (*ādīnavānupassanā-ñāṇa*),
5. in contemplation of aversion (*nibbidānupassanā-ñāṇa*),
6. in the desire for deliverance (*muccitu-kamyatā-ñāṇa*),
7. in reflecting contemplation (*paṭisaṅkhānupassanā-ñāṇa*),
8. in equanimity regarding all formations of existence (*saṅkhārupekkhā-ñāṇa*), which is followed by
9. in adaptation to truth (*saccānulomika-ñāṇa*).

(1) consists in the meditative observation of the three characteristics of existence (impermanence, suffering, no self) in one's own bodily and mental processes. As long as the mind is still disturbed by the ten imperfections (see v), the three characteristics will not become fully clear in their true nature. Only when the mind is free from these imperfections can the characteristics be observed clearly.

(2) When through such repeated practice, knowledge and mindfulness have grown keen and the bodily and mental formations become apparent quickly, at that stage the phase of dissolution of these formations will become prominent.

"Consciousness with (e.g.) materiality as its object arises and dissolves. Having reflected on that object, he contemplates the dissolution of (reflecting) consciousness." (PTS.M. I, 57, quoted in VISM. XXI, 11).

The eight blessings of this knowledge are: abandoning the belief in eternal existence (*bhava-diṭṭhi*), giving up attachment to life, constant right application (of mind to meditative endeavour), a purified livelihood, overcoming of anxiety, absence of fear, acquisition of forbearance and gentleness, conquest of discontent and sensual delight (VISM. XXI, 28).

(3) Knowledge consisting in awareness of terror (or fearfulness) is the seeing of terror in the conditions as well as the continuity of existence. For whoso considers the formations as impermanent, to him the conditions of existence (i.e., the karma-formations producing ever new existence) appear as terror, as driving towards death. Whoso considers the formations as misery, to him the continuity of existence appears as terror, as something oppressive. Whoso considers the formations as impersonal, to him the karma-formations, as well as the continuity of existence, appear as terror, as an empty village, as a mirage, etc.

(4) Contemplation of misery (or danger) is another aspect of the awareness of terror: "The origin (of existence) is terror ... continuance of existence is terror ... arising is suffering', such understanding in the awareness of terror is the knowledge of misery. 'Non-arising is bliss', this is knowledge of the peaceful state (PTS.M. I, 59); i.e., the no-more-arising is safety, is happiness, is Nibbāna.

(5) Contemplation of aversion means: aversion for all formations as terror, therefore its name 'awareness of terror' has come into use. Because it has made known the misery of all these formations, therefore it has received the name of 'contemplation of misery' (*ādīnavānupassanā*). Because it has arisen through aversion for those formations, therefore it is known as 'contemplation of aversion' (*nibbidānupassanā*).

(6) Knowledge consisting in the desire for deliverance means: the desire for freedom and escape from all formations of existence. For feeling aversion for all formations, becoming weary of them, finding no more delight in them, the mind does not cling to a single one of all these formations.

(7) Reflecting contemplation is the repeated meditative discernment of the formations of existence, attributing to them the three characteristics of existence, with the desire to find deliverance from all forms of existence.

(8) Equanimity regarding all formations: "When the meditator (through reflecting contemplation) has discerned the formations by applying the three characteristics to them and sees them as void, he abandons both terror and delight, and becomes indifferent and equanimous with regard to all formations; he neither takes them as I nor as 'mine'; he is like a man who has divorced his wife" (VISM. XXI, 61).

Now, while continuing to contemplate the three characteristics of existence and perceiving the tranquil lot of Nibbāna as the peace, this equanimity-knowledge becomes the triple gateway to liberation. As it is said (PTS.M. II, 48):

"Three gateways to liberation (*vimokkha-mukha*; see *vimokkha* I) lead to escape from the world, namely: that the mind is contemplating all formations as limited, and is rushing forward to the conditionless element (*animitta-dhātu*); that the mind is stirred with regard to all formations of existence, and is rushing forward to the desireless element (*appaṇihita-dhātu*); that the mind sees all things as something foreign, and is rushing forward to the void element (*suññatā-dhātu*)."

At this stage, and through the triple gateway, the diversification of path attainment takes place, according to the seven kinds of noble persons (*ariya-puggala*, q.v.); on this see VISM. XXI, 74ff.

The sixth, seventh, and eighth knowledges, according to VISM. XXI, form really only one single knowledge in its first, middle, and final stages of development. This knowledge is also known as the 'insight leading to path ascent' (*vuṭṭhāna-gāminī-vipassanā*, q.v.).

(9) Adaptation to truth (or conformity with truth) is called that knowledge which, while contemplating impermanence, etc. adapts itself to the preceding eight kinds of insight-knowledge, as well as to the immediately following supermundane path and to the thirty-seven elements pertaining to enlightenment (*bodhipakkhiyā-dhammā*, q.v.). It is identical with adaptation-knowledge (*anulomañāṇa*).

"Whosoever has cultivated, developed, and frequently practised 'equanimity regarding all formations' in him arises very strong faith known as determination (*adhimokkha-saddhā*) and his energy is better exerted, his mindfulness better established, his mind better concentrated, and a still stronger 'equanimity regarding the formations' arises. 'Now the path will reveal itself', thus thinking, the meditator contemplates with his equanimity-knowledge all formations as impermanent, etc., and thereafter that knowledge sinks into the subconscious stream of existence (see *bhavaṅgasotā*). Immediately afterwards there arises advertence at the mind-door (see *viññāṇa-kicca*). And just like equanimity-knowledge, the adaptation-knowledge, too, takes as its object the formations, regarding them as something impermanent, miserable and impersonal. Thereupon, while continuing the uninterrupted continuity of consciousness (*citta-santati*), there arises the first impulsive moment (*javana*, q.v.), called 'preparation' (*parikamma*), taking the same formations as object. Immediately thereafter, with the same formations as object, there arises the second impulsive moment, known as 'access' (*upacāra*). And again immediately after that, there arises the impulsive moment called 'adaptation' (*anuloma*)."

(VII)

Purification of knowledge and vision (*ñāṇadassana-visuddhi*) is the knowledge associated with any of the four kinds of supermundane path-consciousness (see *ariya-puggala*).

"Immediately upon this adaptation-knowledge there arises the 'maturity-knowledge' (*gotrabhū-ñāṇa*; see *gotrabhū*) taking as object the Unconditioned, the standstill of existence, the absence of becoming, cessation, Nibbāna, while at the same time transcending the rank (*gotta* = *gotra*: lineage), designation and plane of the worldling (*puthujjana*, q.v.), and entering the rank, designation and plane of the Noble Ones (*ariya*), being the first turning towards Nibbāna as object, the first thinking of it, the first concentration on it, and the condition for the path ... forming the culmination of insight, and never as such coming back again.

"As the immediate continuation following upon that maturity knowledge (*gotrabhū-ñāṇa*), there arises the first path-consciousness (stream-entry) forever destroying the first three of the ten fetters of existence (*saṃyojana*, q.v.), and closing the entrance to the lower worlds. Immediately after this path-knowledge, there arise, as its result, two or three path-produced states of consciousness, the fruitional consciousness (*phala-citta*).

"Immediately after the sinking of this consciousness into the subconscious stream of existence, the retrospective knowledge (*paccavekkhana ñāṇa*, q.v.) arises, having the path-consciousness as its object" (VISM. XXI).

For the three higher paths, see *ariya-puggala*.

Each of the four kinds of path-consciousness performs at the one and the same time four functions, namely: the function of full understanding (*pariññā*, q.v.) of suffering, the function of overcoming (*pahāna*, q.v.) the origin of suffering, the function of realising (*sacchi-kiriyā*) the extinction of suffering, the function of developing (*bhāvanā*, q.v.) the supermundane Noble Eightfold Path (*magga*, q.v.).

See *Path of Purification*, by Buddhaghosa, tr. by Ñānamoli (BPS); *Path of Freedom*, by Upatissa (BPS).

vitakka: 'thought', 'thought-conception', is one of the 'secondary' (not constant) mental concomitants (see TAB. II), and may be either karmically wholesome, unwholesome or neutral. "There are three karmically unwholesome (*akusala*) thoughts: sensuous thought (*kāma-vitakka*), hating thought (*byāpāda*-~), and cruel thought (*vihiṃsā*-~). There are three karmically wholesome (*kusala*) thoughts: thought of renunciation (*nekkhamma*-~), of hatelessness (*avyāpāda*-~), of not harming (*avihimsā*-~)." The latter three constitute 'right thought', the second link of the Eightfold Path (see *magga* 2).

See 'Removal of Distracting Thoughts' (Vitakka-Saṇṭhāna Sutta), M. 20 (tr. in WHEEL 21).

vitakka-vicāra: 'thought-conception and discursive thinking', (or 'applied and sustained thought') are verbal functions (*vacī-saṅkhāra*: see *saṅkhāra*) of the mind, the so-called 'inner speech (*parole interieure*). They are constituents of the first absorption (see *jhāna*), but absent in the higher absorptions.

(1) "Thought-conception (*vitakka*) is the laying hold of a thought, giving it attention. Its characteristic consists in fixing the consciousness to the object.

(2) "Discursive thinking (*vicāra*) is the roaming about and moving to and fro of the mind. ... It manifests itself as continued activity of mind" (VISM. IV).

(1) is compared with the striking against a bell, (2) with its resounding; (1) with the seizing of a pot, (2) with wiping it. (Cf. VISM. IV.).

vitality: *jīvitindriya*; see *indriya*, *khandha* (corporeality, mental formations), TAB. II.

vīthi (citta-vīthi): 'process of consciousness', see *viññāṇa-kicca*.

vivaṭṭa: 'absence of the cycle of existence' (*vaṭṭa*, q.v.), standstill of existence, is a name for Nibbāna (q.v.).

SOURCE NOTE: as a name for Nibbāna, the term seems to be found only in the com.

vivaṭṭa-kappa: see *kappa*.

V

vivaṭṭānupassanā: 'contemplation of the turning away', is one of the eighteen chief kinds of insight (*vipassanā*, q.v.).

SOURCE NOTE: is already mentioned in PTS.M., together with the remaining seventeen kinds of *vipassanā*. It is not found in the old texts.

viveka: 'detachment', seclusion, is according to Niddesa, of three kinds: (1) bodily detachment (*kāya-viveka*), i.e., abiding in solitude free from alluring sensuous objects; (2) mental detachment (*citta-viveka*), i.e., the inner detachment from sensuous things; (3) detachment from the substrata of existence (*upadhi-viveka*).

In the description of the first absorption, the words "detached from sensuous things" (*vivicc' eva kāmehi*) refer, according to VISM. IV, to 'bodily detachment'; the words "detached from karmically unwholesome things" (*vivicca akusalehi dhammehi*) refer to 'mental detachment'; the words "born of detachment" (*vivekaja*), to the absence of the five hindrances.

viveka-sukha: 'happiness of detachment', or aloofness (see *viveka*). "Whoso is addicted to society and worldly bustle, he will not partake of the happiness of renunciation, detachment, peace and enlightenment" (A. VII, 86).

vodāna: 'cleansing', may refer either to (1) morality (*sīla*), (2) concentration (*samādhi*), or (3) wisdom (*paññā*).

(1) "Cleansing of morality takes place in two ways: by understanding the misery of moral deviation (*sīla-vipatti*; see *vipatti*) and by understanding the blessing of moral perfection (*sīla-sampatti*)" (see VISM. I).

(2) Cleansing of concentration is concentration connected with progress (*visesa-bhāgiya-samādhi*; see *hāna-bhāgiya*). If, for example, one has entered the first absorption, and sensuous perceptions and reflections arise, in that case there is concentration connected with decline. ... If, however, perceptions and reflections free from thought-conception and discursive thinking (second *jhāna*; q.v.) arise, in that case there is concentration connected with progress.

(3) Cleansing, with reference to wisdom, is identical with the 'insight leading to the (path) ascent' (*vuṭṭhāna-gāminī-vipassanā*, q.v.), which arises at the stage of 'purification by knowledge and vision of the path-progress' (see *visuddhi* VI), and is followed immediately by the maturity moment and the entrance into the supermundane paths.

vohāra-desanā: 'conventional exposition', as distinguished from an explanation true in the highest sense (*paramattha-desanā*, q.v.). It is also called *sammuti-sacca* (SKR. *saṃvrti*).

SOURCE NOTE: the terms *vohāra-sacca, paramattha-sacca, sammuti-sacca*: etc., belong as such to the commentarial literature, but their significance is clearly shown in the old sutta texts, e.g. D. 9: '*loka-sāmaññā, loka-vohāra*'; further (D. 33): *sammuti-ñāṇa*, etc.

void-deliverance: see *ceto-vimutti*.

vokāra: see *pañca-vokāra-bhava*.

SOURCE NOTE: *pañca-~, catu-~*, and *eka-~* (*bhava*), occur as technical terms only in the ABH. (VIBH., YAM., PATTH.) and com., e.g. VISM., but their substance is an integral part of the suttas.

volition: *cetanā* (q.v.).

votthapana-citta: 'determining consciousness', is that mind-element (functioning independently of karma; see TAB. I, 70). which in the process of sense-perception performs the function of determining the sense-object. It is one of the fourteen functions of consciousness (*viññāṇa-kicca*, q.v.).

SOURCE NOTE: not found, or not found in this form or meaning, in the oldest parts of the Sutta Piṭaka; see *citta-vīthi*.

vuṭṭhāna-gāminī-vipassanā: 'insight leading to (path) ascent'. It is also called 'cleansing' (*vodāna*, q.v.), and according to PTS.M. II, 64, it is a name for three kinds of insight-knowledge, namely: knowledge consisting in the desire for deliverance (*muccitu-kamyatā-ñāṇa*; see *visuddhi* VI, 6); reflecting-contemplation-knowledge (*paṭisaṅkhānupassanā-ñāṇa*; ib. VI, 7); and knowledge consisting in equanimity regarding all formations (*saṅkhārupekkhā-ñāṇa*; see *visuddhi* VI, 8).

It arises at the stage of 'purification by knowledge and vision of the path-progress' (see *visuddhi* VI), and is followed immediately by the maturity moment and the entrance into the supermundane paths.

"'Ascent' (*vuṭṭhāna*) is the supermundane path (see *ariya-puggala*) since it rises above the object forming the external foundation (of insight; i.e., the external five groups of existence), in which object one's mind was absorbed, and also rises above one's own continuity (one's own five groups of existence, or *khandha*, q.v.) together with its defilements. By reason of its leading upwards to the supermundane path, this insight is called 'ascending insight'. That it passes on to the path: that is the meaning implied" (VISM. XXI, 83ff.).

SOURCE NOTE: the term is probably implied in PTS.M. I, 60, under the name of *vuṭṭhāna-vivaṭṭane ñāṇa*.

vyāpāda: 'ill will', is a synonym of *dosa* (see *mūla*); it is one of the five hindrances (*nīvaraṇa*, q.v.) and one of the ten fetters (*saṃyojana*, q.v.).

W

water-element: *āpo-dhātu*, see *dhātu*.

water-kasina, white-~, wind-~: see *kasiṇa*.

weighty karma: *garuka-kamma*, see *karma*.

wheel of existence: see *saṃsāra*, *vaṭṭa*.

wheel of the law: *dhamma-cakka* (q.v.).

will: *cetanā* (q.v.).

wind-element: *vāyo-dhātu*, see *dhātu*.

wisdom: *paññā* (q.v.).

woeful courses (of existence): *duggati*, see *gati*.

world, the threefold: *loka* (q.v.).

worldling: *puthujjana* (q.v.).

worldly: *lokiya* (q.v.).

worldly conditions, the eight: *loka-dhamma* (q.v.).

world-period, formation, dissolution: see *kappa*.

wrongnesses, the ten: *micchatta* (q.v.).

wrong path: *micchā-magga* (q.v.).

wrong understanding (or view), wrong thought, wrong speech; etc: see *micchā-magga*.

Y

yakkha: in popular belief, a kind of ghost, goblin, or ogre.

Yāma-deva: are a kind of heavenly beings of the sensuous world, see *deva*.

yamaka-pāṭihāriya: 'twin miracle'. "There the Perfect One performed the twin miracle unattainable to any disciple: from the upper part of his body a flame sprang forth, and from the lower part a stream of water. etc." (PTS.M. I, 125ff.).

SOURCE NOTE: the term is perhaps for the first time mentioned and described in PTS.M.

yathā-bhūta-ñāṇa-dassana: 'the knowledge and vision according to reality', is one of the eighteen chief kinds of insight (*vipassanā*, q.v.).

yathākammūpaga-ñāṇa: 'knowledge of rebirth according to one's actions', see *abhiññā* (4).

yathāsanthatik'aṅga: 'the practice of being satisfied with whatever dwelling', is one of the ascetic means of purification; see *dhutaṅga* (12).

yoga: 'yokes, bonds', is another name for the four cankers (*āsava*, q.v.).

yogāvacara (= **yogi**): 'one devoted to mental training,' is in VISM. the usual name for the disciple cultivating mental concentration.

SOURCE NOTE: these two terms belong to the commentarial literature, but the first term appears also in MIL.

yokes: *yoga*, q.v.

yoni: 'modes of generation.' There are four modes: generation from the egg, from the mother's womb, from moisture, and spontaneous birth (*opapātika*, q.v.) in heaven, hell, etc. Explained in M. 12.

yoniso manasikāra: 'thorough attention' or wise consideration': see *manasikāra*.

youth-infatuation: see *mada*.

yuganaddha: see *samatha-vipassanā*, last paragraph.

APPENDIX

Attempt at a chronological fixing of terms not found, or not found in this form or meaning, in the oldest parts of the Sutta Piṭaka.

akusala-sādhāraṇa-cetasika
ānantarika-kamma
ārammaṇa
avacara
āvajjana
avyākata
āyūhana
bhava
bhāva
bhavaṅga-sota, -citta
carita
cāritta- and vāritta-sila
cetasika
citta-lahutā
citta-vīthi
cuti-citta
dhātu-vavatthāna
dhutaṅga
gotrabhū
hasituppāda-citta
iddhi
indriya-samatta
javana
kalāpa
kāma
kamma
kammaññatā
kammaṭṭhāna
kaṭattā-kamma
kāya-lahutā
khaṇa
kilesa
kiriya- (kiriyā-, kriyā-) citta
lahutā, mudutā, kammaññatā
manodvārāvajjana
mudutā
ñāṇa
natthi-paccaya
n'eva-sekha-n'āsekha
Nibbāna
nimitta
nissaraṇa-pahāna
nissaya, nissita
niyāma
niyata-micchā-diṭṭhi
paccaya
pādakajjhāna
pāguññatā
pahāna
palibodha
pañca-dvārāvajjana
paramattha
pāramī, pāramitā
paricchinnākāsa
pariyatti, paṭipatti, paṭivedha
paṭipannaka
paṭipatti
paṭisandhi
paṭisandhika
paṭivedha
pattidāna
rūpa
samādhi
sama-sīsī

samatha-yānika
sammasana
sammuti
sampaṭicchana-citta
samuṭṭhāna
santāna, santati
santīraṇa-citta
sīla
sukkha-vipassaka
tadārammaṇa-citta
tathatā
tatra-majjhattatā
Theravāda
ujukatā
upacaya
upādā-rūpa
vāritta-sīla
vasī
vatthu
vimokkha
viññatti
vipassanā
vipassanūpakkilesa
vivaṭṭa
vivaṭṭānupassanā
vohāra-sacca
vokāra
votthapana-citta
vuṭṭhāna-gāminī-vipassanā
yamaka-pāṭihāriya
yogāvacara, yogi

TABLE I.
CONSCIOUSNESS GROUP
(VIÑÑAṆA-KHANDHA)

Consciousness, from the karmic or moral standpoint, may be classified as of eighty-nine kinds, as follows:

	Karmically Wholesome (*kusala*)
Sensuous Sphere	(1) Joyful, with knowledge, unprepared. (Imp.) (2) Joyful, with knowledge, prepared. (Imp.) (3) Joyful, without knowledge, unprepared. (Imp.) (4) Joyful, without knowledge, prepared. (Imp.) (5) Indifferent, with knowledge, unprepared. (Imp.) (6) Indifferent, with knowledge, prepared. (Imp.) (7) Indifferent, without knowledge, unprepared. (Imp.) (8) Indifferent, without knowledge, prepared. (Imp.)
Fine-material Sphere (Absorptions)	(9) 1st Jhāna (Imp.) (10) 2nd Jhāna (Imp.) (11) 3rd Jhāna (Imp.) (12) 4th Jhāna (Imp.) (13) 5th Jhāna (Imp.)
Immaterial Sphere (Absorptions)	(14) "Boundless Space" (Imp.) (15) "Boundless Consciousness" (Imp.) (16) "Nothingness" (Imp.) (17) "Neither-perception-nor-non-perception" (Imp.)
Super-mundane	(18) Path (-moment) of "stream-entry" (Imp.) (19) Path (-moment) of "once-returning" (Imp.) (20) Path (-moment) of "nonreturning" (Imp.) (21) Path (-moment) of "arahatship" (Imp.)
	TOTAL 21 kinds

	Karmically Unwholesome (*akusala*)
Sensuous Sphere	*Rooted in Greed* (*lobha*) (22) Joyful, with evil view, unprepared. (Imp.) (23) Joyful, with evil view, prepared. (Imp.) (24) Joyful, without evil view, unprepared. (Imp.) (25) Joyful, without evil view, prepared. (Imp.) (26) Indifferent, with evil view, unprepared. (Imp.) (27) Indifferent, with evil view, prepared. (Imp.) (28) Indifferent, without evil view, unprepared. (Imp.) (29) Indifferent, without evil view, prepared. (Imp.) *Rooted in Hate* (*dosa*) (30) Sad, angry, unprepared. (Imp.) (31) Sad, angry, prepared. (Imp.) *Rooted in Delusion* (*moha*) (32) Indifferent and sceptical. (Imp.) (33) Indifferent and restless. (Imp.)
Fine-material Sphere (Absorptions)	———————
Immaterial Sphere (Absorptions)	———————
Supermundane	———————
	TOTAL 12 kinds

	Karmically Neutral (*avyākata*) (a) Karma results (*vipāka*)
Sensuous Sphere	*Result of wholesome Karma* (*with desirable objects*): 1. *Without Root-cause* (34–38) Eye-, ear-, nose-, tongue-, (agreeable) body consciousness. (Adv.) (39) Mind-element (*mano-dhātu*) (Rec.) (40) Joyful mind-consciousness-element (*mano-viññāṇa dhātu*). (Inv. Reg.) (41) Indifferent mind-consciousness-element (*mano-viññāṇa dhātu*). (Inv. Reg.) 2. *With Root-cause* (42–49) = (1–8) (Reg. R. S. D.) *Result of unwholesome Karma* (*with undesirable objects*): *Without Root-cause only* (50–54) Eye-, ear-, nose-, tongue-, (painful) body-consciousness. (55) Mind-element (*mano-dhātu*) (Rec.) (56) Mind-consciousness-element (*mano-viññāṇa dhātu*). (Inv. Reg. R. S. D.)
Fine-material Sphere (Absorptions)	(57) (58) (57) (58) (60) (61) = (9–13) (R. S. D.)
Immaterial Sphere (Absorptions)	(62) (63) (64) (65) = (14-17) (R. S. D.)
Supermundane	(66) Fruit (-moment) of "stream-entry" (Imp.) (67) Fruit (-moment) of "once-returning" (Imp.) (68) Fruit (-moment) of "nonreturning" (Imp.) (69) Fruit (-moment) of "arahatship" (Imp.)
	TOTAL 36 kinds

	Karmically Neutral (*avyakāta*) (b) Independent functions (*kriyā*)	
Sensuous Sphere	1. *Without Root-cause* (70) Mind-element. (Adv: 5d) (71) Indifferent Mind-consciousness-element (Adv.) (72) Joyful Mind-consciousness-element (Imp.) 2. *With Root-cause* (73–80) = (1–8) (Imp.)	Only in the Arahat (72–89)
Fine-material Sphere (absorptions)	(81–85) = (9–13) (Imp.)	
Immaterial Sphere (absorptions)	(86–89) = (14–17) (Imp.)	
Supermundane	——————	
	TOTAL 20 kinds	

TABLE II.
FORMATION-GROUP
(SAṄKHĀRA-KHANDA)

To this group belong fifty mental formations, of which eleven are general psychological elements, twenty-five lofty qualities, and fourteen karmically unwholesome qualities.

Eleven GENERAL formations*

(a) Five **Primary** ones (in all consciousness):

Mental Impression (*phassa*)
Volition (*cetanā*)
Vitality (*jivita*)
Concentration (*samādhi*)
Advertence (*manasikāra*)

(b) Six **Secondary** ones (not in all consciousness):

Thought Conception (*vitakka*)
Discursive Thinking (*vicāra*)
Determination (*adhimokkha*)
Energy (*viriya*)
Interest (*pīti*)
Intention (*chanda*)

Twenty-five LOFTY formations

(a) **Primary** ones (in all wholesome and its corresponding neutral consciousness):

Faith (*saddhā*)
Mindfulness (*sati*)
Moral Shame (*hiri*)
Moral Dread (*ottappa*)
Greedlessness (*a-lobha*)
Hatelessness (*a-dosa*)
Equanimity (*tatramajjhattatā*)
Tranquillity of Spiritual Group (*kāya-passaddhi*)
Tranquillity of Consciousness (*citta-passaddhi*)
Agility of Spiritual Group (*kāya-lahutā*)
Agility of Consciousness (*citta-lahutā*)

* The moral quality of these eleven formations depends upon whether they are associated with a karmically wholesome, unwholesome or neutral state of consciousness.

Elasticity of Spiritual Group (*kāya-mudutā*)
Elasticity of Consciousness (*citta-mudutā*)
Adaptability of Spiritual Group (*kāya-kammaññatā*)
Adaptability of Consciousness (*citta-kammaññatā*)
Proficiency of Spiritual Group (*kāya-pāguññatā*)
Proficiency of Consciousness (*citta-pāguññatā*)
Uprightness of Spiritual Group (*kāya-ujukatā*)
Uprightness of Consciousness (*citta-ujukatā*)

(b) **Secondary** ones (not in all lofty consciousness):

Three Abstinences†

Abstinence from wrong bodily action
Abstinence from wrong words
Abstinence from wrong livelihood

Two Boundless States

Compassion (*karuṇā*); Sympathetic Joy (*muditā*)
Non-delusion (*a-moha = paññā*, knowledge)

Fourteen UNWHOLESOME formations

(a) Four **Primary** ones (in all unwholesome consciousness):

Delusion (*moha*)
Lack of Moral Shame (*ahirika*)
Lack of Moral Dread (*anottappa*)
Unrest (*uddhacca*)

(b) Ten **Secondary** ones (not in all unwholesome consciousness):

Four Hateful Ones

Hate (*dosa*)
Envy (*issā*) †
Stinginess (*macchariya*) †
Worry (*kukkucca*)†

further:

Greed (*lobha*)
Evil View (*diṭṭhi*)
Conceit (*māna*)
Torpor (*thīna*)
Languor (*middha*)
Scepsis (*vicikicchā*)

† The three abstinences and two boundless states, as well as envy, stinginess, worry, conceit, torpor and languor, are called "inconstant" (*aniyata*), as they are only occasionally associated with the states of consciousness in question, and also then only one at a time.

TABLE III.
COMBINATION OF THE TWO GROUPS

KARMICALLY WHOLESOME

(1) & (2) eleven General + twenty-five Lofty	= 36
(3) & (4) above thirty-six – Knowledge‡	= 35
(5) & (6) above thirty-six – Interest	= 35
(7) & (8) above thirty-six – Interest – Knowledge	= 34
(9) and above thirty-six – three Abstinences	= 33
(10) the latter thirty-three – Thought-Conceptions	= 32
(11) the latter thirty-two – Discursive Thinking	= 31
(12) the latter thirty-one – Interest	= 30
(13) the latter thirty – two Boundless States	= 28
(14) to (17) the latter twenty-eight Formations	
(18) to (21) = (9) to (13) but – two Boundless States + three Abstinences	

KARMICALLY UNWHOLESOME

(22) eleven General + four Primary Unwholesome + Greed + Evil View	= 17
(23) = (no. 22) + Torpor§ & Languor †	= 19
(24) = (no. 22) – Evil View + Conceit	= 17
(25) = (no. 23) – Evil View + Conceit	= 19
(26) = (no. 22)	= 16
(27) = (no. 23) – Interest	= 18
(28) = (no. 24) – Interest	= 16
(29) = (no. 25) – Interest	= 18
(30) = (no. 22) – Interest – Greed – Evil View + four Hateful	= 18
(31) = preceding + Torpor† and Languor†	= 20
(32) eight General (missing Interest, Determination, Intention) + four primary Unwholesome + Scepsis	= 13
(33) = preceding, but Determination instead of Scepsis	= 13

‡ (–) is in this column everywhere used only as a minus sign.

§ Inconstant, i.e., only occasionally present

KARMICALLY NEUTRAL

(a) Karma resultant

(34) to (38) five Primary General; Concentration weak
(50) to (54) five Primary General; Concentration weak
(39) & (55) = preceding five + Thought Conception + Discursive = 8
(41) & (56) Thinking + Determination; Concentration weak
(40) nine General (missing Energy and Intention; Concentration weak)
(42) to (49) = (1) to (8), but – two Boundless States – three Abstinences
(57) to (69) = (9) to (21)

(b) Karmically Independent functions

(70) = (39)
(71) = nine General (missing Interest & Intention; Concentration weak = 9
(72) = ten General (missing Intention) = 10
(73) to (80) = (1) to (8) – three Abstinences
(81) to (89) = (9) to (17)

WORKS OF THE AUTHOR

ENGLISH

The Word of the Buddha. 14th ed. Kandy: Buddhist Publication Society, 1967. Abridged Students' Edition. Colombo: YMBA, 1948.

Guide through the Abhidhamma Piṭaka. 3rd ed. Kandy: Buddhist Publication Society, 1971.

Fundamentals of Buddhism: Four Lectures. 2nd ed. Bauddha Sāhitya Sabhā. Colombo: Lake House Bookshop, 1956.

Path to Deliverance. 2nd ed. Colombo: Lake House Bookshop, 1959.

Karma and Rebirth. (WHEEL 9). Kandy: Buddhist Publication Society.

Influence of Buddhism on a People. (Bodhi Leaves A. 2), Kandy: Buddhist Publication Society.

GERMAN

Das Wort des Buddha. Konstanz: Verlag Christiani, 1906.

Aṅguttara Nikāya (tr.). Five vols. 2nd revised edition. Köln: Verlag M. DuMont Schauberg, 1969. First published 1907.

Milindapañha (tr.). Two vols. 1918.

Dhammapada. Pali text, metrical tr. and com. (in Ms.).

Puggala-Paññatti (tr.). 1910.

Abhidhamattha-Saṅgaha (tr.). (in Ms.).

Visuddhi-Magga (tr.). Konstanz: Verlag Christiani, 1952.

Führer durch das Abhidhamma-Piṭaka. (*in Ms.*).

Systematische Pali-Grammatic. 1911.

Pali-Anthologie und Wörterbuch (Anthology and Glossary). Two vols. 1928.

Grundlehren des Buddhismus. (in Ms.).

Pfad zur Erlösung. Konstanz: Verlag Christiani, 1956.

Buddhistisches Wörterbuch (Buddhist Dictionary). Konstanz, Verlag Christiani.

FRENCH

Vocabulaire Pali-Francaise des Termes Bouddhiques. French tr. of the Buddhist Dictionary, by S. Karpeles. Paris: Adyar, 1961.

La Parole du Buddha. French tr. of "The Word of the Buddha". Paris: Adrien-Maisonneuve.

PALI

Sacca-Saṅgaha. Pali text of "The Word of the Buddha", in Sinhala script. 1914.

Buddha-Vacanaṃ. Pali text of "The Word of the Buddha", in roman script. Buddhist Publication Society.

SINHALA

Buddha Vacanaya: Sinhala tr. of "The Word of the Buddha". Rajagiriya (Sri Lanka): Ananda Semage, 1964.